The
Nation-State
and
the Crisis of
World Politics

The Nation-State and the Crisis of World Politics

ESSAYS ON INTERNATIONAL POLITICS
IN THE TWENTIETH CENTURY

John H. Herz

David McKay Company, Inc./New York

THE NATION-STATE AND THE CRISIS OF WORLD POLITICS:
Essays on International Politics in the Twentieth Century

COPYRIGHT © 1976 BY DAVID McKAY COMPANY, INC.

MANUFACTURED IN THE UNITED STATES OF AMERICA

Developmental Editor: Edward Artinian
Editorial and Design Supervisor: Nicole Benevento
    Design: Pencils Portfolio, Inc.
Production and Manufacturing Supervisor: Donald W. Strauss

Library of Congress Cataloging in Publication Data

Herz, John H   1908–
    The nation-state and the crisis of world politics.

    Includes bibliographical references.
    1. International relations. I. Title.
JX1391.H47   327′.09′04   76–7507
ISBN 0–679–30308–1

TO THE MEMORY OF MY MOTHER
1882–1976

ACKNOWLEDGMENTS

The lines from Rilke's poetry on pages 54 and 55 are reprinted from *Sonnets to Orpheus* by Rainer Maria Rilke. Translated by M. D. Herter Norton. By permission of W. W. Norton & Company, Inc. Copyright 1942 by W. W. Norton & Company, Inc. Copyright renewed 1970 by M. D. Herter Norton.

Chapter 2 is reprinted from "Idealist Internationalism and the Security Dilemma," by John H. Herz, *World Politics*, vol. II, no. 2 (copyright 1950 by Princeton University Press): pp. 157–180. Reprinted by permission of Princeton University Press.

Chapter 3 is reprinted from "Rise and Demise of the Territorial State," by John H. Herz, *World Politics*, vol. IX, no. 4

CONTENTS

Introduction   1

1. Power Politics and World Organization   57

2. Idealist Internationalism and the Security
   Dilemma   72

3. Rise and Demise of the Territorial State   99

4. International Politics and the Nuclear Dilemma   124

5. The Relevancy and Irrelevancy of Appeasement   148

6. The Impact of the Technological-Scientific
   Process on the International System   172

7. The Civilizational Process and Its Reversal   195

8. The Territorial State Revisited—Reflections on
   the Future of the Nation-State   226

9. Relevancies and Irrelevancies in the Study of
   International Relations   253

10. Détente and Appeasement from a Political
    Scientist's Vantage Point   279

11. Technology, Ethics, and International Relations   290

12. Prologue as Epilogue: Aristotle's Dream   303

The Nation-State and the Crisis of World Politics

INTRODUCTION

Consider a piece of art—a composition by Bach, for instance. Where, how, in what form does it "exist"? Certainly not, or not only, as the piece of paper on which the notes are written. Music needs performance, but no two performances are identical. Each participant in a performance has his "idea about," his "attitude toward" the piece, and it has equally differing impacts upon the listener. Over the years, the decades, the centuries, approaches and interpretations vary. For the naive "realist" that piece of music is a "given," and there certainly is "something" which underlies the varieties of interpreting it; but more sophisticated analysis shows that, while we have, perhaps, a chance to come close to that "something," it will never reveal itself fully and unequivocally.

What are "international relations"? Here, too, a simplistic

"realism" (denoting, in this context, not the specific international relations approach, so called, but the belief that there exists a world outside us which can be fully grasped and scientifically dissected) takes several assumptions for granted: (1) that international relations consist of certain actions and reactions of actors or units called, say, nation-states; (2) that they reflect their power or influence over one another; (3) that out of these relationships come "systems," such as bi- or multipolarity, or a balance of power, or a collective security system; (4) that there is a certain role played not only by political actors but by economic units such as business companies, or by racial or ethnic groups, or by international agencies set up by states or by nonstate groups; and so on.

A closer look at the situation, however, reveals that here, too, there is an infinity of perceptions of, and approaches to, these "givens." Thus, to some students of international politics competition for power has been and will always be the hallmark of relations among "powers"; others consider "power politics" as a possibly passing phase of specific historical development. Marxians will interpret international politics as a mere reflection of business interests, and the ensuing "imperialism" as something controlled by these interests, clashing, since 1917, with the "socialist" sector of the world. Others will consider as basic the phenomenon of "nationalism" and the striving for "national self-determination." More specifically, for some the United States was (or still is) an "imperial" power; for others, it is one of two (or now three, or even five) "superpowers." For some, the destructiveness of nuclear weapons confronts the world with an entirely unprecedented crisis, while others see nothing fundamentally new in the appearance of yet another weapon. And so forth.[1]

As in the case of "the true version of the St. Matthews Passion," we shall never be able to get at the "true nature" of international relations (or any other political, economic, or social system), although we can try to come closer to the "realities." But these, unlike the unchanging core of a piece of art, are constantly in flux. Thus their analysis must take notice

1. The role of "perception" as such has been a rather recent discovery by analysts of international politics, such as John Stoessinger, one of the pioneers in this area.

of their changing nature, their dynamism. Looking over a lifetime effort to keep track of, and analyze, international politics, I noticed that, in my effort to dig a bit below the surface of things and to account for causes in a changing political landscape, my own approach has frequently tied in with, and reflected, the great transformations in the world of international relations. Thus the essays here assembled are, perhaps, paradigmatic of the way those who spend their lives in observing and analyzing the events of this century have done so, which is one reason for republishing them.

But there is more to it. When drawing the analogy between analyzing works of art and political events we did not mention one great difference, the one that refers to "practical effect." Perceptions on the part of those who are in a position to deal with international affairs in practice may vitally affect developments themselves. Consider the extreme case of a Hitler. Had he remained a little rabble-rouser, he would merely be remembered as a peddler of somewhat absurd theories of the "innate" superiorities and inferiorities of races; but when he happened to come into control of a major power, his acting on the basis of this "worldview" meant tragedy for his country and the world—World War II and the Jewish holocaust might never have happened, the atomic bomb never been invented or developed. . . . But the effect of worldview and perception is not only apparent in totalitarian systems with their set doctrines or "ideologies." It is felt wherever leaders act and interact internationally. Did the postwar world, as in the perceptions of the Western leaders of the antagonistic power blocks, reflect an irreconcilable conflict between the "free world" and communism—the one defensive, the other engaging in world-revolutionary expansionism? Or is it a world where two or more antagonistic systems can coexist? What is "détente" to some is "appeasement" to others. Perceptions, on the part of those in power, are thus bound to be instrumental in shaping "realities," whether the actors like it or not.

Publishing essays of a more or less theoretical nature by a nonpractitioner cannot, of course, vie in effectiveness with the actions of those in charge of world affairs. It rarely happens that a man like Henry Kissinger has a chance to apply theoretical insights gained during an academic career to the actual affairs of nations. And I, of course, have never had this opportunity. But it appeared to me, when going over my literary product of some decades, that one change in approach has become ever more prominent: the one from dealing somewhat narrowly with the power political, strategic, and similar aspects of international relations (nuclear threat, security, etc.) to the recognition of the urgency of additional problems facing the world: the demographic crisis (population explosion) and the ecological ones (depletion of resources, threats to the biosphere). Although I had become aware of these threats at an early point,[2] I had mentioned them in my writings only marginally. Since the early 1960s they have taken equal place besides the more political issues, and by now I have come to the conclusion that the very survival of the human race depends on their speedy solution. Thus the second reason for collecting these essays is a feeling of urgency for contributing my share in "saving a livable world" before departing from it.

To show these changes in attitudes and perceptions I had to leave the articles in their original form with only occasional cuts in order to avoid repetition. Only in this way does their relatedness to changing world conditions become clear. This Introduction, therefore, has the dual purpose of commenting on the pieces here assembled and of describing the development of the chief concepts through which I have tried to get to the roots of international politics. The volume thus constitutes an *apologia pro studia mea* which may elucidate some of the ways in which we theoreticians of a very practical area of study try to find our way through the maze of facts and events, interpretations and analyses. Others who have done so before —whether in this or other fields—have talked of "intellectual pilgrimage" (Michael Howard), "models of my views" (George Schwarzenberger), "conceptual itinerary" (Erik Erikson). In all modesty, I herewith offer a chart of my own journey.

2. Since the late 1940s, I have always started my lectures on international politics with an introduction into "the great revolutions of our times" in which these matters were emphasized; after all, we had already then been warned by Fairfield Osborn (*This Plundered Planet*) and other early prophets of coming events.

I

The scene opens in Geneva in the 1930s, the time of the decisive test case facing the collective security system thought to have been established through the League of Nations. I had gone there on the first leg of emigrating from my native Germany, to study international relations at the outstanding European academic institution specializing in this field, the Graduate Institute of International Studies. I came not entirely unprepared. I had studied in Germany with Hans Kelsen, whose "Pure Theory of Law" constituted what, today, one might call a model for the analysis of law and the state, with international law considered the normative framework of international relations. My doctoral thesis had dealt with a combined problem of political theory and international law; and for a while I was engaged in trying to develop a broader theory of state, law, and politics by combining Kelsen's approach with the ontology of the German philosopher Nicolai Hartmann. Like many young Germans who later came to the United States, I was deeply involved in somewhat metaphysical theory which kept its distance from the more pragmatic Anglo-American approach.[3]

With Hitler came a brutal awakening. Politically, most young German-Jewish intellectuals had been more or less leftist, many of them Marxists, few paying attention to such un-Marxian (because noneconomic) elements of politics as nationalism. Now that the extreme, expansionist nationalism of the fascist countries threatened to destroy the very system of independent nations, our eyes were opened to the brutal role of power in international affairs. To interpret international law in the Kelsenian sense as system applicable to the analysis of international politics appeared more and more dubious,[4] and the hope for a defense of the still "free world" seemed to lie, as

3. As Max Ernst, dadaist and painter, had maliciously remarked: "Les intellectuels allemands ne peuvent pas faire caca ni pipi sans des idéologies."

4. In an essay on international law written at that time I tried to fashion a more realistic doctrine of that law, an effort I resumed decades later in applying what I still considered valuable in Kelsen's "Pure Theory" to the nuclear age (cf. "The Pure Theory of Law Revisited, Hans Kelsen's Doctrine of International Law in the Nuclear Age," in Law, State, and International Order, ed. S. Engel and R. A. Metall, 1964, pp. 107ff.).

it had lain throughout the classical period of the modern state, in fashioning a "Grand Coalition" to oppose and defeat (by war, if necessary) the would-be hegemonial power. Study could no longer be "pure" research; it had to become research committed to warn of the deadly peril and show the way to the necessary action. My first book, published in German but outside Nazi Germany and pseudonymously,[5] analyzed the approach of Nazi "scholars" to problems of international law, organization, and foreign policy, and tried to warn of the deception waged in theories that still painted Nazi policy in peaceful colors. In vain. The book appeared in the year of Munich, when nobody wanted to listen.[6]

Only those who remember the blind appeasement attitudes of the Western powers can fathom the despair of those who understood the aims of the fascist coalition and called for resistance by the nations it threatened. At the time of Mussolini's attack on Ethiopia, matters were "on razor's edge." Public opinion in many countries favored sanctions which, if applied in determined fashion, would have defeated the dictator. The League might this way have proved effective as a system of collective security, and even Hitler might thereafter have hesitated to attack one of its members.[7] As it turned out, a world war was needed to defeat the aggressors. It might have been done more cheaply in 1936.

One of my first essays published in English after coming to the United States reflected one of the three great disappointments affecting me in the 1930s: besides the failure of the

5. "Eduard Bristler," *Die Völkerrechtslehre des Nationalsozialismus* (The National Socialist Doctrine of International Law), Zurich, 1938.
6. Some summaries were subsequently published in English, in journals such as *Political Science Quarterly* and *Social Research*, but that was some years later, when the warnings were less needed.
7. Thus I did not, and still do not, share the utter skepticism in regard to the potentialities of the League's collective security system which Hans Morgenthau recently revealed he had at that time: "I listened to the debates in the League of Nations which were centered upon the revision of the Covenant of the League. I said to myself: 'How inadequate, how utterly out of proportion is this approach to the danger which we are facing. . . . Such and similar experiences have indeed instilled in me a skepticism about attempts to preserve international peace and order. . . . I, indeed, believe that there can be no peace without the existence of a government which can give the law, formulate the law, apply and enforce it. . . ." (*Proceedings*, 68th Annual Meeting of the American Society of International Law, Washington, D.C., 1975, p. 332). Since Morgenthau does not believe in the possibility of world

Geneva experiment to build a more peaceful world order on the basis of collective security and the disappearance of however weak roots of socialism in Russia under the Stalinist terror, it was the apparent success of Nazism to establish a totalitarian regime in a country that had given hope of turning away from authoritarianism to Western-style liberal democracy. I tried to interpret Nazi totalitarianism as a completely nihilistic power system about to solve all the great problems facing industrial societies through the application of pure coercion (something I called the "Gordian knot solution").[8] From then on my scholarly interests and efforts bifurcated: on the one hand, comparative politics, with an emphasis on German affairs, both domestic and foreign; on the other hand, theory and analysis of international politics, the subject matter of the present collection of articles.

II

The first article in this volume, "Power Politics and World Organization," written during the war, was largely inspired by the abundance of plans for a better postwar world propounded at the time. Against the utopianism of the "world federalists," [9] I emphasized the stark fact that in a world which would still be one of sovereign nations not subordinate to higher authority, national power and national interests had to be the guiding principles of action. I had come close to my subse-

---

government, this either-or attitude cannot but lead to the type of extreme realism he is known for. I believe that, depending on time and circumstances, "in-between" systems, such as collective security, *may* have a chance of realization.

8. "Alternative Proposals to Democracy: Naziism," *Journal of Negro Education*, July 1941, pp. 353 ff.

9. Against too, the general, more "idealistic" and moralizing attitude of earlier American international relations research. Whatever impact my attitude, together with that of other Central European émigrés (such as Hans Morgenthau, Karl Deutsch, Arnold Wolfers), had on the development of American thought in this field is part of the intriguing story of the interface of American and European ideas at the time of the great intellectual migrations of the 1930s. This volume thus may prove to be a small contribution to the ongoing study of this interaction. The best writing in this area on some of the respective authors and theories is Stuart Hughes, *Sea Change, The Migration of Social Thought* (New York: Harper, 1975).

quently developed theory of the "security dilemma" when talking of "the compulsion which the system exerts upon each member and the inescapability (that is, of power politics and power competition) which it implies as far as policies of each single unit are concerned." On the other hand, a return to the pre-League, unorganized balance-of-power system would mean ever more total and worldwide wars. This might lead to the demise of man: "Unable to escape the vicious circle of mutual fear, insecurity, and conflict for power . . . the 'victor over Nature' may turn out to have been but another among Nature's abortive attempts to create a species capable of survival." The pessimism characterizing my later writings began prior to the explosion of the atomic bomb.

I was, however, optimistic enough to believe in the practicability of an in-between system, equidistant from world government and power anarchy, provided the powers emerging as victors from the war would learn from the experience of the 1930s how to establish an improved system of collective security. A fundamental requirement of its functioning would be the realization on the part of the leading nations that they would have to subordinate specific national interests to the overriding, long-range interest of all in preserving the peace, and to take action whenever peace was threatened.

But an additional requirement, a multiplicity of not-too-unequal major powers that could apply effective sanctions even after surprise attack, turned out no longer to exist in the postwar period. Instead there emerged bipolarity, rendering any conflict between the two superpowers a fifty-fifty proposition; and nuclear attack seemed to rule out the organization of sanctions to cope with it. This, of course, one could not anticipate prior to the end of the war. When the United Nations was established, it could not (and, as was clear from the veto given to the superpowers, was not intended to) constitute a genuine collective security organization. Looking back from today's vantage point, the article, written in the early 1940s, appears both backward- and forward-looking. It laid the ground for a subsequent, more closely worked-out realist theory of international politics but, with its hope for an improved League of Nations, was still beholden to the ideas and expectations of the preceding decades.

III

When I wrote "Power Politics," I had begun to ask myself some basic questions concerning nations and their interactions. What accounted for their character as "states"? What made it necessary for them to give power and power considerations the prominence they apparently had had throughout history? Why had movements for the betterment of a world of constant conflict failed so often and so consistently? My answer is found in two books from which the two following essays were abstracted. The first, *Political Realism and Political Idealism, A Study in Theories and Realities* (Chicago: University of Chicago Press, 1951; pbk., University of Chicago Press, 1973), primarily dealt with the question of power and its relation to "idealist" movements. Its main concepts had been developed prior to the end of the war, so that bipolarity and nuclear weapons—the two novel postwar phenomena—were remarked upon only briefly. Indeed, the book tried to develop a more general theory of basic types of political attitudes and action applicable not only to foreign affairs but in principle to all levels of political interaction. The second book, *International Politics in the Atomic Age* (New York: Columbia University Press, 1959; pbk., Columbia University Press, 1962), whose publication was also delayed, reflects the earlier postwar period with its emergence of two antagonistic power blocs armed with nuclear weapons. Its main thrust was to show the impact of the new weapon on states conceived as "territorial" units.[10]

The first of the two essays, "Idealist Internationalism and the Security Dilemma," inquiring into the why of a world of powers and power politics, wars, and worldwide movements and ideologies, deals with what I consider a fundamental social constellation, here called "security dilemma," and tries to derive therefrom two opposite types of political thought and action: political realism and political idealism. The security dilemma besets, above all, those units which, in their respective historical setting, are the highest ones, that is, not

10. These two books could not, of course, be condensed in the two articles presented here, and the reader is referred to them for what is missing. However, some highlights are mentioned in this Introduction.

subordinate to any higher authority. Since, for their protection and even their survival, they cannot rely on any higher authority, they are necessarily thrown back upon their own devices; and since they cannot be sure of the intentions of competing units, they must be prepared for "the worst." Hence they must have means of defense. But preparing for defense may arouse the suspicions of others, who in turn will engage in such preparation. A vicious circle will arise—of suspicion and counter-suspicion, competition for power, armament races, ultimately war. The realism of this theory is distinguished from that of Hans Morgenthau, who sees the chief cause of power politics in innate human aggressiveness, or of Reinhold Niebuhr, who finds its deepest ground in human pride and sinfulness. Such factors, to be sure, may constitute additional grounds for conflicts and wars, but the security dilemma remains an inescapable basic condition, even in the absence of aggressivity or similar factors. Thus it is quite possible (and, in my opinion, makes more sense than the usual, mirror-image interpretations of "communist world conspiracy" and "imperialist aggressivity") to consider the cold war of the postwar period as having resulted from the security concerns on *both* sides which, defensive-minded though they may have been, were inclined to interpret the opponent's policies as offensive ones.

Political realism means insight into what the security dilemma implies and awareness of the difficulties to avoid the constant conflict which this constellation creates. Political idealism, on the other hand, lacks such realist insight. Such idealism has informed most of the great historical movements for a better world, and we encounter its characteristics whether we analyze the world-revolutionary internationalism of the French Jacobins or the surprisingly similar expectations of the early Bolshevists, whether we deal with movements for worldwide free trade and free migration or with universal "national self-determination." What distinguished all these movements and their leadership was a typically monocausal interpretation of world affairs. The respective "evil" is always found in one major cause whose elimination, therefore, is bound to lead to the desired ideal.

Thus, according to idealist nationalism, once a policy of

subjecting nationalities to empire or keeping them divided is replaced by one of national self-determination, peace and harmony will prevail in a world of genuine nation-states. According to the Manchester school, once free trade has taken the place of conflict-creating mercantilism, people will peacefully exchange goods and peace will prevail. According to Wilson, once autocratic domestic systems (which by nature are bellicose) are replaced by democracies, the people, whose interest is in peace rather than in wars, will live in peace together. According to Marx, once war-provoking capitalism yields to socialism, the classless societies thus established will live in brotherly harmony. The failure of all these movements shows up their utopian idealism. The reality that eventually took the place of their ideals was expansionist nationalism disregarding the equal rights of other nationalities, or economic imperialism of the politically and economically stronger countries, or conflict and wars even among democracies, or conflicts and tensions even among "socialist" countries.

The emphasis of the article thus was on the utopianism of political idealism. But this was not meant as a defense of, or resignation to, the extremism political realism often meant in practice. Just the opposite. The main thrust of the book (only briefly referred to in the article) is on what I called "realist liberalism"—an attempt, while starting from the recognition of the "realist" facts (security dilemma, etc.), to ameliorate and mitigate its consequences and to devise policies to do so without indulging in unrealizable expectations. Thus the classical balance of power was power mitigating at least inasmuch as it served to prevent the hegemony of one power (similarly, in domestic affairs, systems of "checks and balances" and of setting up independent judiciaries have served to inhibit the rise of one power, e.g., the Executive, to authoritarian predominance). But I did not overlook the difficulties in combining realism and idealism. The facts observed by realism are in agreement with the, so to speak, "natural" inclination of men and societies first to look out for themselves and their survival. Realist liberalism thus, in a way, is "antinatural" and has to trace its way patiently and laboriously through the obstacles caused by realist inclinations. It must be intent on avoiding not only utopian wishful thinking (and acting) but also the extremes to which realists in practice may lead men and nations—an unmitigated struggle for dominance that ends in tension, hatred, confrontation, and war. The "Gordian-knot" solution has always been the easy way out, compared with which the attempt to mitigate power and guide action into the direction of more rational policies of cooperation and balance is a thankless job. But the rewards of the latter, in terms of peaceful solution of issues, are greater. This was particularly so in an age when the confrontation of two, and only two, power blocs, armed with conflicting ideologies and annihilating weapons, was now threatening the survival of mankind. If, in book as well as article, the chief emphasis seemed to be on warning of the pitfalls of political idealism, this was due to the fact that, when I conceived of it, we were still (to quote my Preface to the book) "in an era of greater hopefulness. . . . It seemed then appropriate to stress the 'power facts' slightly more than the 'liberal ideal.' Since then the pendulum has swung to the other side. . . . The public, in the major countries, has become almost cynically ready to play the power game. There is thus ground for reemphasizing the liberal ideal to which a policy of Realist Liberalism must remain committed lest it degenerate into unmitigated, power-glorifying, force-obsessed Political Realism."

But if, in the new nuclear-bipolar age, neither the classical multipartite balance-of-power system nor a genuine collective security system was realizable any longer, what was to take their place? What situation were we now confronting? I tried to answer this question in my second book, of which the article "Rise and Demise of the Territorial State" constitutes a partial condensation.

IV

First of all, I asked: what accounts in history for the emergence of the great variety of units which are, in different periods, the highest ones, engaging in "international relations" and of vastly differing types: tribes, city-states, nation-states, empires, and so forth? While traditional theory emphasized economic factors, cultural development, or the emergence of some great personalities ("empire-builders"), my conclusion was that, ultimately, it has always been the need felt by individuals and groups to be protected from outside attack that induces them to unite—despite internal division in classes or similar, often antagonistic groups—in units that can guarantee at least a measure of protection. The politically basic unit is that which can afford its people protection and security. This, in turn, depends on the defensibility of the unit, i.e., the development of the means of defense: military and weapons technology. Recognizing that economic and similar developments certainly had an impact on the emergence of the respective units as well, I did not intend to indulge in a "strategic determinism" comparable to Marx's economic determinism concerning the "means of production"; however, to some extent, developments in the field of politics, and here especially in that of international affairs, seemed to be interpretable as "superstructure" over the development of the "means of destruction."

My chief emphasis was on the transition from the relatively weak and small political units of the European Middle Ages (fortified castle or manor, walled city) to the larger units that became known as territorial or nation-states. The "gunpowder revolution" enabled rulers, with the aid of artillery and standing armies, to eliminate feudal powers within larger areas which they now could protect by surrounding them with a "hard shell" of fortifications, making them, to some extent, impenetrable to similarly established neighbors. Impermeability, of course, was not absolute. In war even big powers might prove penetrable. Smaller ones had anyway to rely on alliances with stronger powers. On the whole, however, a surprisingly stable system emerged. Despite the absence of a recognized superior authority (such as pope or emperor in the Middle Ages), balance-of-power diplomacy (engaged in, above all, by England as the "holder of the balance"), by preventing the emergence of hegemony (of France under Napoleon, for instance), enabled a system of "sovereign," independent powers to coexist for centuries. Its basis was "territoriality" of units in the sense of military protectedness and impermeability. Contributing to its effectiveness were relatively limited means of warfare (favoring defense) and hesitancy completely to wipe out units even through successful war—a hesitancy that, initially, was based on the common interest of dynasties in preserving a system of monarchical legitimacy and, subsequently in the age of nationalism, on a hesitation to destroy "nation"-states.

But the nineteenth century witnessed developments that foreshadowed a transition from sovereignty to interdependence, from impermeability to penetrability. I refer to the article for nonstrategic examples. The two decisive strategic developments were air war and the atom bomb. With the advent of "vertical" penetrability, the roof was off the formerly protected "hard shell" units. The end effect, now that two so-called superpowers had acquired sufficient nuclear power mutually to annihilate each other, seemed absolute insecurity through absolute exposure to destructive penetration. The territorial state seemed to have lost its protective function. Was there anything to take its place? Would "international" relations still be possible in the nuclear age? If so, what would they be like?

According to my theory of (relative) "strategic determinism," what actually happened in the nuclear age had a certain logic: increased vulnerability of even the strongest nations caused them to replace a multiplicity of now "too small" lesser states by blocs where the hard shell formerly girding nation-states would be extended to the outer reaches of the blocs. There would now be two halves of the world, each under the leadership of one of the superpowers, each trying to establish its control wherever there was still space left by the other, through bases all around the world, stationing troops and installations (including nuclear ones) at the respective rim. This is what characterized the new-style postwar alliances established by West and East: NATO, Warsaw Pact, etc. What this meant for, and was new in the relations between the blocs and, within the blocs, between "leading power" and "allies" (which, in reality, were now becoming client-states, or "satellites") is discussed in more detail in my book.

But it would have been a mistake to analyze the new situation as merely a repetition, on a higher level, of what had happened before in history: the substitution of larger territorial units (the two power blocs) for the obsolete, pre-World War II nation-state. Now, even control of half the globe no longer offered security because of the capacity of the new weapon to carry annihilation from center to center. The world had become too small for traditional territoriality and the protection it had provided. Only temporarily, so it seemed, could some balance of sorts, a bipolar balance, be established on the basis of what seemed to prevent the nuclear holocaust: nuclear deterrence (hence, "balance of terror").

Indeed, the effect of the mutual threat of nuclear annihilation, in the opinion of many, would guarantee permanent peace. Who would be foolish enough to initiate a nuclear war when he had to expect deadly retaliation? It is true that the system, contrary to the fears of many at the beginning of the atomic age, *has* so far prevented the use of the nuclear weapon. Still, the optimism thus created seemed rather facile. In "International Politics and the Nuclear Dilemma" (chapter 4) I tried to list, among others, the numerous "gaps" in the system of mutual deterrence: political (in what case of attack, by conventional means or only nuclear ones; attack only on one's own territory or also on that of an ally—even the term "attack" or "aggression" remained undefined—would one retaliate, and how?); psychological (e.g., would one react by nuclear means in case of impending defeat in conventional war: "nuclear war of desperation"?); technical (wrong interpretation of some radar signal: "nuclear war by mistake"); or plain human failure (disregard of orders, insanity). Judging from the tensions of the cold-war situation, its recurring crises and confrontations, its widening range of competition for power and influence (especially in the emerging Third World of newly independent countries), and even from the multiplying conflicts within the blocs between superpower and clients (which in the case of the communist bloc, with the defection of China, meant actual splitup of the camp), it seemed unlikely that the world could escape nuclear devastation indefinitely. Thus I concluded that only a radical change in attitudes and policies could, in the long run, save the world from disaster. I called that attitude "universalist"; it would be based upon a realization that would impose itself eventually on all. To wit: that which in earlier periods had to be considered utopian, namely, to subordinate national interests to internationalist ideals, now, with the total threat of demise to all, had itself become an overriding interest. Giving up national controls over nuclear weapons as well as an international approach to the solution of demographic and ecological problems were now in the interest of nations and men exactly as much as defensibility, national wealth, etc., had been before.

As a realist, however, I had to give due attention to the obstacles in the way of such radical attitudinal reversal. I therefore proposed a kind of "holding operation" that would give mankind a chance to stop and reflect: a chance to inaugurate arms control and reduction of armaments as well as prevention of nuclear proliferation in the strategic sphere; also, so I hoped, there would be an agreement on what constitutes aggression and a more clear-cut definition of the *casus belli nuclearis,* i.e., of the circumstances in which there would be nuclear retaliation. In the political sphere one might recognize the de facto boundaries between the two blocs as delimitation of bloc spheres in which each side would agree not to interfere—in other words, recognition of the territorial status established after the war. One might try to reduce ideological tension by scaling down charges of "communist conspiracy" and "capitalist imperialism" and similar mutual recrimination, and to substitute for a spirit of crusade more sober policies of détente and "peaceful coexistence."

The reader may conclude from this by no means exhaustive list how much (or how little) has been realized so far in practice: little, if anything, in the field of weapons and armaments; on the contrary, proliferation despite nonproliferation treaties; increase (not only quantitative but qualitative) of weapons and delivery systems in a by now meaningless effort to achieve, or maintain, nuclear "superiority"; and so forth. On the other hand, after, and in consequence of, the most dangerous confrontation of all, the Cuban missile crisis, an amount of détente combined with some measure of deideologization has reversed, at least temporarily, the cold-war rush into oblivion. As a result, nation-states as units of protection seem to have gained a new lease on life. Perhaps because of a misinterpretation of the word "demise" used in the title of my article I had caused some readers to assume that I had predicted the impending disappearance of the nation-state.

This, of course, was not so. Still, the apparent stabilization of the nation-state system in the 1960s caused me to "revisit" my earlier theses on territoriality, which I did in an article ("The Territorial State Revisited"; chapter 8 in this volume) I shall briefly deal with here outside the chronological sequence of the essays.

V

The first reason for a restrengthening of territoriality I distinguished in this article was the end of empire, i.e., of colonialism, with its concomitant emergence of large numbers of territorial states in the now so-called Third World. Many of these were imbued with a strong sense of national identity and thus less amenable to inclusion in either of the bloc spheres; they tended to be nonaligned. This trend coincided with a turn toward deradicalization by the communist countries, in particular, the Soviet Union. Even in cases of "wars for liberation" they now refrained from direct interference or participation, leaving it to the respective people to gain their "freedom from colonialism and imperialism" through their own efforts. The United States, as has become clear from the elaborate documentation now available on intervention in Vietnam, Chile, Greece, etc., was less inclined to leave nations and regimes—in this case, left-leaning ones—alone.[11]

11. Something, perhaps, should be said at this point about Vietnam. In the immediate postwar period, when the struggle against colonialism had begun in many parts of the world, my personal view was that, not only morally but for very practical reasons, Churchill's well-known statement that he "was not to preside over the liquidation of Her Majesty's Empire" disregarded the "winds of change" his successor was to recognize, to the benefit of a generally peaceful transition from British rule to self-determination. Not so others, such as France and, particularly, the U.S. We have here a supreme illustration of the impact of "perception." The U.S. came to see the postwar world in ideological, bipolar colors, free world vs. communism. What happened in the Third World was perceived chiefly under these viewpoints. The overlooked force was nationalism, the urge everywhere in the colonial world to be free from the rule of the white man and the economic exploitation and racist indignities this rule implied. Vietnam, right from the beginnings of its fight against French rule, was an example of this urge. That Ho Chi Minh, a communist, controlled the movement, was secondary to most Vietnamese. Eisenhower, in 1954, knew that a vast majority of the Vietnamese, North and

Even so, a second factor favoring statehood intervened, something I called the "unavailability of force," in particular, nuclear force. The weapon was just too massive to be used in guerrilla warfare. In addition, doubts whether they could actually rely on the nuclear deterrent in the case of threats to them rather than to the superpower rendered bloc countries on both sides more autonomy-minded. In some cases, such as France, it caused them to build their own *forces de frappe,* which, while certainly not very convincing as deterrents against the big ones, heightened national confidence. Gaullism, in this more general sense, spread through both blocs. Furthermore, détente between the superpowers by its very nature caused the bloc systems, NATO and Warsaw Pact, to appear less vital, and its members to feel less in need of protection. If only, so I argued, the vastly increased number of nation-states, and especially the new ones, could be rendered more "legitimate," both in terms of internal structure and of boundaries, a world of territorial states could still be expected to become more stable in respect to units themselves and their interrelations. I did not fail to recognize the lack of such legitimacy in many of the new states, often artificial units established within the arbitrary boundaries carved out by former colonial rulers and beset with tribal and similar struggles. But I expected much from their modernization, which would involve "nation building" on a large scale. More will be said below about the problem of their "legitimacy." Suffice it to say here that today I regard the chances as well as the blessings of "development," "modernity," and industrialization more skeptically. The ability of nations—both new and old—to fulfill the minimum

---

South, saw in Ho a *national* leader. We might have backed him against the ineffective and corrupt regime set up by the French, and created a Tito. Instead, when the French had finally seen the light and given up, we gradually slipped into their role as white colonial oppressors, complete with backing up corrupt and oppressive regimes. Imagine we had decided to back up the Dutch when they were trying to resist the Indonesian fight for independence; we would have gotten into the same "quagmire" as we did in Indochina. But ideological blinders prevented U.S. leadership—military and civilian—from seeing the real issue. Even today, the discussion of the "why's" (why did we get involved, what caused defeat?) for the most part remains strangely remote from the real reason, indigenous nationalism, with the "fish-in-water" situation created by nationalism and benefiting the liberation forces in their guerrilla warfare.

functions lending them internal and external legitimacy has become more questionable; in particular, my assumption that industrialization would render nations more independent from outside resources has been drastically disproved (oil and energy crises!). Reading over that piece, I am tempted to write a third one on "The Territorial State Re-revisited"! It would have to take into consideration the whole gamut of nonstrategic and nonnuclear factors that now imperil the functioning of states big and small, from food and energy crises to the pollution of the environment in which we live, threats that do not respect either boundaries or the sovereignty of states.

VI

My concern turned toward these problems in the 1960s, but before discussing the corresponding essays, I shall refer briefly to some of the political problems involved in power polarization, cold-war crises, and "détente." They were first dealt with in "The Relevancy and Irrelevancy of Appeasement," which I discuss here in conjunction with a more recent piece, "Détente and Appeasement from a Political Scientist's Vantage Point," that pursues the arguments surrounding appeasement and détente up to the present.

Since the dawn of the nuclear age, or at least since the acquisition of the H-bomb by the Soviets, the world has been in a permanent state of emergency, its survival depending on the pushing of a button. No wonder that realizing this fact led not only to the pursuit of an accumulation of power and its concentration in two power poles but also to an increasingly acrimonious debate and an ideological antagonism reinforced by the conflict between two worlds endowed with opposed political, economic, and social systems. In such a situation each side is tempted to see in any policy or step not entirely antagonistic to the other side a retreat that, in view of the appeasement policies of the 1930s, would encounter the stigma of a "Munich." One seemed to have learned a lesson: never give in to an "aggressor." The question was: was the lesson correctly applied?

In the first of the two articles I tried to develop a theory of appeasement in historical perspective. Appeasement is one possible reaction in a continuum of attitudes in a conflict situation that ranges from the use of force over intransigence ("stand-pattism"), compromise-readiness, to concessions to "appease" the opponent, joining him to share in the spoils, and, finally, unconditional surrender. In the age of the "classical" balance-of-power system, appeasement was the "wrong" policy whenever an insatiable power or leader was striving for hegemony; here, only stand-pattism (or, if it was too late for that, joint use of force) could restrain the "aggressor." This was the lesson of Munich. Was the postwar world comparable?

I believed, and still hold, that it is not. There was, first, the new nature of war. The cost of "general," i.e., all-out nuclear war, had become unacceptable for would-be aggressors. Even a Stalin, supposing he was bent on world conquest, could not act like Hitler without risking his own demise. He might go to the brink (as might his Western opponents, such as Dulles) but, as Berlin and similar crises showed, would refrain from going over it. In addition, as indicated earlier, both sides were primarily intent on keeping, and defending, what they had gained in the war, that is, the maintenance of the bipolar balance, and not, in contrast to the expansionism of the Axis powers in the 1930s, in overthrowing the balance. Thus the tacit agreement not to interfere with what was going on in the opponent's realm (noticeable long before the turn from cold war to détente, e.g., on the Soviet side, noninterference in the postwar Greek civil war or in Berlin, and on the Western side, noninterference in cases like the East German uprising of 1953 or the Hungarian revolution). Hence the symmetry of mutual "appeasement" reproaches in the Cuban missile crises. In the U.S. some felt that Stevenson "wanted a Munich"; the Chinese thought that Khrushchev had "capitulated." In a situation of stalemate, any concession, no matter how slight, is bound to be called appeasement by extremists; but as long as those in charge are interested in balance rather than expansion, it is bootless to talk of appeasement or "giveaway" when concession is balanced by counter-concession. The only meaningful alternatives are stand-pattism and détente.

When, under the impact of the Cuban crisis, stand-pattism,

hallmark of the policies of the powers up to that time, yielded to an effort to relax tension and solve issues by compromise, the new "détente" policy, unsurprisingly, ran into even more violent charges of "appeasement." The term détente seems to have acquired the same pejorative meaning as the term appeasement (which originally had meant a bona fide effort to come to terms with compromise-ready opponents) acquired in the 1930s. This seems to me unjustified. Despite SALT and similar agreements, détente has achieved little in the field of arms control, and yet cries of "surrender" have accompanied each small step forward (the incomplete nuclear test ban, the largely unsuccessful nonproliferation treaty).

In the area of political relationships the main thrust of détente has been toward recognizing of de facto regimes and de facto territorial settlements. The United States has normalized its relations with Communist China, and this recognition of the PRC lends itself to potentially increased stability in East Asia, with four major powers being mutually interested in, e.g., keeping the peace on the Korean peninsula. But the major effect of détente has been in Europe. The one factor that threatened postwar stability there had been the "German Question," i.e., the partition of Germany and the question of its eastern boundaries. The aforementioned tacit recognition of the postwar settlement had conflicted with Western insistence on the right of Germans to be reunited "in freedom," that is, through Eastern abandonment of the GDR. But a situation is never really stable where a major actor is revisionist. Attesting to the sober realism that spread in West Germany in the 1960s was Chancellor Brandt's *Ostpolitik*; initiative could finally be taken to reverse revisionist policy, recognize the existence of a second Germany, accede to the boundaries established after the war, and thus enable East and West to ratify formally (at Helsinki) the status quo that had emerged from that war.[12] There was no "appeasement" in this. "Nothing—as Brandt had said at the signing of the Moscow Treaty—is given up that was not gambled away long ago" (that is, through Hitler's follies). If some Western voices still bemoan the "legitimization of the

12. For details, see my chapter on "Germany" in *Divided Nations in a Divided World*, ed. G. Henderson, R. Lebow, and J. H. Stoessinger (New York: David McKay, 1974), pp. 3–41.

Soviet empire" allegedly implied in *Ostpolitik* and détente, this merely reflects the unrealistic nature of the attitudes and policies of "nonrecognition" where there is no actual chance (that is, in our times, without risking nuclear war) to redress the "nonrecognized" situation. This applies to Poland or the Baltic states as it did to the GDR or the PRC. Such pragmatic recognition does not, or should not, imply moral approbation. Both sides should feel free to criticize, and détente leaves at least a hope to prod the Eastern regimes into alleviating the crudest and, under liberal standards, most objectionable features of their systems.

Does the Near East disprove the expectations of the détentists? This is not the place to go into details, but in my view, as long as the Soviets recognize Israel's right to existence it is a question of boundaries, and of how best to secure her safety. Nothing, so far, has indicated a desire on the part of the Soviets to join forces with those who would wipe out Israel. Thus here, as in the general area of the Near East (and, indeed, beyond—in the Indian Ocean, for instance), it is a problem of how best to maintain power equilibrium, and therewith stability. Interventionist tendencies exist on *both* sides, and it is above all the question of oil and the powers' energy policies that destabilizes the situation in the area. About this, more will be said below.

VII

I started this introductory essay with a reference to the changes in the perception of the world which underlie one's attitudes toward international relations. The most radical turn in my own perceptions occurred in the early 1960s when I became more fully aware of the phenomenon of "acceleration" of events and developments that, in an entirely novel way, affects radically *all* fields of human relations and thus must affect the political ones, too.

True, acceleration had already been observed in the field of armaments (rise in the rate of the destructiveness of weapons, etc.), and I had stressed its results (on statehood, for instance) in previous writings. I now conceived of it as a general process that, for the first time in history, renders the "civilizational process," the progress of science and technology, the overriding one, eclipsing all else in cultural, political, or similar (often not one-directional but cyclical or random) processes. I had tried to analyze this J-curve acceleration process in its effect on such diverse fields as population rise, rise in volume of information, speed of transportation and communication, intermingling of people, use and depletion of nonrenewable resources, and pollution and similar environmental degradation in a book-length study tentatively called "International Politics in the Technological Age, An Analysis of the Role of Acceleration and Petrification in World Affairs" which, for personal reasons, could not be completed in publishable form. I have, however, included here its somewhat shortened concluding chapter, "The Civilizational Process and Its Reversal." In this collection it is printed *after* "The Impact of the Technological-Scientific Process on the International System," an essay I wrote later that summarizes the more strictly political conclusions of my manuscript, because some of the basic terms used in it are explained in the last-named piece.

For reasons of space, I cannot go into details of "The Civilizational Process." Basically, however, it is concerned with the impact an unchained, relentless, and one-directional technological progress has on minds and attitudes. The essay constitutes what Germans call *Kulturkritik,* an indictment of the impoverishment of feeling, the loss of diversity and individuality, the disappearance of interest in the "human" features of an ever more mechanized environment that threaten man and his societies as we have known them. In this, my thesis resembled Herbert Marcuse's criticism of "one-dimensional man," which I had not read at that time. It calls for a "great reversal," one that, in contrast to Marcuse, was to occur in general attitudes rather than in specific political action. I tried to develop a new ethic of how to behave humanely under the pressures of the ongoing technological process. In some respects the essay still reflected assumptions of the 1950s, e.g., that economic "abundance" was possible at least in industrialized societies (although I already doubted whether such "affluence" actually meant improvement of what today is discussed under the heading of "quality of life"). I was, however, fully aware of the global threats involved in regard to the developed as well as the underdeveloped portions of mankind and of the global survival problems posed, e.g., by exploding populations and exploding cities. I therefore called for a "great reversal" in man's reaction to the civilizational process, for a "conservative liberalism" (conservative in the sense of "conserving" and "preserving" the humane traditions of human civilizations), and for a campaign of "technological disobedience" in the face of technological conformism. Remember that all this was written prior to the "great revolt," especially of the young, that occurred in the later 1960s, which evinced many of the attitudinal features I had called for. Whether that revolt—considering the new conformism of the 1970s—will prove to have been more than a transitory phenomenon is one of the fateful questions of the future.

In "The Impact of the Technological-Scientific Process" I tried to trace some of the impacts of the process on international relations. Thus, the technological-scientific process had for the first time rendered true "world politics" possible through establishing one planetary universe of communication and concerns. Speed of communication renders distance almost nugatory; "remote sensing" and scanning, as from orbiting satellites, enables one to observe in minute detail what is going on anywhere on earth (e.g., enabling nuclear powers to "inspect" each others' installations without entering their territory—another instance of "penetrability"—but also "snooping" into the affairs of everybody). It involves the speeding up of diplomatic processes, foreign-policy decision making, crises and their solution—something positive if it leads to peaceful solutions, negative if it leaves only minutes to decide between peace or war. It likewise means concentration of ever more power in ever fewer power centers and decision makers. So much about processes.

In regard to technology's impact on systems (internal as well as international ones), the article distinguishes two opposite trends. One I call "petrification," that is, increasing uniformity of life styles and institutions in the world, a "rush into the conformity of modernity" that is about to transform nature all over the world into the synthetic habitat of a technologized world. This affects East and West alike, and also the world's "South," whose overriding objective, even ideology, is that of modernization through economic growth. In regard to East-West relations I believed at that time in "convergence," at least as far as style of life of man in mass society was concerned. If this would bring about a rapprochement in political relationships (détente), this might be all to the good; but I now have doubts in regard to some of its effects. It may also mean—and has already meant—that the big ones, having eliminated some of their conflicts, jointly lord it over the smaller ones, in particular (under the principle of nonintervention into the other's sphere) those included in one's own bloc (as one observer has said, apropos the Soviet invasion of Czechoslovakia in 1968, "the only country a big power can still attack with impunity is one of its allies"). Among many non-superpowers there is a fear of a coming "condominium" of the United States and the Soviet Union over the world.[13]

The paradox is that, beneath uniformity and apparent stability, loom instability and the threat of utter chaos. This is the result not only of the ongoing process of armaments and armament races but also of the destabilizing effects of unchecked population increase (with rural people flocking to the shantytowns of the cities); threats of exhaustion of scarce resources; and, above all, the widening gap in living standards between the (still) rich and the poor, the world's "North" and the "South." These developments threaten the legitimacy and even the cohesion of nations, the authority of their governments, the rationality and consistency of their policies. The growing incidence of violence (both from above and below), terrorism, and similar phenomena point up the brittleness of what, on the surface, appears as stability. The reality spells rapid change and accelerating transformation. It is with the problems thus created that the world has now to cope.

13. Alastair Buchan speaks of "adversary partners" ("The Indochina War and World Politics," Foreign Affairs, July 1975, p. 642); William T. R. Fox, of "enemy brothers who cannot make war and cannot make peace" ("Pluralism, the Science of Politics, and the World System," World Politics, July 1975, p. 600); Henry Kissinger, of "being doomed to coexist" (on "Meet the Press," 12 October 1975). Jonathan Schell ("Reflections," New Yorker, 23 June 1975, p. 77), referring to the Nixon-Brezhnev détente at the time Nixon was blocking Haiphong Harbor to Soviet vessels, remarks: "The two behemoths were fusing at the head while continuing to kick one another with their feet."

VIII

Concern with the fact that the study of international relations seemed to pay little attention to these increasingly urgent problems caused me to write the only article dealing with method included in this collection, "Relevancies and Irrelevancies in the Study of International Relations." Indeed, it appeared to me in the late 1960s that for some ten years I had become somewhat separated from the main thrust of what my coworkers in that vineyard, especially the younger ones, were doing. They claimed that they were substituting "scientific" investigation based on quantifiable data and systems models derived therefrom for the traditionalist, historical "impressionistic" approach. I decided to select at random a number of pieces reflecting the new methods from one of the best-known readers for courses in international politics and to assess their findings. The results were disappointing, and this not so much because of the methods used (there is much that is helpful in data collection, systems analysis, gaming, simulation, content analysis) but because of an apparent inability to distinguish the trivial from the relevant. Apparently, what can be counted will be counted, what can be measured must be measured. Counting the number of times some delegate to some international convention talked with another one (without even knowing what they talked about) seemed as important as analyzing alliance relationships. In view of the urgency of finding solutions to the great world problems, this kind of enterprise seemed not only worthless but also a waste of funds, time, and expert talent, of which we are in critically short supply.

I suggested instead to consider political science a result-oriented effort ("policy science") which, in this respect comparable to medicine, would base itself on all available findings of sociology, economy, psychology, etc. (exactly as medicine is based on biology, etc.) and then propose solutions for the problems confronting us in the political arena. How, in this respect, distinguish the "relevant" from the "trivial"? I admit that, in previous periods, people (including scholars) might honestly differ in normative evaluations of this sort but suggest that, where the survival of the human race is at stake, relevance can be defined as that which, directly or indirectly, is concerned with survival problems. This embraces not only the power relations of nations, the future of nation-states, the increasing role of nonstate units (such as MNEs, or multinational enterprises), questions of arms and how to control them, and the like, but also ecological, demographic, world economic, and related questions. I drew up a list (necessarily incomplete) of problem areas which, it seemed to me, had been neglected, and I am proud to have mentioned in this respect a field of study that was in its infancy at the time but now has captured the imagination of many an excellent researcher, namely, how foreign policy decisions are arrived at (I may perhaps be allowed to remark critically that too much emphasis is still being placed on so-called bureaucratic impacts and inputs, while, despite ITT–Chilean-type revelations, those by business and other interest groups are largely neglected). I may, perhaps, also claim that, in view of more recent revelations about the pervasiveness of the "covert" activities of intelligence agencies, my call for studying these agencies was timely.

Our efforts in the international relations field, I concluded, must be future-oriented. "Futurology," in this instance, turns into conflict theory and peace research, two interconnected areas ever more prominent of late. But we have little time. And the question arises: how to make sure that study remains "objective," i.e., keeps the overriding interests of "survival" on a global level in mind. Planning the future depends on who controls the research topics and the priorities, who selects the researchers, etc. Futures, too, can be preempted, and the "establishments" (e.g., government agencies, foundations) that have most of the funds and exercise most of the controls may thus determine the outcome of the research. Here lies the importance of influence-free academic and similar endeavor wherever such freedom is still available.

IX

The last essay included in this collection, "Technology, Ethics, and International Relations," is a *pièce d'occasion* in which I tried to sum up much of what I had said in earlier pieces, but this time chiefly in terms of normative standards that now must guide policy makers if survival is to be assured. Formerly—as I had pointed out before—"universalist" or internationalist ethical norms had usually to be disregarded in favor of what the "national interest," the preservation and security of the group for which the policy maker felt responsible, required. Thus there was the traditional conflict between "ethics and power politics," with the latter prevailing in practice. But now that the continuance of the human race (or, perchance, all life on earth) is at stake, a "minimum ethic of survival" must override individual or group ethical standards. Thus, to mention just one example, where in former times a catastrophe such as famine might hit an area included in a colonial empire, say India, and the non-British countries of the world could dissociate themselves from dealing with the problem, it could now no longer be considered "somebody else's" problem but must be dealt with in the comprehensive context of the entire world's food supply. Such a minimum ethic may well clash with norms of traditional ethical systems that, for instance, prescribe improving health, combating epidemics, fighting infant mortality, prolonging individual life. But in a situation of population outrunning food supplies and other necessities, priority (e.g., in foreign assistance) must be given to family planning, birth control, providing agricultural machinery and technology, fertilizers, and so forth, over programs for improvement of health, hygiene, etc. If this sounds immoral under traditional standards, it is the emergency situation that renders it necessary. Would it not be even more cruel to allow infants to survive only to be condemned later to almost certain death through malnutrition? [14]

Survival ethic thus has two dimensions which traditional ethical systems lack: in terms of space it must embrace the

14. At this writing the papers report a "triumph of medicine": smallpox is about to be eradicated from the earth. The paradox of mankind's plight is marked by the fact that the last cases of smallpox now being dealt with are occurring in Bangladesh, "basket case" among the poor countries of the world (as Kissinger so elegantly called it), where millions of an exploding population are likely to be "eradicated" through famine, malnutrition, and nutrition-related diseases in the near future. In the health field, of course, priority should be given to eradicating debilitating but nonkilling diseases.

community of mankind as a whole and overrule particularist interests; in terms of time it must take the interests of future generations into consideration to make sure that there will be any future for man. It is thus an issue of the long term vs. the short term, humanity vs. the smaller groups it embraces. It is not an ethic of "starry-eyed idealism." On the contrary, it must try to utilize for its purposes what has been proved practicable. Thus, institutions already tested, such as international peacekeeping forces, may be applied to the enforcement of rules for the protection of the environment; an international sea patrol, for instance, might be established to control the oceans beyond territorial waters and to seize and punish polluters or those who overexploit the living resources of the sea. Such steps, of course, require new rules of international law; new international agencies or increased powers of existing ones; and also, in view of lack of time, agreement on new rule-making procedures that are speedier than the ones developed by diplomacy in more leisurely times. Survival ethic, to be effective, must and can be both realistic and practical.

X

Having summarized the essays assembled in this volume, I could leave it at this; however, at the risk of repeating myself, I propose, on the remaining pages of this Introduction, to delve further into the nation-state system as it appears to me today and study its functioning (or malfunctioning) in the face of the world crisis.

The first impression that imposes itself upon anyone who surveys the present, approximately 150 self-styled independent states is that of utmost variety, if not incongruity. What has a superpower in common with, for instance, the growing number of "micro-states," most of them barely viable, frequently little islands or island groups inhabited by less than 100,000 people, lacking skills, resources, means of defense? Clearly there has been failure to cope with the inheritance left by decaying old-style empires. In the latest, still ongoing, case of Portugal, for instance, there has emerged one—so one may hope—viable unit, Mozambique; Angola was threatened with strife and disintegration even prior to official independence; so is Timor. Others, such as the island of Sao Thomé, may become alluring to some power as naval bases or may otherwise fall victim to external manipulation if strategically located or "fortunate" enough to have some exploitable resources. The rest will rot and decay. On the other hand, some of the oil-rich countries of the Near East try to build a new power status upon the dependence of the old industrialized countries on their resources; but even here, nationhood is often in doubt. Some of the new units in the area are hardly more than stretches of desert sand covering pools of oil, and the inhabitants do not know whether they are "nations" individually or part and parcel of one overarching "Arab nation." One of the prime shortcomings of decolonization has been the failure, on the part of the emerging units, to define the "self" in claimed or achieved "self-determination." Once liberated from colonial rule, populations frequently do not know whether and how to live together (or apart). And even some of the oldest and most uncontested nation-states (France, with her Corsicans or Bretons; Britain with the Scots; Belgium; Canada) find themselves suddenly confronted with threats to their coherence, if not their national identity.

We may refer to the problems raised so far as those of "external legitimacy." A unit is legitimate in this sense when its population feels that it should live together within its established boundaries, i.e., that it should not be integrated into a larger unit or divided into smaller ones. If it is one of the functions of the nation-state, besides protection and welfare, to provide people with a group sense of identity, external legitimacy performs this task by setting them off from other people. But the process of "nation building" in this sense took a long time even in the home of nationhood, Europe. Even in the first of the "new" nations outside Europe, the United States, it took a civil war finally to establish one Union, and it took the originally artificial units of Latin America about a century to develop a sentiment of integrated nationhood. It would be asking too much to expect this to happen overnight, as it were, for most of the recent nations. And the attempts to render numbers of the less viable nations viable through federation have so far failed. Thus it will take a long time

before they will settle down in well-defined "national" units—
if at all. In the meantime their contribution to international
politics will consist in large measure of conflict, strife, destabil-
ization.[15]

If, thus, the impact of external legitimacy (or illegitimacy)
is pretty obvious, that of "internal legitimacy" (or its absence
or decline) is more elusive but no less real. Since, in my
opinion, it will have a growing impact not only on domestic but
also on international relations (and, there, in particular upon
the solution of the great global problems) it is discussed here in
some of its more important ramifications and effects.[16]

We may define the internal legitimacy of the state as the
feeling, or consensus, on the part of the vast majority of the
people living within a state's confines that those who rule fulfill
the functions of protection and welfare in the name of and for
the people as a whole; this, at least, is the presently accepted
version, a democratic one (in contrast to a formerly widespread but now almost extinct oligarchic, feudal, or dynastic
legitimacy). Even autocratic or totalitarian regimes pay tribute
to democratic virtue by erecting façades of democratic institutions and procedures (pseudo elections, pseudo parliaments,
etc.) that are meant to conceal a reality where force is the
primary foundation of rulership. One can thus use Max
Weber's famous formula (according to which the modern state
is characterized by having "a monopoly of the legitimate use of
force" in a given territory) by ranging countries from a pole of

15. This has been a major failure of the United Nations. Membership in
the world organization having become a status symbol among nations, each
new one aspires to be admitted right away. The organization (as did the
League of Nations) should have made membership dependent on minimum
requirements concerning size, population, perhaps even defensibility. This
would have avoided the oftentimes grotesque discrepancy between actual
strength and formal equality of members, whose consequences threaten the
effectiveness of the organization.

16. I have dealt with this in some more detail in a section of a book
published in Germany, to which the German readers are referred ("Gedanken
über Legitimität, Gewalt und die Zukunft des Staates," in John H. Herz,
Staatenwelt und Weltpolitik [Hamburg, 1974], pp. 183 ff.). What follows here
is more "impressionistic" than "scientific." A more scholarly study of
legitimacy would have to analyze sentiments and attitude structures of the
various strata of the respective societies in much more detail. It is here that
empirical political science (study of "political socialization," "political mobili-
zation," public opinion, etc.) could make a valuable and "legitimate" contribu-

genuine legitimacy to the pole of out-and-out coercion, with force the stronger (because more needed to uphold rule) the weaker is the legitimacy.

My thesis is that we live in an age of declining legitimacy even in regard to the traditionally most legitimate units. One reason—and here we meet the world problems again—lies in their inability to cope with problems of well-being that are now generally included in the term "welfare of the people": urban crowding and decay; environmental problems such as providing clean air, clean water; etc. But the process of loss of legitimacy goes farther back. I propose to analyze it briefly by reference to the United States.[17] In a country generally considered one of the most liberal and democratic there has occurred, over the last decades, a process of frozen socioeconomic status that is favorable to a majority but neglects disadvantaged minorities. One reason lies in the American political-constitutional framework. Never has a governmental system been more perfectly designed to inhibit governmental action. Its great achievement has been in its check on the concentration of power (as most recently illustrated by Watergate which, in essence, reflected an attempt to concentrate power in the Executive). A system of "constitutional limitations" enabled American society not only to preserve individual liberties but also to perform the task facing it during the first century of independence: to penetrate an entire continent through private enterprise uninhibited by state power. But with the end of the frontier and with new tasks confronting an industrialized country (regulating industry, protecting and integrating labor, etc.), a system favoring governmental *in*action has proved a

tion to predictive efforts concerning the future of the nation-state. But it must be a much more "in depth" study than the usual voting and survey research. It matters less, e.g., how people voted in certain elections; what matters is the degree of their political involvement or political alienation (who, which groups are indifferent or hostile to traditional politics, why, when, etc.). Comparative study of different countries (and/or classes and other groups in countries) is likewise of the essence. So is "longitudinal" research, such as legitimacy feelings at times of democratic decline (e.g., Weimar Germany, 1930–33), or initial periods of authoritarian or totalitarian control (e.g., Germany, 1933 ff.).

17. Here, too, I refer readers of German to a piece of mine, dealing with America: "Amerika—Land ohne Alternative?", first published in *Politische Vierteljahrsschrift* (1969), pp. 170 ff., and reprinted in Herz, *Staatenwelt und Weltpolitik*, pp. 143 ff.

major obstacle in the path toward the democratic "welfare state." It would belabor the obvious to list here the institutions and procedures which account for the difficulty to have great reform legislation enacted. Only in one of four constellations in the relations between the Executive and the Legislature, namely, when a reform-minded President could rely on an equally progressive congressional majority, could this be achieved: e.g., the New Deal under Franklin Roosevelt.[18] It hardly ever happened before or after. President Johnson's war against the poverty besetting (as it still does) at least a third of the nation, though supported by a congressional majority, was deflected toward foreign war, and therewith aborted.

But there is more to it, and this is where the American experience is, perhaps, paradigmatic of other industrialized democracies. As long as the masses of the people, such as an industrial proletariat, are economically underprivileged and/or socially not fully equal, it has been the function of democracy to integrate them into society through peaceful reform. But with the achievement of equality and a minimally comfortable living standard of a majority consisting of a middle class plus large portions of labor, democracy tends to become the political instrumentality for the defense of this status quo against the demands of still underprivileged strata. Even labor, once it has "arrived," tends to become conservative. This is true not only in America but also in a Europe where, at least in the traditional labor movement, there used to be a feeling of solidarity with *all* disadvantaged groups. In Europe the majority now tends to neglect those who correspond to America's "nonwhites" or "poor whites," such as foreign workers migrating from the Mediterranean countries northward or colored immigrants in Britain. Democratic legitimacy of such systems becomes questionable.

In America the process tends to split society into a functioning major portion and an inactive, at best welfare-

18. The other three, reform-preventing ones are: a reactionary or "do-nothing" President facing an equally conservative Congress; a do-nothing President facing, and inhibiting, a reformist Congress; a reformist President facing a conservative Congress. A "do-less-than-nothing" President, restraining a mildly progressive Congress through "rule by veto," is the present constellation.

recipient, "underclass" (Myrdal) living on a subsistence level (even actual hunger exists in many pockets) where unemployment is chronic and joblessness in the ghettoes becomes inherited. In addition, there now emerges a split within the majority itself. With "stagflation," or recession, becoming permanent or recurrent, the corporate system, under which wealth and income tends to become concentrated at the upper level of society, threatens others—workers, lower-level employees, small businessmen—with impoverishment and the end of the "affluence frontier." The top level, consisting of corporate executives plus a bevy of hangers-on (corporation lawyers, tax experts, accountants, lobbyists, etc.) manages to escape the effects of both inflation and depression by maintaining a system of "administered prices," high income of the top group, more or less corrupt practices (such as avoidance of taxation through tax loopholes), and securing favorable legislation and/or executive action through campaign financing or by opening its ranks (through promise of lucrative employment) to government officials in key positions. More and more, the state becomes a controlled rather than a controlling factor.[19]

Concentration of purchasing power in the upper class favors production of what appears, from the viewpoint of the community at large, as luxury and involves waste not only of the unproductive manpower of the hangers-on but—through the "throwaway system," the huge apparatus of unnecessary advertising, the "built-in obsolescence" of shoddy products—of raw material and energy resources. Hand in hand with this goes neglect of maintenance and proper repair of the "infrastructure" in housing, transportation, etc., that previous, more industrious generations erected. Moreover, with a large proportion of corporate production going into "defense," the system's tie-in with the state becomes complete. The degree of the subservience of the state to these new-style "feudal" powers is revealed whenever one of them meets financial difficulties: they can safely rely on being bailed out by the

19. For a couple of particularly "juicy" examples, see the article by James R. Phelan on Howard Hughes in New York *Times Magazine*, 14 September 1975; hardly exaggerating, Phelan sums it up by stating: "Equality under the law is an American ideal, but some Americans are more equal than others."

government. But when cities like New York, on whose services the lower classes and the poor depend in particular, encounter difficulties, there is neglect and punishment for "welfarism."

No wonder that this kind of political community faces a loss of legitimacy. This is expressed in widespread feelings of general "malaise," anomie, political apathy combined with contempt of "politics" and "politicians," drug addiction, vandalism, crime waves, and a steady rise in individual and group violence. This, in turn, impels the "establishment" to place increasing emphasis on, and spend ever larger funds for, the maintenance of "law and order," which, in turn, means "improved," increasingly militarized police forces; private guard systems; neglect of individual and group rights in cases of search and seizure, arrest and internment; inroads into citizens' privacy through "surveillance" by uncounted branches of intelligence, security, police, and similar authorities. Revelations in the wake of Watergate have shown how far police-state action patterns have gone even in traditionally free societies. Some of these actions, indeed, take on totalitarian coloration: medical experiments on humans with lethal drugs; plans to assassinate foreign (or even domestic?) leaders, etc.[20]

Matters have not (yet?) gone quite that far in other democracies; but the malaise is there, too. Thus, in the face of tiny groups of "urban guerrillas," West Germany, where "illiberalism" is never far from the surface, has engaged in a witch-hunt of "radicals." Even in England, mother of "bills of rights," we witness illiberal action patterns in the Ulster situation. In almost all parliamentary regimes with two major party groupings the public seems to become weary of an "alternation in power" that leaves the great problems of stagflation, environment pollution, etc., unsolved by either party. After both are given their chance and found wanting, there lurks the danger that democracy will decline and a "benign authoritarianism" or a "friendly fascism" will take

20. Even communist systems (probably less for moral than for doctrinal reasons; Marx's rejection of individual terror engaged in by Bakunin and the anarchists) have generally abstained from killing off foreign leaders. Fascists, however, did set precedents (Hitler and Austrian Chancellor Dollfuss, Mussolini and French Foreign Minister Louis Barthou, as well as King Alexander of Yugoslavia).

over (only that it might turn out to be much less benign and friendly than some foresee). History seems to teach that groups which have attained a certain living standard and social status but feel squeezed between still higher groups and proletarian lower strata (such as the lower middle class in Weimar Germany between upper bourgeoisie and workers, or American organized labor in between bourgeoisie and "subclass") are particularly susceptible to fascism. It may thus happen first in America.

The corporate system projects its legitimacy-destroying effect to the world of the "less developed countries" (LDCs) through its "multinational enterprises" (MNEs). "Multinational" is really a misnomer since these corporations, though active in all parts of the world, usually are national in terms of ownership, management, capitalization, etc.; that is, they are American, British, Japanese, or what not. A better term, therefore, would be "transnational enterprises." Anyway, instead of "modernizing" Third (or now Fourth) World countries so as to benefit the impoverished masses of their populations, most of what they invest, for example through practices of avoiding taxation, is returned to them, while the "export of technology" generally benefits a small emerging "native" upper class, in part consisting of MNE-bribed middlemen or government officials, that develops high living standards and endows its "modernizing" countries with modern cities complete with air-conditioned office buildings, Hilton hotels, jet airports, etc. The impoverished rural masses flock to these cities' inevitable shantytowns only to find worse living conditions and more misery there. At "best" the multinationals export the sweatshops of the Old World to countries like South Korea or Taiwan, whose cheap labor they prefer to higher-cost labor at home.[21]

21. How, especially in the case of the smaller countries, legitimacy vanishes when their "independence" is placed in jeopardy, may once more be illustrated by reference to Howard Hughes. Before moving to the (independent) Bahamas he told his handyman, Maheu: "I would expect you really to wrap that government up to a point where it would be—well—a captive entity in every way." Phelan, New York *Times*. It proved to be so when Hughes successfully avoided extradition requested by U.S. authorities. So, to this day, has another fraudulent business figure, Robert Vesco, who now seems to control another small LDC, Costa Rica.

Foreign aid programs conducted by governments rarely have had more desirable effects because most of them have similarly wrong priorities (nuclear plants or steel mills instead of slum-clearing or irrigation projects) and because over the years they tend to place the LDCs in debt for loan repayment and amortization, the sum total of which outpaces the aid input; anyway, governmental aid has been declining steeply of late. In sum, there has been little of that "poor-oriented, social-equity-focussed strategy of developmental assistance" [22] that is needed to salvage or create legitimacy in the LDCs.

The "new rich" (OPEC countries and others which manage to use oil or other resource monopolies to extract funds from the "old rich" consumer countries) have abused their new-found wealth in comparable fashion. Instead of improving their backward agricultural systems and their overcrowded metropolises or industrializing in a way that would benefit the living of their poor majorities (not to mention aid to their Fourth World brethren, who suffer most from an increase in energy prices), they try to imitate, if not outdo, the old rich by building up their armed forces (acquiring the most advanced weapons systems and in this way fulfilling ambitions to become at least regional "big powers") and, in the civilian sector, by putting a veneer of Western-style modernity on old-style Oriental misery. The Shah builds a new luxury Teheran with golden gates and palaces next to the old Teheran that still lacks a sewer system.

Even more than in the old developed countries, this type of modernization destroys traditional community loyalties and life styles. Thus there tends to be even less legitimacy sentiment than elsewhere, especially in new "nations" with artificial boundaries, tribal conflicts, and lack of "national" leadership. Indeed, after the overthrow of colonial rule and the demise of whatever charismatic and integrating leadership there may have been in the period of the struggle for independence, follow-up regimes tend to be so weak and inefficient that legitimacy declines rapidly; rule of force, that is, military rule, prevails even where originally there had been a genuine effort

22. L. A. Dunn, "Past as Prologue," *World Politics*, July 1975, p. 622.

to develop processes of democracy. Military, or military-backed (praetorian) dictatorship, that rock-bottom type of rulership, spreads throughout the less developed world, leaving few islands of democracy. Even in some older countries, like Argentina, or now Lebanon, the result of constant feuding and battling of forces threatens to be anarchy in the literal sense of "absence of government."

If the foregoing sounds like "vulgar Marxist" interpretation, this may be due to developments of the capitalist system that by now actually do lend themselves to such interpretation. Hardly ever before have business interests had so strong an impact on governments all over the world. But let us reemphasize that in communist systems it is the very nature of their coercive regimes that makes for lack, or loss, of legitimacy. This is especially noticeable in the more recently established systems of Eastern Europe; but even in the Soviet Union, where the regime has had more than half a century to become "rooted," the astoundingly strong resurgence of dissidence points toward the same conclusion. In addition, attitudes toward resource depletion, population increase, and environment destruction resemble those found in the rest of the world. True, the motive of profit maximizing that impels private enterprise into expansion regardless of waste of resources and damage to environment is absent. Instead, a veritable euphoria of "growth" as well as ideological commitment to anti-Malthusian doctrine has meant neglect of population planning, resource conservation, and environment protection. The sky is as dark over East Germany as it is over West Germany. Only the Chinese seem to be an exception: Marxian anti-Malthusianism notwithstanding, they engage in apparently effective family planning (need it, too, with their more than 800 million people) and place the economic emphasis on agricultural production, decentralization of industries, avoidance of further urban sprawl, and the like. Only in the armament sector do they behave like the others (with the "security dilemma" playing its customary role, especially in regard to the perceived Soviet threat).

XI

We thus find a loss of legitimacy by nation-states all over the world and a corresponding turn toward the use of force and rule by force. The nation-state can regain its legitimacy qua state only if it turns from being more and more a "warfare state" into a genuine "welfare state"; and qua nation, even where it is integrated as a unit and thus has external legitimacy, only if it turns from ego-centered identification with itself toward becoming—in sentiments and action of leaders and people—a member of a worldwide community of nations, each feeling responsible for the future of all. Let us discuss the chief obstacles in the path of such a reversal and what can, perhaps, still be done about them.

Ill-defined boundaries create conflict and strife over territorial possessions—something that could well be ameliorated by referring more cases to the neglected jurisdiction of the International Court of Justice or other institutions of arbitration and adjudication. Additional conflict areas are created by growing economic interdependence (or unilateral dependencies) with ensuing temptations to resort to force. Thus the dependence of industrial countries on oil has led to OPEC "blackmail" and counter-threats to take over oilfields by force. But threats or the use of force are not restricted to nations. Developed societies, in particular, with their interconnected systems of energy supply, have become so vulnerable to sabotage that individual terrorists can stall their functioning through action upon key centers (power stations, telephone networks). Add to this the danger of "nuclear terrorism," rendered possible by countries with nuclear facilities neglecting to prevent diversion of waste material easily convertible into "little" bombs; the future harbors additional, and even more horrible, threats of plutonium diversion. This opens vistas not only of domestic but also of cross-boundary terror. It is one of the reasons why developed countries no longer have the option to withdraw into "fortresses" of their own (exactly as within the United States affluent suburbs can no longer seal themselves off from the effects of decaying or exploding inner cities). Even if the vast majority of the destitute outside the fortress were ready to starve in silence, there would still be those who would vent their despair and their hatred in violence. And they may well get away with blackmail—not the relatively mild type now in vogue of extorting money through kidnapping an occasional diplomat or wealthy business heir, but the nuclear-terrorist type. What if some group threatened to blow up an entire city unless a million tons of food were immediately shipped to a famine region? Of course, governments can play the same game, once they are in possession of the material needed. Population explosions, too, may render the walls of "fortresses" penetrable. With Mexican "wet-backs" already flooding parts of the United States, how can the tide be stemmed when, at the turn of the century, Mexico's population will have doubled to over 100 million?

Before asking what the role of the state can be in demographic and similar areas, let us briefly return to a problem that looms larger than the others in the writings here presented: armaments and security. Here, too, the picture is growing more somber. Despite its "gaps," the system of mutual deterrence did offer some "stability" that was based, politically, on de-ideologization and détente, and strategically on second-strike capacity and the nonproliferation of nuclears beyond the five great powers, three of which had remained inferior to the big two. It now seems that this (relatively) stable system is endangered. For one, mutual deterrence is in jeopardy. The United States is building a system of "cruise missiles" sufficiently accurate to deliver warheads to targets such as enemy missiles in their silos. Defense Secretaries Laird and Schlesinger have talked about using nuclear weapons in case of an opponent's "conventional" attack. A change of strategic doctrine toward counterforce targeting might well induce an opponent to strike "preemptively" to prevent his adversary's first strike. We would be back at utmost nuclear instability.

Second, nuclear capacity is spreading to nonnuclears through the export of nuclear technology officially designed for peaceful purposes but without the necessary safeguards to prevent receiving countries from using the acquired knowledge and/or facilities for producing nuclear weapons (this has happened already in Canada and India, and may well happen in cases of West Germany delivering to Brazil and South Africa, the United States to Egypt, the Soviet Union to Libya, France to South Korea, and so forth).

Third, we have an ongoing and accelerating armaments race in the field of conventional weapons, chiefly activated by the profit motive of competing defense industries in weapon-producing countries. It vividly illustrates the predominance of corporate interests over the "national" interests of their countries, since by now even the former rationale of assisting allies no longer applies. In almost absurdly irrational fashion one arms one's "friends" *and* their opponents, Israelis *and* Arabs, Iranians *and* Saudis, and so on. This enables increasing numbers of countries to engage in violent solutions of conflicts, and it also serves to strengthen the usually oppressive and dictatorial regimes internally. And, in the Fourth World in particular, it tempts governments that can afford arms only at the expense of the lamentably low living standards of the vast majority of their people to waste scarce funds and resources.

But even more wasteful and dangerous is the nuclear arms race among the superpowers, which continues unabated. Their piling of one nuclear weapons system on the other has become as senseless and irrational as the race in the sale of nonnuclear arms, for, once one possesses "overkill" capacities, there is no sense in striving for "superiority" (or being "Number One"). A former UN specialist on nuclear affairs thus could advocate convincingly an ultimate "cutback of all deterrent forces to ten percent of the present fleet of nuclear submarines" which would leave the United States, for instance, with 640 warheads, "a quite adequate deterrent. . . . Land-based missiles and bombers would be eliminated. This might even be done unilaterally, with the U.S., for instance, saying: 'We have enough. You go waste your money if you wish.' " [23]

23. See New York *Times*, 24 August 1975. Dr. Epstein also argued that "the powers tend to agree on problems with little immediacy," such as demilitarization of the Antarctic, the seabed, and celestial bodies, while failing to come to grips with "the overriding danger" of stockpiling vast quantities of nuclear weapons and fissionable material. The major trouble, of course, is that the voice of reason is not heard by the many, including most members of Congress. For instance, according to the New York *Times* (11 June 1974), in a debate on the defense budget, "fewer than a dozen senators understood the subject-matter"; Senator McIntyre, opposing Pentagon requests, had a dif-

We still talk of "unacceptable damage" in regard to nuclear war, but the tone of the discussion has become so "hard nosed" that one easily forgets what is involved: the extinction of hundreds of millions of persons. Some believe that present-day insensitivity and brutalization go back to the impact of the—until then—unheard-of slaughter of World War I. If so, it explains much in similar insensitivity toward other abominations of our century: genocides (the first of which, that of the Armenians by the Turks, happened during that war; the Jewish holocaust during World War II; since then, in Indonesia, West Bengal, Burundi); torture, in particular of political opponents, which, according to Amnesty International, is engaged in by over one hundred governments; not to mention the war crimes committed by all sides in "conventional" wars such as World War II, Korea, Vietnam. Human life has become cheaper than ever. Perhaps one reason is that there are "so many of us." Perhaps another one is destructive technology run wild.

The foregoing illustrates the dangers of international conflict involved in, and partly caused by, the present state system: dangers arising from the mere possession of overly ample nuclear and nonnuclear arms; dangers arising from territorial and boundary conflicts that abound especially among the newly established states; conflicts over the extent of territorial waters and other claimed rights concerning use and exploitation of the oceans and the ocean bed; conflicts arising from the shaky nature of units lacking legitimacy, whose (usually dictatorial) rulers are tempted to divert internal trouble toward external issues; civil wars affecting other countries and thus involving the threat of international war; quite generally, the increased danger of revolutions occurring in developed and developing countries alike under the impact of the illegitimacy caused by maldistribution of income and wealth for which the corporate system is responsible and which may affect even the relative "stability" of international "balances," whether bi- or multipolar, worldwide or regional; dangers involved in nonrecognition (mutual or one-sided) of

---

ficult time getting a dozen senators to listen to his arguments. The military and the defense industry, in league with part of the academic crew of "strategic doctrine" specialists, manages to obfuscate the obvious.

existing units (the basic issue in the Arab-Israel conflict, but also underlying conflict situations of divided nations, such as North and South Korea, or China-Taiwan); conflicts between countries of the Third and the Fourth World over issues of supplies desperately needed by the latter; conflicts over boundaries and/or ideological supremacy among communist countries (the present Soviet-China conflict perhaps constituting the most dangerous of all).

The case of the two Koreas offers an example of how the big powers might try to defuse or at least localize such conflicts. Overcommitments threaten to involve them in every local strife. Limitation of commitments to what is considered most vital is of the essence. Vietnam might have been avoided this way. The first Korean war, perhaps, was justified by the objective of containing an aggressive unit, but the present U.S. commitment to defend South Korea (with 40,000 American troops plus "tactical" nuclear weapons there) would involve it, and possibly other big powers, in any military conflict between the two Koreas. South Korea, with two-thirds of the Korean population and armed to the teeth, should be able to fight it out by itself. So should the Western Europeans, if assured of American nuclear retaliation against nuclear attack. Berlin is an exception; there the Western garrison is required as a "trip-wire" because of the indefensibility of the city.

So far we have dealt with traditional, "power-political" problems and situations, and with the customary strategic considerations and policies originating from such situations. Equally as important and urgent, however, are the less purely political-strategic problems—which we have referred to as global-survival problems. If, according to Robert McNamara, "some 900 million people are now subsisting on incomes of less than $75 a year" ("they are the absolute poor, living in situations so deprived as to be below any rational definition of human decency"), we must agree with Henry Kissinger, who (according to James Reston)[24] has argued that the larger debate in Washington (and, we may add, in Moscow and other capitals as well) should not merely be about "ICBM's, cruise missiles, and force levels" but should involve the realization

24. New York *Times*, 12 September 1975.

that "poverty levels may be more of a threat to the security of the world than anything else," and that "the startling disparity between the rich nations and the basket cases" is, in the long run, more vital to all of us than concerns about alleged military disparities.

Thus we must return to the role of nations in the solution of the global economic, demographic, and ecological problems. As for exploding populations, enough has been said about the urgency to come to grips with the problem of world population outrunning food and other resources and thus impeding progress in any of the other fields.

As for food, one problem is how to cope with emergency situations like crop failure or famine, which are bound to occur more frequently in the future. To engage in a policy of "triage" (that is, simply writing off entire countries as hopeless) would not only be shocking to every moral sentiment but also unnecessary as long as the food-producing nations are willing to do what, in ancient times, Joseph in Egypt already knew: establish an ever-ready granary of sufficiently large grain reserves for bad times. But an effective policy to balance the bad years and the good requires replacing a system where production, pricing, and distribution of such basics as grain and other commodities are determined by market speculation and the "free play" of private enterprise (often interacting with communist trade monopolies, as in U.S.–Soviet grain deals) with governmental and international planning. Such planning must include attempts to improve backward agricultural systems, such as agrarian reform to free farmers in countries like India from permanent indebtedness to, and exploitation by, land owners or usurers.[25] The developed countries, in turn, must devise priorities under which meat production, for instance, takes a back seat behind the produc-

25. Just one more example of how, even in the area of the oldest, most elementary, and still pretechnological need fulfillments, such as using firewood for cooking and heating, population increase threatens to destroy the food-producing environment. At this writing, the papers report that a rapidly increasing need for firewood causes ever larger areas to be deforested which, in turn, causes erosion, decreasing fertility of land used for food production, in many instances turning the land into desert (see New York *Times*, 3 October 1975). As we know, deforestation and erosion were prime causes of the downfall of such civilizations as the Greco-Roman.

tion of wheat or corn, or strip mining for coal behind conservation of acreage for food production. This may involve economic sacrifice in the global interest and changes of ingrained consumption habits; but, as stressed before, no solution of emergency problems can be had without sacrifices, individually and by nations, and without a reversal of respective attitude patterns.

This applies equally to economic resources and environment problems. The world is running out of replenishable resources, especially where their consumption rises in exponential fashion, as it does in the developed countries. But it is exactly here that one encounters the usual, fallacious argument: *because* consumption (let us say, of oil) has been rising annually by a factor of so many percentage points, we *will* have to increase production (especially if we are to become self-supporting) by so much per annum. This argument must be turned around: if, in all likelihood, only so much is available by way of reserves, and if, at the current rate of depletion, nothing will be left within so many decades, we must curtail use by certain percentages in order to have what is essential for basic needs and to leave enough for future generations. This, again, requires changes in consumption habits and life styles; it may further require investment controls and controls of at least the higher ranges of profits. It may even require internationalization of resources not yet actually exploited, such as the ones on the ocean floor and, perhaps, off-shore resources located beneath territorial waters and on the continental shelf. The plan to make the wealth of the ocean floor a "common patrimony of mankind," plus international draft agreements to preserve the living resources of the sea and to prevent further pollution of the oceans, points up the vital importance to have the ongoing sea-law conferences succeed in securing a fairer distribution of wealth among industrialized nations and LDCs. My additional proposal to place what so far has been in the sovereign domain of states under an international regime will meet with objections on the part of sovereign nations and the MNEs, but there is really no reason why the accident of uneven natural distribution of vital resources should favor one coastal country over another or over land-locked ones. It may, indeed, become necessary to internationalize the management of *all* basic raw materials, wherever located. If this be called "utopian," hope for mankind's survival must likewise be considered utopian.[26]

What has been said does not, of course, imply an "antitechnological" attitude. On the contrary. All science, all available technology must be applied, but with the right priorities, that is, for the solution of the overriding global tasks. Neither does it involve an antigrowth (or "zero growth") approach, because growth is necessary to provide for more equitable distribution of goods and services in the developed countries and for improvement of conditions in the developing ones, lest they cease—as some have already—to be "developing" at all.

Clearly nation-states can still have ample functions and great importance in all these respects. Provided that, under the pressure of the majority of their people, governments revamp their systems so as to be able to fulfill their basic needs (elementary material wants and a livable environment), the state will regain legitimacy. Especially in the Fourth World, should governments, instead of becoming or remaining stooges of MNEs and /or "aiding" countries, turn against the economic dominance involved in "neoimperialism" and convince the developed nations that, in the interest of bridging the gap (and the conflict) between North and South, they must assist them in meaningful ways, this would endow them with the legitimacy many of them so woefully lack today.[27]

This would also mean the end of policies of constant

26. In another area, that of nuclear installations, a similar proposal for internationalization has been made by Lincoln Bloomfield in an important article in *Foreign Affairs*, "Nuclear Spread and World Order," July 1975, pp. 743 ff.

27. This does not mean that one must support all the demands made by the LDCs for a "new economic order." Many are based on the idea of indemnification for past injustices and exploitation. But for the world as a whole it is more important to look ahead and find solutions for common survival problems. In that respect, Third or Fourth World countries must realize the importance of doing something about population explosion and environment pollution exactly as the industrialized countries must recognize claims for more favorable terms of trade and for technical and economic assistance. The LDCs' present strategy of overwhelming the developed countries through bloc voting in the UN and elsewhere can only be counterproductive. It may eventually destroy the organizations, especially if these nations monomaniacally insist on tying up all their strategies and demands with the problem of Palestine.

intervention on the part of the big, whether in the interest of their MNEs or for alleged political or strategic reasons. As the resistance of the weak against being swallowed up or controlled has shown recently (in Indochina, for instance, or in Eastern Europe), there remains considerable latent strength in the idea and sentiment of nationhood. Using it for solving global-survival problems might restore importance to nations and legitimacy comparable to what they enjoyed in times of "impermeability."

Indeed, the last hope for common survival lies in states becoming better organized for cooperation in the solution of global problems and the performance of global tasks. We cannot, for the foreseeable future, count on their being replaced by world government. We must work with what we have. But we must hope that even the big, rich, and powerful will come to realize that those tasks must be given priority over traditional concerns with shifting power relations, balances and imbalances, alignments and nonalignments. What good "tilting" this or that way? What real U.S. concern, for instance, is there with India's leaning more or less toward the Soviets? (The cynic might assert the opposite: who wants to be responsible for getting India out of her perennial mess?) Better engage in a policy of what, in the final essay in this book, I call the "power surplus." That is, once a power like the United States has satisfied itself that it has done whatever is necessary for its own security (and, as noted, this involves even under nuclear conditions much less by way of armaments than commonly asserted), it would then use its influence and resources (1) to assist the LDCs in efforts of survival and development, and (2) to aid in whatever way necessary those that share its values (such as Western Europeans, Israel, Japan). This would be done instead—as has been American policy all too long—of propping up all sorts of semifascist, authoritarian, dictatorial regimes whenever they claim to be anticommunist, or for less and less meaningful strategic purposes (such as bases).[28] This kind of policy has proved

28. According to the New York *Times* (11 September 1975) the U.S. House of Representatives approved a foreign aid bill going in the right direction. It denies aid "to the government of any country that engages in a consistent pattern of gross violation of internationally recognized human

counterproductive whenever the respective regime was over-thrown.

Thus we must place our hopes on an improved system of international cooperation. Leisurely meeting in international conferences (such as the seemingly self-perpetuating sea-law conferences, or Rome on food, Bucharest on population, Stockholm on the environment) which, perchance, give birth to new international bureaucracies employed by old or newly established agencies and, after another couple of years, produce some international treaty or other, clearly is not enough. Pressure must be generated for speedier and more substantial agreements and their implementation. It is also not—or not primarily—a matter of further research. The basic facts and figures, for the most part, are known and widely disseminated through individual governments, conferences of the type mentioned, as well as through the UN and its affiliated agencies. Also there is no dearth of discussion of these issues in the media, through organizations such as the Club of Rome, among environmentalists or groups concerned with family planning, and so forth. And in many countries, especially the advanced ones, clean air, clean water, and similar legislation has been enacted.

But the obstacles are great. One lies in the fact that states, if they are to regain legitimacy, must cooperate much more, and much more intensively, than ever before and thus rely on increased powers and increased effectiveness of international organizations. But the international agencies that are to be entrusted with the implementation of common tasks are themselves now facing a general loss of prestige and credibility. If the present trend to make the UN and other international agencies arenas of confrontation (Third World vs. Western World, West vs. East, etc.) is allowed to continue, they will lose their ability to function as centers for the solution of the global survival problems. Legitimacy of nations and legitimacy

---

rights, including torture or cruel, inhuman, or degrading treatment and punishment . . . . or other flagrant denials of the right to life, liberty and the security of a person." For once, I said to myself, progress—until I read (New York *Times*, 12 December 1975) that, under the pressure of the administration, the Senate had added to this stipulation a clause that the President can waive the restriction!

of international organizations are interdependent; one reinforces the other. Loss of legitimacy on one or the other level weakens the whole system.

Another great difficulty lies in the conflict between the long-range and short-range interests and concerns. Governments in particular, in such conflicts, under the pressure of interest groups, tend to give preference to what seems most urgent in the short run. Thus environmental-protection legislation is revoked or watered down, or the law remains unapplied, whenever—as in an energy crisis—it interferes with the immediate needs or proves expensive. Such resistance is clearly related to unwillingness on the part of the *possidentes* to make sacrifices in their living style. But if we want a livable world for all, the waste of resources involved in the "conspicuous consumption" by the affluent upper crust (both in the advanced and the developing countries) must yield to austerity and, especially in the industrialized world, to a willingness to work harder and more productively. I refer, of course, not to the already overly hard-working and driven miner, or rural worker, or even most factory workers, but to the "coffee-break" type of office worker and bureaucrat (both West and East) and the unproductive or even counterproductive crew of tax-shelter advisers, admen, and the like. The simpler, more Spartan life style of some of the young people would seem to point the way.

There are many other obstacles to the new world order that is needed in order to cope with the global problems. Some are listed in the last essay in this collection and need not be detailed here. Instead I would like to emphasize once more the need for a "great reversal" in attitudes and policies, especially on the part of decisive elites. What are the chances that their perception of our world will agree with what an increasing but still small and relatively powerless number of people are beginning to perceive as a situation of global emergency? The signs are far from encouraging. People all over the world, baffled by the complexity of their problems, without guidance by moral standards, leaderless, and unable to find answers by themselves, are yearning for standards of conduct for their own lives and for the group or groups to which they belong. As one has remarked, "Nobody's got a plan. Nobody knows the way out." Respect for traditional institutions and leaders is down, and there is "no fresh allegiance to positive beliefs." [29] Perhaps our situation is comparable to the decay of previous civilizations, such as the Greco-Roman one; but in those instances only one part of humanity, not all of it, was at stake. Now, as the present secretary of the UN has aptly put it, "the civilization that is facing such a challenge is not just one small part of mankind—it is mankind as a whole."

Few charismatic leaders are left in the world, and those few apparently do not know how, or want, to use their charisma for calling on their people to engage in a great new venture to solve their most urgent problems. One might forgive Indira Gandhi's installing something akin to a personal dictatorship if, in view of her people's utter destitution, she would—in the manner of Franklin Roosevelt's "fireside chats" during the Great Depression—address them in simple terms, outlining the situation, urging them to limit the size of their families, assuring them that, in a stable and developing economy, they could then live in security in their old age. She might then urge other nations to help those who would prove willing to help themselves. True, this would also require a revolution of Indian agrarian structure, as well as of deeply ingrained attitudes, but it would at least have some promise of success with people yearning for leadership and meaningful programs. The radicalism of measures presently tried out to stop the population explosion (compulsory sterilization, etc.) is the result of previous indecisiveness and neglect.

As the case of India shows, revolutions affecting socioeconomic structure (perhaps not necessarily violent but fundamental ones) must occur before attitudinal reversal has a chance to affect policies. Revolutions, in turn, are destabilizing in the international environment, so the path to global improvement may well lead through valleys of danger and death. We even lack those great "movements" (like revolutionary internationalism, or socialism), whose chiliastic idealism, to be sure, turned out to be utopian (see chapter 2) but at least was aware of the need for the "altogether different."

Today, more sober, rational-realist insight must do,[30] per-

29. See Christopher Lydon in the New York *Times*, 7 September 1975.
30. Might we expect it from Henry Kissinger? This elusive leader occasionally talks in terms that sound encouraging; e.g., in his interview with

haps imbued with that sense of "compassion" which, in my
Political Realism and Political Idealism I called the basic,
underlying trait of all political "idealists." [31] We may, perhaps,
use this concept also for an ethic that, in addition or as an
alternative to the "minimum ethic of survival," would probe
the requirements of an ultimate "ethics of a decent demise." *If*
survival should prove impossible or unlikely, should we, as
human race, not prepare ourselves for an exit that would at
least minimize the worst of the slaughter and the suffering, the
cruelties and "inhumanities" that can otherwise be expected in
a rapidly decaying and disintegrating world of chaotic deterioration? This must not imply schizophrenia; we must try to
combine what survival ethic prescribes with the demands of an
alternative ethics of demise. While preparing for the worst, we
must also work for the better. Thus we might stop the
slaughter of cattle and the hunting of other animals—with the
dual benefit of avoidance of suffering of living beings and
increased grain production. We might, through supplying
those who desire them with means for ending their lives,
enable people who confront only misery (for instance, in their
old age) to decamp from this world in peace (again, through
diminishing "surplus population," serving both ethics). We
might even hope that, should the "unthinkable" happen—
namely, an all-out nuclear first strike—those in a position to
retaliate would forego a by now useless counter-slaughter and
thus enable part of mankind to survive—if only for a while.
This, of course, could only be an unannounced, momentary
reaction, since otherwise the credibility of "mutual deterrence" would lose its deterrent effect. But such considerations
concern an "ultimate" where, to quote Herbert Butterfield,
"the mind winces and turns to look elsewhere."

It has sometimes been remarked that the countries and
people on this planet would forget their different ideologies,
bury their quarrels, and join together if an enemy from

James Reston (New York *Times*, 13 October 1974), he spoke of a new
international structure "built not on the sense of the preeminence of two
power centers, but on the sense of participation of those who are part of the
global environment. . . . There is no doubt in my mind that, by the end of the
century, this will be the dominant reality of our time."

31. Pp. 6ff.

"abroad," say, from Mars, threatened them all. If they would recognize that there now *is* such a common enemy in the shape of the deadly perils which threaten that tiny, slim biosphere in which we must live, there might still be time to unite in a common last effort. But only constant prodding can help. Otherwise, I am afraid the chances that the end will come, sooner or later, in some way or another, are rather overwhelming. It may come with the bang of an apocalyptic nuclear exchange or with a whimper (pandemics; starvation; poisoning of body, air, or water; man-made climatic changes; fluorocarbons destroying the ozone layer or similar atmospheric deterioration; spreading insanity or stunting of brains because of malnutrition in children; or any other of the innumerable possibilities extant or as yet unknown)—an *embarras de richesse* enabling everybody to select his own "preferred way to doom."

What is awaiting us is in the balance. We must place behind the word "survival" that question mark which is implied in "Prologue as Epilogue: Aristotle's Dream," at the end of the book. But we should not fatalistically embrace the inevitability of doom. On the contrary. All I have written (and taught), despite its pessimism, was meant to challenge my fellow humans to resist and try to reverse the trend toward extinction.

The journey that led from my early attempts to construct a logical system of norms for a world of powers to more realistic findings about the nature of states and the complications and dilemmas of their interrelations in a nuclear age, and thence to an insight into the accelerating rush of mankind into a multiplicity of threats to its survival has truly been a long one, full of turns and contrasts, and not always without contradictions. The jolt that drove me out of my European environment healed me forever of utopianism, but it took place when it still seemed that a somewhat more rational structure of world affairs could be based on systems of states characterized by their territoriality and ensuing defensibility. Then came Hiroshima. The question: *Security—Can We Retrieve It?* (the title of a book published in the 1930s), had now to be answered in the negative. Further developments in the field of arms and strategy, from the "baby bomb" to the Trident nuclear submarine, were only a matter of degree (although, once again, demonstrating exponential increase). The impenetrability of nations had yielded to utter vulnerability, and nothing was taking the place of their former protective function. This was the second jolt. The third did not come with the sudden flash of the first atomic explosion; it was the more gradual realization of the deadly peril into which (in addition to the nuclear threat) an unchained and undirected technology had placed humanity together with all its organized establishments, such as nation-states. In this latest perception the particularist "national" or "security" interest of individual units or actors merges with the supranational interests of mankind as a totality. A student of "international" politics had become one of the "universal-ist" approach to global problems and an advocate of an ethic of supranational survival.

At the outset of this Introduction I used the artistic simile to show the relation between perceptions and realities. Now, at the end, I resort to creative art and literature again, to search for indications of what the future holds in store. Oftentimes the imaginative capacities of the human mind have proved to be in advance of the intellectual ones. Franz Kafka's uncannily correct forecast of how a completely technified world would look is an outstanding example. I have come across one book (in German, but its illustrations speak a universal language) that sets forth in detail how, beginning at the turn of the century, artists, composers, and writers began to have visions of an atomic doom; and some paintings and sculptures that the author uses for exemplification in an otherwise somewhat fuzzy and exaggerated line of argument are stunning indeed.[32] We can, perhaps, say that, since the height of modern indus-trial civilization was reached around 1900, all serious creative effort in the aesthetic fields has been tinged with a sense of foreboding. At that time, Rainer Maria Rilke, one of the most profound lyrical poets of this century, spoke of the beautiful being but the beginning of the frightful ("das Schöne ist nichts als des Schrecklichen Anfang").

32. Walther Krüger, *Das Gorgonenhaupt—Zukunftsvisionen in der mod-ernen bildenden Kunst, Musik, Literatur* (Berlin, 1972).

This, of course, had not always been so. We can trace what great writers expected from the future in an industrial age from Goethe, who in his old age witnessed its beginnings and welcomed them enthusiastically, to Thomas Mann who, hardly more than a century later, used the same Faust figure Goethe had used to lament the frightfulness of what it had wrought. Goethe had his Faust, symbol of man "forever striving," die with the optimistic vision of something we today would call "modernizing development toward freedom." The dying Faust sees himself presiding over great technical works that will create "space for millions": swamps are drained and land is gained for "vast throngs" no longer peons but "free people on free ground."

> To such a vision I would say:
> Stay on, you are so beautiful!
> The traces of my earthly days
> Would not in eons fade away.

This vision of the blessings of growth and development (we might, perhaps, say, by Faust, chief of the U.S. Army Corps of Engineers) may be set against the much more skeptical analysis made of the human and ecological effects of a forever expanding technological culture less than half a century later by John Stuart Mill. Since he is quoted at length at the end of essay 6, I refer the reader to what Mill has to say there. Another half century later, Rilke put his finger on where the real wound inflicted by technology is found—not in the machine per se but in its having become the master instead of the servant of man:

> All we have gained the machine threatens, so long
> as it makes bold to exist in the spirit, instead of obeying,
>
> . . .
> It is life,—thinks it knows best,
> which, with equal resolve, arrays, produces, destroys.[33]

A few decades after that, Thomas Mann, watching in horror

33. Rilke is almost untranslatable. The above translation is taken from M. D. Herter Norton, *Sonnets to Orpheus* (New York: W. W. Norton, 1942).

from his exile how Nazism, in "hellish drunkenness," used the most advanced technology to destroy humans by the millions, saw Germany destroying itself and its entire cultural heritage. *His* Faust's fictitious composition, the "Lamentations of Doctor Faustus" ("Dr. Fausti Weheklag"), was meant to be the "revocation" of the Ninth Symphony with its "Ode to Joy"; it bemoans Götterdämmerung, the end of everything.

But a couple of decades later we see Germans prosper, having joined the Western world (and, in part—perhaps to atone for their previous abominations—the East, too), still there to partake in the world's problems. Does it mean that artists and writers can also misread the future? They are certainly not infallible and, like all of us, are liable to be torn between hope and despair. As René Dubos has reminded us, "Trend is not Destiny." [34] In the same sonnet in which Rilke indicts the overbearing machine he also sounds a more encouraging note:

> But to us existence is still enchanted, at a hundred
> points it is original still. . . .
> And music, ever new, out of most tremulous stones
> builds in unusable space her deified house.

Utter pessimism, on the other hand, marked the Western world's greatest playwright's leave-taking from *his* world. Perhaps it was no coincidence that Shakespeare, standing at the beginning of the scientific age, which was to bring about ever more spectacular transformations of traditional life and society, in his last play (after having conjured up with considerable irony a utopia of plenty for all without state, force, and war) has Prospero abjure magic,[35] drown his magic

34. See his remarkable musings in the New York *Times*, 10 and 11 November 1975.

35. In the early stages of the scientific-technological era, the exploits of science were often considered akin to magic. Thus Prospero's "rough magic" had enabled him " 'twixt the green sea and the azur'd vault" to

> Set roaring war: to the dread-rattling thunder
> Have I given fire and rifted Jove's stout oak
> With his own bolt: the strong-bas'd promontory
> Have I made shake; and by the spurs pluck'd up
> The pine and cedar: graves at my command
> Have wak'd their sleepers, op'd, and let them forth
> By my so potent art.

book, and resign himself to the vision of eventual *global* doom. Did he foresee what man's new-won power over nature would bring about?

> The cloud-capp'd towers, the gorgeous palaces,
> The solemn temples, the great globe itself,
> Yea, all which it inherit, shall dissolve
> And, like this unsubstantial pageant faded,
> Leave not a rack behind.

If this, then, be our likely fate, let us yet be guided by the admonition of another poet of our age, Dylan Thomas, who summoned us to resist the looming darkness to the very end:

> Do not go gentle into that good night.
> Rage, rage against the dying of the light.

1

POWER POLITICS AND WORLD ORGANIZATION

This chapter appeared a third of a century ago in the *American Political Science Review* 36, no. 6 (December 1942): 1039–52. It reflects my developing views on the role of power in international politics and my attitude toward the numerous plans for a better world order developed during World War II. For an analysis of this essay, see pages 7–8 of the *Introduction*.

Reprinted by permission of the American Political Science Association.

Le Pouvoir est la manifestation suprême de la peur que l'homme fait à lui-même par ses efforts pour s'en libérer. Là est peut-être le secret le plus profond et obscur de l'histoire.

Ferrero, *Pouvoir*

I

The current discussion of a future world order[1] has made it plain that the problem of coming international relations is of a magnitude surpassing even that of winning the war. It is not intended here to add to the rising tide of concrete plans in this field, but rather to elucidate certain proposals in the light of some basic features of the present system of international relations and, starting from a clearer picture of what is, to seek to discriminate between what is desirable and undesirable, possible and utopian. Wrong concepts of the forces underlying

1. Cf., for example, the very thorough investigations of the Commission to Study the Organization of Peace, results of which have been published in Nos. 369 and 379 of *International Conciliation* (April 1941 and April 1942). An excellent bibliography is contained in the *Bulletin* of the Commission, vol. 2, nos. 5 and 6 (May–June 1942), prepared by Hans Aufricht.

the present system have too often produced "peace plans" built on the sands of wishful thinking, and therefore bound to be wrecked on the rocks of reality. Disappointment caused by the failure of ill-conceived devices, in turn, is apt to produce a "realism" which ridicules any attempt to discuss international relations in terms of a possible evolution toward a more integrated stage.

Power, in modern international relations, has been the ultimate means of deciding issues and adjusting relationships among the units constituting international society. The states have regarded themselves as "sovereign" entities, not subordinated to any superior political power nor guided in their power politics by considerations of an apolitical, i.e., power-alien, nature. True, power-alien elements such as economic interests of a particular group or considerations of religious, moral, sentimental, or purely personal nature have from time to time diverted policies from purely power-mechanical lines, thus, e.g., lining up a Catholic country, against its own power interests, with another Catholic country, or having a state interfere with policies of another country not for reasons of power politics, i.e., out of self-interest, but because that country persecuted certain minorities or social classes whose interests the other state strove to defend. In spite of occasional "deviations," however, power politics has asserted itself in the long run as predominant in the international realm. Exactly as economic competition *within* states once created "economic man," eventually tending to drive out all economy-alien motivations, power-competition *among* states has created "powers," tending to drive out power-alien considerations and policies. Once power has entered the field at all, this must be the necessary result. For, should any single member of the system try to replace power politics quite generally by policies based on humanitarian or similar power-alien ideals, it would merely play into the hands of its competitors and thus weaken and eventually destroy itself. Any proposal for a reform of the system has to start from a realization of the compulsion which the system exerts upon each member and the inescapability which it implies as far as the policies of each single unit are concerned.

Power competition among several units of a system eventually leads either to the predominance of one of them or to the establishment of a system where the political units balance each other, and thus can continue to exist side by side. It was this latter alternative, the existence of an equilibrium—highly precarious and ever shifting though it has been—which has enabled the "modern state-system" to govern international relations in the last centuries.

In the time of its flowering, the balance-of-power system fulfilled two main functions: (1) to enable a plurality of autonomous political units to exist side-by-side, and (2) to allow these units internally to develop their own culture as "nations," a culture based mainly upon the values of individual and group autonomy within the state. Today, however, the system not only has become unable to fulfil these two main functions, but results in the contrary of what it had achieved in its "classical" period.

Let us first regard the "external," or international, side of the problem. Here, the event which led to the destruction of the balance system was the growing, and now worldwide, inter-connection of economic and other relationships in the indus-trial age and the ensuing interdependence of states. Under the compulsion of power-competition, each major power unit, in order to avoid dependence on any other unit, sought now to dominate ever larger regions in an effort to become "self-sufficient" and thus "secure." These attempts failed because in a shrinking world no single power can satisfy its security interests without doing harm to those of another power. The world is no longer large enough to harbor several self-contained powers. Thus the growing interdependence of the nations of the world led to the contrary of what "internationalists" had hoped its result would be; instead of making for peace and world order, it brought a struggle of powers to dominate the world in order to be secure from the world. The trend toward world domination or hegemony of a single power is but the ultimate consummation of a power-system engrafted upon an otherwise integrated world.

Within the states, an international system which allowed nations to develop an at least partly "civilized" peacetime society and economy of plenty has now resulted in what is called the totalitarian organization of state and society. Whatever the other roots of totalitarianism may be, it is easy to see what bearing power competition must have on its development. To compete successfully with other powers, states had to subordinate every realm of life and society to the requirements of war and "preparedness." Wars which used to be localized and not interfering with "ordinary civilian" life have become "total" wars which no longer recognize regions and spheres outside war, and are characterized by the destruction of mankind's accumulated wealth ("scorched earth policy," etc.) and the extermination of entire populations. But "total war" means also obliteration of any distinction between times of "peace" and of "war." Any period outside actual warfare necessarily becomes one of war preparation, since not using it for this purpose means giving an advantage to a potential enemy who does so. The relentless consequence is that states had to be organized not only so that foreign policies are conducted with an exclusive view to the furtherance of power interests, but so that every realm of the political, economic, and cultural life of individuals and groups is regulated with this same view in mind. Therefore more and more "living standards" are sacrificed for war production and war potential. Moreover, since every moral or other "inhibition" might weaken defense requirements, more and more "standards of civilization" and cultural values are discarded in favor of the fascistization of man and mind. Thus an age of liberal and individualistic tendencies in the internal life of countries has been replaced by that of régimes which consolidate populations into iron *blocs* ruled through managed and centralized mass-control, and where all of economy becomes *Wehrwirtschaft,* cultural life *Wehrkultur,* religious life *Wehrgottesdienst.* Power competition drives remaining nontotalitarian states into entering the same route. All this means the *reductio ad absurdum* of our present societal organization: Man may starve (both physically and spiritually) while in the possession of the most costly and most formidable machinery ever created for the protection of lives and goods.

History, so far, has not meant progress toward less war and conflict and more peace and harmony, but only the transfer of competition and strife from smaller to ever larger social groups. The perpetuation of this system on the world-level not only would mean that the bottom is out of our civilization (which, like every previous one, has been built on mitigation, or at least canalization and balancing, of power in certain realms and spheres), but might well signalize the decay of man as a race. Unable to escape the vicious circle of mutual fear, insecurity, and conflict for power and to eliminate the life-and-death struggle from the societies formed by his own kind, the "victor over Nature" may turn out to have been but another among Nature's abortive attempts to create a species capable of survival.

Some problems of future international relations will now be examined in the light of these facts. Provided that world-domination on the part of the totalitarian powers has been successfully averted, it must first of all be realized that the postwar world will still be one of powers. More than that, it will be a world of "total suspicion," worse than at any time before; for what happened in the years preceding the war will not so soon be forgotten. Totalitarian conduct of foreign affairs, with its utter disregard of traditional standards and its uninhibited use of any means furthering the end, lying and betraying, "fifth columnism," ideological warfare, will have left its impact, and there will probably be less confidence among individuals and nations than at any time in history. We must face the fact that this will be the basis on which to erect a better world order.

II

The various proposals for a new order of world relations can be divided roughly into three categories:[2] first, one which

2. Among these we need not include proposals which, though sometimes under high-sounding new names such as geopolitics, are nothing but elaborations of the existing system of limitless power politics. It is significant that *Geo-Politik* has been the ideological basis of Nazi foreign policy. Its adoption by the victors of this war would not make the system any different from what it was when Haushofer inspired Hitler. However, it must be recognized that such proposals contain the only *realistic* alternative to a more integrated international system. Future wars for supremacy would be wars between a few superpowers organized in *Grossräumen*. There is no going back to the system of sixty independent nation-states.

leaves the "sovereignty" of states basically intact while providing for their voluntary engaging in what may be called "negative obligations"—certain duties of abstention in order to eliminate or diminish the danger of war. Second, at the opposite extreme, one which would abolish nations in their capacity as independent powers and replace them by some superstate authority or government. A third category of proposals, while retaining the system of coexisting powers, would combine them in a system with one particular "positive obligation"—their duty to concur in collective prevention of the individual use of force, a system of "collective security."

1. The first, and least ambitious, view holds that the danger of war can be ended or greatly diminished if only the nations of the world would enter into all or some of the following undertakings: in the field of military preparation, not to arm too heavily, or to renounce the use of certain weapons—in short, to reduce armaments; in the economic field, to renounce certain instruments of "economic warfare," such as high tariffs, raw material monopolies, etc.—in short, to establish free, or freer, international trade relations; in the political and diplomatic field, to renounce the right to have recourse to war, at least for certain types of conflicts, and instead to settle disputes peacefully—a system of mediation or arbitration.

These are the steps and procedures commonly proposed by "internationalists," and partly tried in the practice of states during the last hundred years. Surveying these practices means surveying their failure. This could not be otherwise, since all imply an at least partial renunciation of power, while, on the other hand, the system of power politics, with power competition and ensuing individual and collective insecurity, is left intact. These proposals thus mean putting the cart before the horse. Even a simultaneous and entirely "equal" renunciation of certain uses or instruments of power on the part of all states (if ever practicable) would in its continued fulfilment be guaranteed only by the goodwill and honesty of each power, overconfidence in which, on the part of those to whom the conduct of affairs is entrusted, might be considered a dereliction of their duty toward those whose lives and goods are to be protected against foreign spoliation. In a system of power politics, any major concession can be due only to temporary forgetfulness of the necessities of the system, constituting, as it would, a gratuitous favor to those who would not take part in the engagement or were least faithful in its execution.

Disarmament, in particular, which so often has been said to constitute the main prerequisite for the abolition of "insecurity" in the world, could in reality be obtained only *after* the establishment of a firm security system, since only a lessening of the feeling of insecurity could bring about a general reduction of power instruments. Moreover, war *potentials* constituting the backbone of modern preparedness, mere reduction of actual armaments would eliminate neither war's possibility nor its root, the competition of states for power.

For the same reason, any large amount of economic internationalism cannot be preparatory for, but only consecutive to, a state of lessened political tension. Recent events have shown that the requirements of power politics, in this realm, prevail even over strong tendencies and interests of an economic nature which in themselves would be in favor of increased and freer trade relations. In the nineteenth century, an even higher degree of economic internationalism and of corresponding vested interests in the continuation of the peace which makes these relationships possible was not enough to change basic power policies. "In the long run power politics demands power economics." [3]

As for arbitration, its apparent success in certain instances has been due to the fact that recourse to it has been had mainly in the case of minor issues or minor countries, while *maxima non curat praetor*. Under the prevailing system, similar efforts to take out of power politics certain issues or regions and to administer them in a depoliticized way, e.g., "international" control of "backward" regions, "neutralization" of strategically important areas, straits, canals, etc., or "technical" management of minority or migration problems, likewise ended in failure. In times of international crisis, these realms were regularly reoccupied by power interests. With the extension of the power system all over the world, any power-alien latitude still open to earlier periods has become impossible. As long as this system lasts, it cannot be restored.

3. G. Schwarzenberger, *Power Politics* (1941), p. 271.

2. Those disappointed with the aforementioned procedures are today, for the most part, looking toward the establishment of "world government" in the form of a genuine federal government over and above existing states. In order to understand the implications of this scheme, one must first realize that it would by no means abolish "power," or even mitigate it, but would merely transfer its central seat from the "sovereign" states to a new higher unit of governmental power, the federal union (or whatever its name). Whatever the details of such a setup, there must be a central authority with legal competence and actual power to monopolize the use of force in the world, thus depriving the member-"states" of their real power (whatever secondary competences might be left to them).

A like scheme cannot from the outset be called utopian. History has witnessed many shifts from one kind of societal organization to another, involving a transfer of the seat of ultimate power, e.g., from tribes to the *polis*, from feudal groups to the "state." Such changes, however, require also shifts of ideologies and transfers of "allegiance." Besides all organizational changes, there would, in the case here discussed, be one fundamental prerequisite: the shift of allegiance, by at least a politically effectual number of individuals, from nation-state to world-state, thus replacing national loyalties with an entirely new loyalty toward the new highest unit of authority. Where comparatively small groups are politically decisive, similar transformations might imaginably take place without too great difficulty, but in an age of politically activated masses whose ultimate loyalties have come to be molded almost exclusively into one toward the nation, the change from nation-state to world-federation would require more than ever a tremendous political effort. Nothing short of an ideological and spiritual revolution would be required in order to eradicate "nationalism" from the minds in favor of "world patriotism." This, however, is not likely to happen in a world of still mutually suspicious "powers."

It would be illusory to think that the new allegiance might simply be added to existing loyalties. Eventual decisive power cannot be expected where loyalties are divided. Since the main function of the new world government would for a long time be to prevent recourse to force on the part of member-units (outlawry of war and monopoly of coercion by the federal government), such division of loyalties would in all likelihood fatally hamper the functioning of the highest authority. In a test case, the federal authority would be revealed as either a sham, with one or more old-style "powers" really controlling it,[4] or else as a pseudo-authority with no actual power at all, in which event, at a critical juncture, it would simply disintegrate into its component parts, the founding powers. Thus, a lack of ideological and psychological prerequisites, not politico-organizational difficulties, would appear to make this plan impracticable. This does not mean that, once the problem of security and power-competition has been solved, federalism or some similar form of more integrated world-government might not gradually evolve from the new basis. But, for the reasons stated, it seems too radical a step from the existing system of power politics toward a new order of international relations.[5]

3. A system of "collective security" would be midway between impracticable superstate government and ineffectual obligations of abstention from certain activities. It means the establishment of a system of general security through collective sanctions against the use of force. Recourse to force on the part of any individual state as a means of power politics would immediately encounter the active opposition of a coalition of all remaining states which would have committed themselves beforehand to the enforcement of peace in such an event. Apparently, this system would increase the range and possibilities of war instead of diminishing them, because it would replace the individual power's "right" to make war by a duty to make war, and a worldwide war at that, in the event of individual aggression. The underlying idea, of course, is to eliminate total wars by the threat of a still more total one, since each state resorting to war or other violence would have to

4. This would probably appear first of all in the sphere of military organization regarding the control of the "international army" or "federal police force," which, after all, must be stationed somewhere, with ultimate command emanating from somebody, etc.

5. The foregoing discussion has been concerned with federalism as a proposal for *world* government, and not with the various plans propounded for one or another *regional* federation of existing states. Such schemes may be entirely practicable, but obviously would leave the major problem, that of competing power units, unsolved.

face a worldwide coalition, with the result—so it is hoped—that the very threat of such opposition would deter it from starting such a venture.

This scheme would not do away with the existing society of states as such. It would not even eliminate the "power" of states as a basis of international relationships. However, it would organize the use of power in such a manner as to avoid the vicious circle into which traditional power politics, with its ever-increasing "insecurity because of mutual dependence," has run. Organized collective use of force, or the threat of its application, would be made the instrument for preventing or suppressing its individual application. The deadlock of a system under which insecurity makes for wars, and wars—since they cannot give any power that real security which today could come only from world-domination—engender more insecurity, would be broken. It would mean the adaptation of the balance-of-power principle to modern conditions. Since every war today, through the mechanism of power-competition, tends eventually to involve all powers, these would ultimately have to take part in an attempt to reestablish the balance anyway. Therefore, each of them would seem to have more interest in preventing such "unorganized" wars than in its own continued right to make, or abstain from, wars whenever it pleases. Since today no single power is independent enough to play the role which Great Britain traditionally played vis-à-vis the Continent, namely, that of the decisive weight which could be thrown into the balance to turn the scales one way or the other, a balance creating general security can be established only through collectivization of the force to be thrown against its attempted individual use. This presupposes that the system be worldwide, and that the outlawed individual recourse to force, if occurring at all, remain limited to single cases and powers. Otherwise the result would be merely the formation of another system of antagonistic *blocs* and alliances.

What are the chances for the working of such a scheme, if ever adopted? As one knows, it has not worked during the League of Nations period. But the difficulties encountered were not those mentioned by most of the more skeptical observers. Thus the determination of the aggressor in a particular situation—a problem often pictured as one of insuperable difficulty —in practice proved easy, at any rate so far as technical standards of determining who "first started it" were concerned. Here, the situation used to be clear and unequivocal.[6] Although certain standards of determination will have to be worked out, along with the whole machinery of the system, this problem seems to be of comparatively minor difficulty. A further objection was that collective sanctions would require common preparation for hypothetical wars of every imaginable combination—grand strategies, so to speak, against every state by all remaining powers. This, it was said, would defeat the whole scheme, since the potential aggressor would have to cooperate in, and thus know, the plan for its own defeat. In reality, this means only that plans for sanctions would have to be adopted after the aggression has occurred and the aggressor has been duly determined. While this would give the aggressor the advantage of time gained by surprise, it would not appear likely that even in an age of *Blitzkrieg* all or the major part of the other states could be overwhelmed before having a chance to react. If all states are ready to participate in sanctions, even after the immediate victim of aggression has been overrun, permanent success of the aggressor seems scarcely possible.

The fundamental difficulty is not technical or strategic, but political and psychological. Beyond organizational, institutional, and legal requirements, the system presupposes for its successful working one main politico-psychological *datum:* the realization, on the part of political leadership and public opinion in the various countries, that each country in the world, be it geographically or politically "near" to or "remote" from the location of immediate conflict and aggression, has exactly the same, and a superlative, interest in its suppression. Any rational analysis of recent developments of power politics makes it clear that from the viewpoint of each state's very existence, its interests are equally involved by any breach of

6. The problem of identifying the aggressor has to be distinguished from the question of who, with respect to the underlying conflict, is right or wrong. This latter problem involves that of how "fair" and "just" decisions of international disputes can be obtained—a question touched briefly at the end of this article.

peace wherever occurring. This conclusion is based upon a realistic appraisal of such facts as the changed nature of war and the universalism of the mechanism of power competition. Just as there are "no islands any more" (nor hemispheres for that matter), there are today no longer "producers" of security as opposed to "consumers," as a writer in the 1920s[7] characterized the then allegedly diverging interests of powers regarding the fulfilment of the sanctions and obligations contained in the Covenant of the League of Nations. Any attempt to avoid this conclusion by "appeasing" aggressors or "isolating" oneself either leads to one's self-destruction or merely defers one's involvement to a moment when the situation has become more dangerous through the strengthening of the adversary. Turning from power politics to collective security, therefore, means the adoption of a more rational scheme of international relations, just as balance-of-power politics at one time meant a comparatively rational system based on the elimination of certain power-alien elements in favor of *raison d'état*.

Collective security, then, rests on the realization, with appropriate action, of what the states' common interests in their continued existence require today. However, the rationality of a scheme is in itself no guarantee of its adoption or application. The basic problem confronting a plan for collective security is whether people throughout the world are likely to realize the fact and are ready to act in a bold and novel way. More skeptically inclined persons will probably pronounce this requirement fatal. They will doubt whether people at large will suddenly adjudge necessary, and even advantageous, what for centuries has run counter to the actual or imaginary interests of their countries and still today appears to many as nothing but self-denying sacrifice. To this, one can reply only that men sometimes learn from bitter experience. While it took the average Englishman from World War times to 1940 to comprehend that the airplane had changed his country's strategic, and therewith political, position, actual bombardment, coupled with the threat of immediate invasion, caused him to learn in a few days what he failed to learn in twenty years. Similarly,

7. S. de Madariaga.

Pearl Harbor and what may ensue will have opened the eyes of many an American who failed to realize earlier that sanctions against a Japan still at the boundary of China proper might have been preferable to a "war of survival." The question, of course, remains whether the impact of experience will be sufficiently strong and general, and not too quickly forgotten. Without engaging in futile prophecies, it can at any rate be stated that there is no inevitability in provincialism, considering that, e.g., the man from Oregon (and even the Kansan) well understands that an attack on New York or Florida is of immediate concern to him, while New Zealanders (and even some South Africans) view similarly an assault on Britain. Lack of these politico-psychological prerequisites, it is true, accounts for the failure of the League's system of sanctions; nor was Ethiopia the only or nearest of those "far-away countries" of which the leaders of the decisive powers pretended to "know nothing." But those studying the details of the first and only sanctions experiment also know that success was actually nearer than commonly realized. The people, or at least those parts of public opinion uninfluenced by Fascist or pro-Fascist propaganda, were in most countries more advanced in grasping their real interest than were their leading statesmen. After the experience of another world war, a better understanding of the failures committed during its prehistory may bring the case for collective security sufficiently near to common people of all groups and countries to make the scheme practicable. Still, a sudden reaction toward isolationist and provincialist illusions, brought about or exploited by groups with vested interests in the previous system, may neutralize and destroy the impact of this experience on the future world settlement. If this should happen, nothing could then prevent the world from becoming the victim of the only alternative: renewed power politics, with recurring worldwide wars on a probably accelerated scale, produced by the necessity felt by one power or another to bring about a situation in which alone it could have real "security": world-dominion. Some day this aim may be achieved by somebody; but it would be in a world where the last remnants of a diversified civilization had disappeared.

The establishment of collective security, on the other hand, would by no means herald the millennium. It would have to take shape in an atmosphere still full of suspicion, since competing powers, just emerging from a life-and-death struggle, would still exist at its start. There would be armaments and economies geared for war; and these national systems would have to be organized for sanctions-preparedness instead of individual warfare. It might even be dangerous to change the system too quickly into one of more peaceful activities, because the new collective system would first have to stand the test of its real working, either by introducing a period of prolonged absence of violence due to general preparedness for sanctions, or by a successful application of sanctions in an actual case of aggression. One such practical application of the system would probably be sufficient to ensure peace for a long time.

Then, after a rather lengthy period of trial and transition, those policies could be inaugurated which are necessary for the transformation of the existing system into a substantially more peaceful one, but which presuppose existing security for their successful working. Thus, in the same measure as suspicion of ever-present danger of attack and the prepossession of minds and actions with war-preparedness and security would lessen, a gradual return to more genuine peacetime activities would become possible. This would apply to all realms, internal as well as international, cultural and economic as well as political. Then, and then only, economic preparation for war could be replaced by economic and social planning for plenty within states—something which under conditions of power politics only meant weakening one's potential war strength. At the same time, an attempt could be made to establish closer international trade relations also. Step by step, with the enlargement of such activities, some reduction of armaments could be mutually agreed upon, although military preparedness could not be allowed to lapse altogether as long as the threat of effective sanctions must be maintained.

Even so, a collective security system would still be confronted with one grave challenge. It would be necessary to find a procedure for the solution of those problems which in the age of power politics were solved by force, and which now would no longer be amenable to such solution. For it must be realized that the mere elimination of force as an instrument for the settlement of international issues and relationships at first would necessarily, and only, mean freezing the existing status quo. Since it would be based on victory and defeat in a world war, this status quo would be rather arbitrary, even though based on the victory of the less totalitarian and the defeat of the more aggressive powers. Unless an effective procedure for "revision," i.e., some kind of international legislation, were devised, not even sanctions could in the long run prevent the countries of the world from rallying again in camps of real or alleged "haves" and "have nots." Changes which under prevailing power politics were brought about by use or threat of force must have a chance to be effectuated in a peaceful way. "Just" decision must replace what formerly was decision by force. Among formidable problems would be such ones as the status of colonial territories and populations, the position of minorities, the shift of populations from country to country. The fundamental issue would be nothing less than finding rational solutions for what rarely, so far, has been regulated in other than irrational ways. It would be more than optimistic to hope that "inherent justice" rather than compromise would be the main device in the adjustment of still clashing interests of still more and less influential, stronger and weaker, parties, at least for a long time to come. This will, then, still be an age of relative fallibility, not of accomplished rightfulness. But it must again be emphasized that all these experiments and procedures require the previous solution of the most urgent problem, the organization of power for general security. Not before mankind has achieved "freedom from fear" can any stable basis be laid for a progressive realization of its age-old aspiration for "freedom from want."

IDEALIST INTERNATIONALISM AND THE SECURITY DILEMMA

This chapter was first published in *World Politics* 2, no. 2 (January 1950): 157–80. A partial condensation of my *Political Realism and Political Idealism* (Chicago, 1951), it deals with the role of the two attitude patterns indicated in the book's title, analyzes political movements that had a high impact on international relations, and applies the concept of the "security dilemma" to the question of why idealistic movements have usually failed and ultrarealistic power politics has usually turned out the winner. For further analysis, see pages 9–12 of the *Introduction*.
Reprinted by permission of Princeton University Press.

The heartbreaking plight in which a bipolarized and atom bomb-blessed world finds itself today is but the extreme manifestation of a dilemma with which human societies have had to grapple since the dawn of history. For it stems from a fundamental social constellation, one where a plurality of otherwise interconnected groups constitute ultimate units of political life, that is, where groups live alongside each other without being organized into a higher unity.

Wherever such anarchic society has existed—and it has existed in most periods of known history on some level—there has arisen what may be called the "security dilemma" of men, or groups, or their leaders. Groups or individuals living in such a constellation must be, and usually are, concerned about their security from being attacked, subjected, dominated, or annihilated by other groups and individuals. Striving to attain security from such attack, they are driven to acquire more and more power in order to escape the impact of the power of others. This, in turn, renders the others more insecure and compels them to prepare for the worst. Since none can ever feel entirely secure in such a world of competing units, power competition ensues, and the vicious circle of security and power accumulation is on.

Whether man is by nature peaceful and cooperative, or domineering and aggressive, is not the question. The condition that concerns us here is not a biological or anthropological but a social one. This *homo homini lupus* situation does not preclude social cooperation as another fundamental fact of social life. But even cooperation and solidarity tend to become elements in the conflict situation, part of their function being the consolidation and the strengthening of particular groups in their competition with other groups. The struggle for security, then, is merely raised from the individual or lower-group level to a higher-group level. Thus, families and tribes may overcome the power game in their internal relations in order to face other families or tribes; larger groups may overcome it to face other classes unitedly; entire nations may compose their internal conflicts in order to face other nations. But ultimately, somewhere, conflicts caused by the security dilemma are bound to emerge among political units of power.

Such findings, one might agree with Henri Bergson, "ont de quoi attrister le moraliste," and men have reacted to them in dissimilar ways. The two major ways of reacting will here be called Political Realism and Political Idealism. Political Realism frankly recognizes the phenomena which are connected with the urge for security and the competition for power, and takes their consequences into consideration. Political Idealism, on the other hand, usually starts from a more "rationalistic" assumption, namely, that a harmony exists, or may eventually be realized, between the individual concern and the general good, between interests, rights, and duties of men and groups in society; further, that power is something easily to be channeled, diffused, utilized for the common good, and that it can ultimately be eliminated altogether from political relationships. The distinction is thus not simply one between thought concerned with the actual and the ideal, "what is" and "what ought to be." It is true that Realism, frequently, is more concerned with description and analysis of what is than with political ideals, while Idealism often neglects factual phenomena for political ideals. But Realism may well, and often does, glorify "realist" trends as the desirable ones, while Idealism may take notice of power phenomena. The distinction is rather one of emphasis: Realist thought is determined by an insight into the overpowering impact of the security factor and the ensuing power-political, oligarchic, authoritarian, and similar trends and tendencies in society and politics, whatever its ultimate conclusion and advocacy. Idealist thought, on the other hand, tends to concentrate on conditions and solutions which are supposed to overcome the egoistic instincts and attitudes of individuals and groups in favor of considerations beyond mere security and self-interest. It therefore usually appears in one or another form of individualism, humanism, liberalism, pacifism, anarchism, internationalism—in short, as one of the ideologies in favor of limiting (or, more radically, eliminating) the power and authority which organized groups claim over men. As one author has expressed it, if "the children of darkness" are realists, pessimists, and cynics, the "children of light" sin through a facile optimism that renders them blind and sentimental.[1]

The distinction here suggested, while frankly inadequate in the realm of more refined political theory, seems to be a fertile one for the study of the great social and political movements of history. Its importance becomes evident when one starts to analyze the characteristic attitude-patterns and emotions of leaders and followers in such movements. Either the approach has been expressive of a utopian and often chiliastic Political Idealism, or—when disillusionment with the ideal's ability to mold the "realist" facts frustrates expectations—it has taken refuge in an equally extreme, power-political and power-glorifying Political Realism. This fatal reversal time and again has constituted the tragedy of Political Idealism, which, paradoxically, has its time of greatness when its ideals are unfulfilled,

1. Reinhold Niebuhr, *The Children of Light and the Children of Darkness: A Vindication of Democracy and a Critique of Its Traditional Defense* (New York: Scribner, 1944).

when it is in opposition to outdated political systems and the tide of the times swells it toward victory. It degenerates as soon as it attains its final goal; and in victory it dies. One is tempted to sum up the history of the great modern social and political movements as the story of the credos of Political Idealism and their successive failures in the face of the facts observed and acclaimed by Political Realism. Nowhere, perhaps, has this been more striking than in the field of the relations among the "sovereign" units of organization and power, i.e., in modern times, in the "international" realm.[2]

I

There is some typical "Idealism" in the very exclusion, or comparative disregard, of international problems from political thought. Unlike thought regarding form and structure of government, theories in the realm of international relations have traditionally formed a side issue. Systems and theories centered around units of government were considered in isolation from their international milieu. A state of peace, in which the fact of international relationships could be eliminated from theoretical consideration, was assumed to be "normal." Thus, most of the well-known utopias located their ideal commonwealth upon some island, wilderness, or similarly isolated place, and even less utopian theorists devoted their main attention to problems of internal politics and the internal improvement of the community.

A lover of the paradoxical might say that the absence of theories of international relations constitutes in itself the most typical idealist theory of international relations. It implies, indeed, that with the solution of the internal political problems no other problems remain; interrelations of political units then automatically become harmonious. But with the passing of the relative self-sufficiency of the highest political units, with their increasing interdependence in a worldwide international society, theories of international relations have at last been given

2. The following, under I through VII, condenses a chapter of a larger manuscript, entitled "Political Realism and Political Idealism, A Study in Theories and Realities."

more significant expression and have come to constitute the basis of political movements and political action. Among them, nationalism and internationalism will be analyzed here with regard to their basic idealist assumptions and their failure in the world of "realist" phenomena.

II

With the rise of sovereign nation-states there emerged the idea and ideal of a system of equal, free, and self-determining nationalities, each organized into its own state, and all living peacefully side by side in harmonious mutual relations. This "idealist" nationalism stands in contrast to the nationalism that developed with the rise of exclusive, aggressive, expansionist, and imperialistic national policies, and which will be called here "integral" nationalism. Integral nationalism represents Political Realism in its extreme: a Realism which starts by analyzing political tendencies in order to evaluate them, and which, through their glorification, then becomes the ideological foundation of the resulting movements. Idealist nationalism, on the other hand, has proved to be utopian in its expectation of an ideal international society which runs counter to actual tendencies of international politics.

As is well known, nationalism as an "ism" hardly existed prior to the French Revolution. The Revolution established the People as a self-conscious unit; foreign attack upon the Revolution created the nation-in-arms and, thereby, French nationalism, revolutionary, missionary, and visionary; resistance to French Caesarism on the part of subjugated countries created a love of nationality in these countries; and in the Wars of Liberation the revolutionary principle of national self-determination was victor over the very nation which had made the Revolution.

Idealist nationalism as a system of thought amalgamated pacifist-humanitarian with liberal-democratic elements. The doctrine of national self-determination had as its source the same ideology that produced the idea of the right of individual self-determination. Rationalistic individualism was opposed not only to restrictions enforced upon the individual but also to "cabinet politics" that disposed of populations without their consent. Thus, the "fundamental" rights of nationalities were considered to be the same as those of man, namely, freedom from interference and oppression. Once such freedom had been achieved in a system of self-determining nation-states, there would no longer be any reason or justification for international friction and war. Freedom of nations was to be the common concern of all humanity; witness the famous decree of November 19, 1792, in which the French National Convention declared that France would "come to the aid of all peoples who are seeking to recover their liberty." But the most significant spokesmen of humanitarian nationalism came from nationalities which were still seeking unification. Because of the later transformation of Germany and Italy from nationalities seeking redemption in a worldwide humanitarian nationalism to power states that were violently aggressive and authoritarian, early nationalists such as Herder, Fichte, and Mazzini, have been widely misrepresented as forerunners of integral nationalism; this obviously does them great injustice. Yet in a deeper sense it may not be without significance that the countries whose early aspirations expressed themselves in these authors later produced a Treitschke and a Hitler, a Corradini and a Mussolini. In both countries it reflects the transformation of idealist utopianism in the realm of theory into the stark reality of power politics for which integral nationalists like Treitschke merely shaped the ideology and the apologetics.

Although in Herder's concept of nationality, nationalism was mixed with elements of romanticism (each nationality having its peculiar "soul" and worth among the "flowers in God's garden"), the emphasis put on the necessity of political freedom was as strong as the expectation that self-determination would make for peace and harmony: It is the cabinets that make wars upon each other, but not so the *Vaterlaender*.[3] One and a half centuries later, with the history of the coexistence of these *Vaterlaender* in mind, a French author, sadder but wiser,

3. See *Ideen zur Philosophie der Geschichte der Menschheit* (Riga and Leipzig, 1784), bk. 9, chap. 4.

could speak of them as "these merciless fatherlands, full of greed and pride." [4] But it was Fichte in whose political philosophy the idea of peculiar "missions" of nations assumed a central importance. In conformity with his philosophy of history, which conceived that an age of utilitarian individualism was being succeeded by one of rational freedom under law and moral norms, Fichte ascribed to Germany a mission to become the model of a *Kulturnation,* a country which for the first time in history would combine political liberty with that social and economic equality without which the dignity of man as a rational being cannot be realized. Patriotism was still the means toward the higher end of the realization of free man and free humanity. To Mazzini, likewise, nationality was not only the natural unit in as association of free peoples, but also the only unit in which the internal task of emancipation from tyranny and exploitation could be performed. God, he maintained, has, in a kind of preestablished harmony, divided humanity into distinct groups on the basis of language. This natural division has been disfigured by the arbitrary boundaries of the "countries of Kings and privileged classes." National unification thus simply means restoration of preordained harmony; and between nations so established "there will be harmony and brotherhood." [5] The battle symbol, so often applied by Political Realists for their own purposes, is utilized by Mazzini for such harmonizing conclusions:

> Humanity is a great army moving to the conquests of unknown lands, against powerful and wary enemies. The Peoples are the different corps and divisions of that army. Each . . . has a special operation to perform, and the common victory depends on the exactness with which the different operations are carried out. Do not disturb the order of battle.[6]

The unanswered question as to whom these divisions were to do battle with was soon to be answered by history itself: not

4. Georges Bernanos, *Journal d'un curé de campagne* (Paris, 1936), p. 300.

5. *The Duties of Man* (New York: Everyman's Library, Dutton, 1907), p. 52.

6. Ibid., p. 55.

perceiving a common enemy, they would turn against each other.

This turning against each other had as one of its major reasons the security dilemma of politically unintegrated units, and their ensuing competition for power. Nationalities inevitably became competing units after having abandoned their state of innocence and established themselves as nation-states. Nationalism in the major nation-states now became allied with ideas of national or racial inequality and superiority; liberal-humanitarian nationalism wandered to the East. Theories of integral nationalism, which now blossomed, had forerunners in certain earlier theories, especially political romanticism, which had ridiculed the concepts of "man" and "humanity" as mere abstractions. Thus the same author who had opposed Rousseau's ideology of the spontaneous formation of the general will with an emphasis on an elite's capacity for "instilling the right prejudices" opined: "I have seen, in my time, Frenchmen, Italians, and Russians; I even know, thanks to Montesquieu, that one may be a Persian; but as for Man, I declare that I have never met him in my life; if he exists, it is without my knowledge." [7] It was through this elimination of the concept of humanity that the universalist ideology was taken out of nationalism.

What remained was either pseudo-Realism, such as that found in theories of racialism (of white, or Nordic, or Aryan superiority, etc.), or genuine Political Realism with a recognition of the inevitabilities of power politics in an age of sovereign states. How did it happen that earlier nationalism, with its vision of international peace and harmony, could have so completely overlooked this central phenomenon? Some explanation may be found in the chiliastic character of all Political Idealism, its inclination to expect the millennium, the "totally and radically different situation" on the other side of the great divide which in such thought separates the present evil world from the brave new world of the future. Thus, the "heavenly city of the eighteenth-century philosophers" (which turned out to be the bourgeois revolution) was expected to follow the abolition of feudalism and absolutism. Socialism

7. Joseph de Maistre, *Considérations sur la France* (Lyon, 1843), p. 88.

expected, and still expects, the "altogether different" to become real, once the capitalistic regime is overthrown. And humanitarian nationalism expected the golden age of international brotherhood to come true once nationalities were set free to determine their fate in liberty. Final victory over the power policies of "kings and privileged classes" was supposed to constitute these nations' "leap into the realm of freedom." But in some respects the mechanical balance-of-power politics of the absolutist cabinets, which nationalists blamed for most international evils, was more suitable for safeguarding peaceful, if not permanently stable, relations than was a policy based on the more emotional impulses, aims, and claims of nation-states whose foreign policy was influenced by the nationalism of the masses.

III

Among movements expressive of idealist internationalism we may count those revolutionary movements which were genuinely universalist, those which, in the conception and programs of their leaders as well as during the early stages of their implementation, tended to bring about a general transformation of society. In the cases of the French or the Bolshevik Revolutions, birthplace and actual theater of the movement were regarded as merely accidental starting points of what was conceived as a world-embracing development; such movements were thus world-revolutionary in the strict sense.

The Puritan revolution in England did not, in the main, conceive of itself as a world-revolutionary movement aimed at changing feudal-monarchical institutions all over the world. Similar ideological isolationism characterized the American Revolution, where even the appeal to "the opinions of mankind" was made for what was considered the cause of one single nation. But world-revolutionary appeal and propaganda were of the essence of the French Revolution. It is true that, except for some radical cosmopolitans like Anacharsis Clootz, neither Girondists nor Jacobins advocated internationalization of world society in the sense of blotting out countries and people; but they all foresaw an impending expansion of the revolutionary ideas over the world; it was France's mission to help other nations to achieve their freedom and to join with France in a society of free nations. "The Revolution is a universal religion which it is France's mission to impose upon humanity." [8]

This religious fervor was characterized by two convictions: one, that the revolutionary ideas, being the expression of undoubted truth, were bound to prevail, so to speak, by themselves, by the sheer force of their truth and reason; the other, that the total transformation of society, which these ideas were bound to bring about, was imminent. This belief in the absolute truth of the gospel and the imminence of the coming of the Savior puts French revolutionary enthusiasm alongside similar universalist-idealistic movements of chiliastic utopianism. This attitude, in the first stage of the Revolution, was common to all groups, leaders, and factions. Said Brissot: "The American Revolution engendered the French Revolution; the latter one will constitute the sacred spot whence will spring the spark that shall put all nations to fire." [9] And Lebrun wrote to Noel: "It is without doubt that our principles will spread everywhere by themselves sooner or later, simply because they are principles of pure reason for which the major part of Europe is now ripe." [10] Robespierre, in the Convention, exclaimed: "What! You have an entire nation behind you, reason as your aid, and you have not yet revolutionized the world? . . . In England, the party of freedom awaits you. . . . If only France starts marching, the republicans of England will reach out their hands to you, and the world will be free." [11] Adherents of the revolutionary gospel in other countries were imbued with the same chiliasm. An address of English republicans to the Convention contained this statement:

> Frenchmen, you are already free; the Britons expect to be free soon. The Triple Alliance, not of crowned heads, but

8. Albert Sorel, *L'Europe et la révolution française* (Paris, 1889), 2:109.

9. 10 July 1791, quoted in F. Laurent, *Histoire du droit des gens* (Paris, 1868), 15:24.

10. 11 November 1792, quoted in Sorel, *L'Europe*, 3:165.

11. 10 March 1793, ibid., p. 344.

of the peoples of America, France, and Great Britain, will bring liberty to Europe and peace to the world. After the example set by France, revolutions will be easy. We should not be surprised if very soon an English National Convention will likewise receive congratulations.[12]

In the unhistoric fashion characteristic of chiliastic movements, conditions prevailing elsewhere were considered as mere replicas of those in France, hence bound to undergo the same development. While overestimating fantastically the importance of revolutionary movements and sympathizing groups abroad, however insignificant or isolated, one vastly underestimated the hostile reaction the Revolution was bound to evoke in a Europe still largely feudal and monarchist. The war against the coalition thus appeared as a fight against toppling old powers, while appeals to the masses of the people would suffice to win them as allies on the side of the Revolution. The war would thus become one of propaganda:

Let us tell all Europe . . . that the battles which the people fight at the orders of the despots resemble blows which two friends, incited by a mean instigator, exchange in the dark; as soon as they see the light, they will drop their arms, embrace each other, and punish their deceivers. So the peoples, when suddenly at the moment of the battle between the enemy armies and ours the light of philosophy strikes their eyes, will embrace each other before deposed kings and a satisfied heaven.[13]

And Robespierre, in 1793, intoned: "Might heaven at this moment allow us to have our voice heard by all peoples: Immediately the flames of war would be extinguished and all peoples would form a nation of brothers." [14]

Thus the Dutch, the Belgians, the Germans were addressed as potential allies. The war against the tyrants was to be the last war. But until ultimate victory was won, there could be no neutrals: "The Republic recognizes only friends or enemies!" [15]

12. 7 November 1792, ibid., 2:214.
13. Isnard, quoted in Laurent, Histoire, p. 82.
14. Quoted in Laurent, Histoire, p. 174.
15. Kersaint, 1 January 1793, quoted in Sorel, L'Europe, 3:244.

Ideological movements carry their own idea of legitimacy, and the established order appears as mere brute force, without foundation in law or morals.

The new movement claimed a "legitimate" right to carry the war to those whose only title was force. Then, when the peoples of Europe failed to respond to the message, disillusioned revolutionaries claimed the right to force them to be free. Expectation of universal revolution was postponed: "Prejudice, unfortunately, spreads like a torrent, while truth arrives at a snail's pace." [16] Napoleon had to report from Italy: "Love of the people for liberty and equality has not been my ally. . . . All this is good for proclamations and speeches but it is imaginary." [17] Propaganda was now used as a weapon of national warfare, a sure sign that the stage of universalist idealism was over and *Realpolitik* had taken its place.

The rejection of the principle of revolutionary intervention by the declaration of the National Convention of April 17, 1793—a declaration which stated that France "will not interfere in any way in the government of other powers" [18]— marked the real end of the world-revolutionary period and the beginning of national *Realpolitik*. Nothing makes clearer this transformation than Danton's explanation of the new policy:

> It is time that the Convention makes known to Europe that it knows how to ally political wisdom with Republican virtues. In a moment of enthusiasm, you issued a decree whose motive was no doubt beautiful, and which obliged you to assist peoples desirous of resisting the oppression of their tyrants. This decree would have involved you if some patriots had wanted to make a revolution in China. But we must think above all of the preservation of our own body politic and of laying the foundation for French greatness.[19]

16. Baraillon, 13 January 1793, quoted in Albert Mathiez, *La révolution et les étrangers* (Paris, 1918), p. 88.

17. Quoted in Laurent, *Histoire*, p. 268.

18. See Vernon Dyke, "The Responsibility of States for International Propaganda," *American Journal of International Law* 34 (January 1940): 61.

19. Jules Basdevant, *La révolution française et le droit de la guerre continentale* (Paris, 1901), p. 164.

Genet now was instructed, in the typical terms of classical diplomacy ("government," "party," etc., as compared with the revolutionary vocabulary of "sovereign peoples," "tyrants," etc.) "to treat with the government, and not with a faction of the people; and to be the representative of the French Republic at the [American] Congress, not the head of an American Party." [20] The Revolution had now become the "revolution in one single country," and, with Bonaparte's appearance quite definitely "le jour de gloire est arrivé," with the glory and might of one's own country as the aim. Napoleon coolly denied that the French Republic had ever "adopted the principle of making war for other peoples. I would like to know what philosophical or moral rule demands the sacrifice of 40,000 Frenchmen against the well-understood interest of the Republic." [21] With the establishment of French hegemony over Europe, propaganda became of the well-known "co-prosperity sphere" type, as when it spoke of France's mission to unify Europe in "one family," where "civic dissensions constitute attacks on the common weal." [22] The oppressed nations, on the other hand, having started a war of conservative intervention, ended by taking over much of the original French revolutionary ideology, which they now were able to turn against its creator. A Prussian general could now appeal to the people in the name of the liberties of 1789: "It is for Germany's freedom that we shall win or die. . . . Any distinction of rank, birth, or origin is banned from our ranks. We are all free men." [23] The circle had become complete.

IV

The history of the Workers' Internationals is yet another confirmation of the prevalence of power-political, "realist" phenomena over too facile assumptions of a utopian Political Idealism. The idea of a classless society, which was to result from the concerted international action of the proletarians of

20. Sorel, *L'Europe,* 3:431.
21. Ibid., 5:66.
22. Laurent, *Histoire,* p. 308.
23. Ibid., p. 467.

all countries, combined internal and international utopianism in one comprehensive structure. The Second International conceived the task of the different Socialist parties as one of opposing "capitalistic" wars or of turning them into struggles for the overthrow of the capitalistic system:

> If war threatens to break out, it is the duty of the working class in the countries concerned, and of their parliamentary representatives, with the aid of the International Socialist Bureau, to do all in their power to prevent war by all means which seem to them appropriate, and which naturally vary according to the sharpness of the class struggle and the general political situation. Should war, nevertheless, break out, it is their duty to cooperate to bring it promptly to a close and to utilize the economic and political crisis created by the war to arouse the masses of the people and to precipitate the downfall of capitalist domination.[24]

But despite its apparent strength on the eve of the World War, the Second International, with its millions of well-organized adherents, proved impotent in 1914. The great majority of workers' representatives in practically every country concerned, with only feeble and scattered resistance, voted for war. Even if it were true that this *volte-face* was engineered by bureaucratized and "treacherous" leaders against the will of the masses, this would only prove the impotence of "party democracy" in the face of oligarchic tendencies in the organization. But such an explanation is of doubtful adequacy. What Socialist party could, in good conscience, have assumed the responsibility of paralyzing the war effort in its own country, unless it could be sure that its "opposite number" in the enemy country would be equally successful? Might not the outcome then simply have been the sacrifice of the independence of one's own country, including its proletariat, in favor, not of the cause of international revolution, but of the capitalists of the enemy country? The allegation of self-defense was certainly

24. Resolution adopted by the Congress of the Second International at Stuttgart, 1907; see Lewis L. Lorwin, *Labor and Internationalism* (New York: Macmillan, 1929), pp. 91 ff.

more than a mere fraud. It was indicative of the profound dilemma connected with the security factor.[25]

While the realities connected with the security and power factors led the Second International to founder in impotence, they eventually turned the Third International, and the movement it carried, into instrumentalities of power politics. There is a striking similarity between the structure and fate of the world-revolutionary ideology of the French revolutionaries and that of its counterpart, the Bolshevik ideology. Even prior to the October Revolution this ideology had been fully established. In April 1917 Lenin declared that, owing merely to historical accident, the Russian proletariat would be chosen to be the "skirmishers of the world proletariat," and that its action would be only a "prelude to and a step toward the socialist world revolution." Worldwide expansion of the revolution he considered as imminent, the preconditions for its outbreak being present in all countries, and the responsibility of the Russians for the fate of the oppressed everywhere was stressed. [26] In striking parallel to the French decree of November 19, 1792, a Bolshevist party resolution of August 1917, stated that "with the liquidation of imperialist domination the workers of that country which will first set up a dictatorship of proletarians and semi-proletarians will have the duty to render assistance, armed, if necessary, to the fighting proletariat of the other countries." [27] Even more striking is the fact that the revolution itself was undertaken only because worldwide revolution was considered a certainty,[28] a fascinating example of how ideologies, by the very fact of being accepted by leaders of a movement, create world-historic events. Even after the establishment of Soviet power in Russia, the interest of the Bolshevist party was considered as subordinate to that of the

25. Nowhere, perhaps, has the tragic situation confronting internationalists during those days been more poignantly portrayed than in Martin du Gard's Les Thibaults.

26. See V. I. Lenin, Selected Works (London, 1936), 6:17f., 230, 288, 297.

27. Resolution on "The Present Situation and the War," adopted by the Sixth Party Congress. I owe this and the following references to Ossip K. Flechtheim, who kindly made available to me a manuscript entitled "The Struggle of Bolshevism for World Dominion." See now his book Bolschewismus 1917–1967, Von der Weltrevolution zum Sowjetimperium (Vienna, 1967).

28. Cf. resolution of the Central Committee of the Party of 23 October 1917.

world-proletariat. Indeed, it was thought the duty of any particular revolutionary movement or party to sacrifice its specific interests if and whenever broader international interests demanded such sacrifice.

Inevitability as well as imminence of world revolution were taken for granted even when events seemed to shatter such belief. The slightest indications became proofs; some strikes in Germany and Austria in early 1918 were taken as sure signs of imminent revolution, not only in these countries, but in England, France, and Spain. The year 1919 constituted the peak of utopian enthusiasm. Following events in Germany, Austria, Hungary, Lenin predicted the imminent birth of an "All-World Federative Soviet Republic"; in July he promised that that month would be the last of the "difficult" July's, and that July 1920 would witness the final victory of the Communist International. About the same time an article by Zinoviev expressed the chiliastic hopes of that period:

> As these lines are being written, there exist already three Soviet Republics as the main basis of the Third International: Russia, Hungary, and Bavaria. Nobody will be surprised if, when these lines are published, there will be not three, but six or even a greater number of Soviet Republics. With dizzying speed Old Europe rushes toward the proletarian revolution.[29]

When the article appeared the number of Soviet Republics had been reduced to one. But its author, not to be discouraged, now predicted a development of such speed and dimensions that "a year hence we shall already begin to forget that Europe once witnessed a fight for Communism; for a year hence all Europe will be Communist, and the fight for Communism will have begun to extend to America and perhaps also Asia and other continents." [30] It took about thirty years, and the transformation of the regime into the autocratic rulership of a country which now had become one of the two poles of world-power, to bring this prediction to a beginning of truth, though in a very different sense. Stalinism adapted the interna-

29. Quoted in Flechtheim MS cited above.
30. Ibid.

tional ideology of Bolshevism to the "realist" fact that the one country in which the revolution had succeeded was forced to live in the same world with its non- or counterrevolutionary neighbors. Realistic appraisal of power phenomena led the regime to abandon its world-revolutionary ideology, except for propaganda purposes. As a unit in international affairs the Soviet Union now acts with at least the same degree of insistence on self-preservation, "sovereignty," security, and power considerations as do other countries. Whereas world-revolutionary ideology upheld the primacy of international over "national" proletarian considerations, Stalinism acts on the assumption that no interest anywhere can possibly be above the existence and maintenance of Soviet rule in Russia. Whatever appears today as Soviet internationalism has in reality become subservient to a primarily "national" cause, or rather, the maintenance of the regime of one specific "big power." From the point of view of genuine internationalism, this attitude, with its cynical and unabashed misuse of internationalist idealism, constitutes Political Realism in the extreme. Moreover, the facts and the struggle connected with the phenomenon of "Titoism" tend to refute the allegation that this Realism is going to last only as long as the entire globe is not yet Communist, and that with the transformation of all countries into Soviet or "popular-democratic" republics, genuine federation on the basis of equality will replace insistence on Russian predominance. The Political Idealism contained in this "federalistic" ideology seemingly is foundering upon the rock of realities inherent even in a system of plural Communist entities. Such questions as "Who will be industrialized first and at whose cost in regard to living standard of the masses?" or "Who will form the 'colonial' raw material basis for exploitation by a more 'advanced' comrade-republic?"—questions which are at the very basis of the Tito conflict—show that the security and power dilemma would have its impact on actual policies in a collectivized world as it has had in capitalistic and pre-capitalistic aeons.

V

Besides the universalism of "world-revolutionary" ideologies, internationalism in the field of political thought has even more commonly taken the form of a general idealism, which has been relatively independent of specific social-political creeds and movements and has centered around what may be broadly described as pacifism. Arising in an age that witnessed an increasing international integration of society in a wide variety of fields, such as communications, trade, finance, this type of Political Idealism had the same traces of rationalist utopianism as were characteristic of humanitarian nationalism. Its chiliastic nature is apparent from its assumption that international integration in certain fields of society will inevitably be followed and implemented by the sociopolitical integration of mankind into one community. All the more radical among the well-known recent schemes for world government assume the "directedness" of history, as progress toward internally ever more democratic, internationally ever more comprehensive societies, which will eventually constitute one great community. Belief in the desirability of the political oneness of the world leads to the assumption of its virtual oneness in fact. All that remains to be done is to lay technical-organizational foundations. Wars and power politics are considered as anachronisms. The philosophy of this school is perhaps nowhere more neatly expressed than in a resolution passed by the North Carolina legislature in 1941:

> Just as feudalism served its purpose in human history and was superseded by nationalism, so has nationalism reached its apogee in this generation and yielded its hegemony in the body politic to internationalism. . . . The organic life of the human race is at last indissolubly unified and can never be severed, but it must be politically ordained and made subject to law." [31]

This was said at the time of the greatest and most "total" war in history, a war which resulted in the polarization and concentration of power in "superpowers" to an extent never witnessed before. The theory of the anachronism of state and sovereignty, of wars and power politics, simply overlooks the opposite tendency growing out of the technical interdependence of the sovereign units in the world: Faced with this

31. Text in *International Conciliation*, No. 371, June 1941, pp. 585 ff.

growing interdependence but also with the security dilemma, their attempted way out is to expand their *individual* power, economically (in order to be self-sufficient in war), strategically (in order to safeguard its defense requirements), etc. This may be international provincialism, but it is hard to see how to escape it in a still anarchic international world. The facile proposal of the world federalists that all that is needed is to abolish sovereignty by *fiat* of international law, simply "takes legal symbols for social realities." [32] Such an unrealistic attitude is responsible for what has been aptly called "the unreality of international law and the unlawfulness of international reality." [33] In view of the security dilemma of competing powers, attempts to reduce power by mutual agreement, for instance through disarmament, were bound to fail, even if there had not been additional, economic factors driving them into the direction of imperialism. If Marxism maintains that political relations and developments form the "superstructure" over the systems and developments of the means of *production,* for the sphere of international relations it might rather be said that political developments have constituted a superstructure over the developments of the means of *destruction.*

VI

It was partly these additional factors driving states in the direction of imperialism that accounted for the failure of yet another type of idealistic internationalism, the one connected with economic, or laissez-faire, liberalism. Whenever and wherever the trading class with its commercial interests came to the fore in competition with feudal groups, it developed an internationalist-pacifist ideology based on the assumption that once the "irrational" monopolistic, militaristic, and nationalist obstacles to free exchange of goods among nations were eliminated, all nations would readily realize their common

32. Reinhold Niebuhr, "The Myth of World Government," *Nation,* 16 March 1946.
33. Gerhard Niemeyer, *Law Without Force* (Princeton: Princeton University Press, 1941).

interest in peace. We hear even before 1400 from a contemporary observer of Florentine policies that these policies were "not determined by ambitions, which are typical of the nobility, but by the interests of trade; and since nothing is more hostile and detrimental to merchants and artisans than the disturbance and confusion of war, certainly the merchants and artisans who rule us love peace and hate the waste of war." [34] England in the seventeenth and eighteenth centuries was filled with the pacifist ideology of commercialism; and similar enthusiasm was expanded, in the work of an early poet of a nation whose very origin was a fight for freedom of trade, into the vision of a world federation "by commerce joined":

> Each land shall imitate, each nation join
> The well-based brotherhood, the league divine,
> Extend its empire with the circling sun,
> And band the peopled globe within its federal zone.
>
> Till each remotest clan, by commerce join'd,
> Links in the chain that binds all humankind,
> Their bloody banners sink in darkness furl'd
> And one white flag of peace triumphant walks the world.[35]

While philosophers such as Comte and Spencer later developed this ideology into a more general philosophy of history—according to which an age of science, technology, industrialism, and peace would follow upon eras of more warlike traditionalism, militarism, and aristocracy—it found its more factual-economic, though more pedestrian, elaboration in the theories of economic internationalism of the Manchester School. Thus Cobden was an active protagonist of the peace movement, which he tried to ally with his anti-colonial free trade crusade: "The efforts of the Peace Societies, however laudable, can never be successful as long as the nations maintain their present system of isolation. . . . The Colonial System of Europe has been the chief source of war for

34. Salutati, quoted by Felix Gilbert in his chapter "Machiavelli," in *Makers of Modern Strategy*, ed. Edward M. Earle (Princeton: Princeton University Press, 1943), p. 21.

35. From Joel Barlow's "Columbiad," as quoted in Hans Kohn, *The Idea of Nationalism* (New York: Macmillan, 1944), p. 299.

the last 150 years." "I see in the Free Trade principle that which shall act on the moral world as the principle of gravitation in the Universe—drawing men together, thrusting aside the antagonism of race and creed and language, and uniting us in the bonds of peace." [36]

The reality was imperialism and world war. The economic system of industrial capitalism, while internationalist in its early theory, was put into practice in national economic units: "Economic theory is cosmopolitan, but political fact is nationalistic." [37] But it was in the economic as well as in the political realm that the "realist" obstacles to the implementation of the laissez-faire gospel were found. Exactly as in internal economies accumulation of economic power by monopolies, etc. has prevented a genuinely "free enterprise" system from functioning, so in the international realm complete freedom of interchange of goods, of migration, etc. could not prevail over the tendencies of monopoly and exclusiveness. Thus tariffs (while at first perhaps justified in certain countries in order to protect rising industries from older ones in other countries—such as England, which otherwise might have frozen the economic status quo in her exclusive favor just by utilizing the free trade principle) became powerful instruments for the preservation of vested economic interests. Also, liberal economic theory overlooked the fact that, side by side with trades and industries interested in peace, such as export or investment banking, there are powerful interests in actual war or at least in conditions under which war always threatens, such as those of the armaments manufacturer. Even with regard to foreign investments, which apparently flourish better in peace than in war, need for protection and desire for better exploitation have often resulted in conflicts among countries backing the respective interests. Political and economic causes here are inextricably intertwined. Just as economic interests would induce governments to intervene on behalf of business, alleged business interests would be used by governments as a pretext for power politics, for instance for strategic aims.[38]

36. From addresses in 1842 and 1846, quoted in Lorwin, *Labor*, pp. 21 f.
37. Frank D. Graham, "Economics and Peace," in *The Second Chance: America and the Peace*, ed. John B. Whitton (Princeton: Princeton University Press, 1944), p. 126.
38. While liberal economic theory has tended to play down the economic factor, Marxist criticism of "finance capitalism" and imperialism has tended to

For, even if capitalism had not developed inherent oligarchic and imperialistic trends, the security dilemma inherent in the system of sovereign nation-states as such would have prevented capitalism from forming a genuinely free-enterprise system on an international basis. It seems unnecessary to enumerate all of the different power-political factors connected with "security," "defense," etc. which have borne upon the national economic policies of the various nation-states.

VII

If the theory of economic liberalism in its international aspects proved to be utopian, one might assume that its opposite, the theory of economic collectivism, with its strong and realistic criticism of liberal fallacies, would be expressive of Political Realism. But an analysis of collectivist assumptions shows that, as in the case of nationalism and internationalism, opposed ideologies may *each* partake of realist and idealist elements. Realistic in their criticism of the opponent, they turn utopian-idealist when their own positive program is involved. Thus a laissez-faire liberal like Hayek criticizes the collectivist for believing that in a system of planned economies the causes of international friction and wars would be eliminated, pointing with good reason to the fact that "if the resources of different nations are treated as exclusive properties of these nations as wholes . . . they inevitably become the source of friction and envy between whole nations. . . . Class strife would become a struggle between the working classes of the different countries." [39] Positively, however, his brother-in-arms among latter-day specimens of "classical" liberalism, von Mises, asserts that "within a world of pure, perfect, and unhampered capitalism" there are "no incentives for aggres-

---

overlook the power factor. Both are realistic in their critique but reveal the harmonistic tendencies of their general doctrines by their respective deemphasis. Cf., e.g., the writings of Eugene Staley, notably his *War and the Private Investor* (New York: Doubleday, 1935); and Wolfgang Hallgarten's book *Vorkriegsimperialismus* (Paris, 1935).

39. Friedrich A. Hayek, *The Road to Serfdom* (Chicago: University of Chicago Press, 1944), p. 221.

sion and conquest." [40] To this the collectivist, Laski, retorts, also with good reason, that "in any capitalist society which has reached the period of contraction every vested interest must be aggressive if it wishes to maintain its ground," and yet he simultaneously denies that the same factor can play a role in a system of planned economy: "The motive of aggression, except on grounds of external security, is ruled out by the nature of the Russian system." [41] This, of course, is begging the question; for it is plain that the "exception" embodies the very problem, that of the impact of security and competition factors on the policies of collectivist societies. It has been observed above (section IV) that, in view of recent development within the Soviet "sphere" itself, there is no reason to assume that even in a system of socialist commonwealths all causes for friction among the units of the system would suddenly disappear. But those among the ideologists of collectivism who now bewail the unbrotherly power politics of a socialist fellow-nation,[42] may take some consolation in the fact that even in classical antiquity the representative of economic materialism had been color-blind with respect to the power and security factor facing a Communist state, an omission for which he was criticized by no less a critic than Aristotle.[43]

VIII

The foregoing may have created the impression that the two extremes—utopian idealism, with its chiliastic approach

40. Ludwig von Mises, *Omnipotent Government: The Rise of the Total State and Total War* (New Haven: Yale University Press, 1944), p. 5.

41. Harold J. Laski, *Reflections on the Revolution of Our Time* (New York, Viking, 1943), p. 245.

42. Thus Moshe Piyade, of the Yugoslav Politbureau, complains: "They have betrayed socialism . . . They accuse us of meddling in their internal affairs, but they have brought back their diplomacy . . . to the line that existed in Russia before the October Revolution . . . We have learned that even the great principles of Socialism and international Socialist solidarity can become business phrases in the mouths of Socialist statesmen. We have learned that behind the phrases of Socialist internationalism there can be hidden the most selfish interests of the great powers toward the small." (From a speech made 7 July 1949, as reported in *New York Times*, 9 July 1949.)

43. Aristotle, *Politics*, bk. 2, chap. 7, with regard to the theories of Phaleas the Chalcedonian.

and its failure in practice, on the one hand, and cynical realism, with its cool acceptance or even idealization of power, on the other hand—were the only existing and possible approaches to the problem of politics. If so, a corrective statement in a however brief paragraph is called for. True, time and again these approaches and corresponding movements have been recurring in the history of the last few centuries, or even millennia, one leading to, and provoking, the other in what appears as an endless chain or a vicious circle. But there have also been possibilities and actualities of synthesis, of a combination of Political Realism and Political Idealism in the sense that the given facts and phenomena were recognized which Realism has stressed, coupled with an attempt to counteract such forces within the realm of the possible on the basis of the ideals of Political Idealism. We suggest to call such an approach, and the policies based upon it, Realist Liberalism. The term "Realist" indicates that the system or policy in question must start from, and accept, the factual insights of Political Realism as its firm basis and foundation, lest it turn into unrealizable utopianism. The term "Liberalism," on the other hand, points to the type of aims or ideals which are to be the guiding stars of such an attitude. As proposed here, the term "Liberalism" is broader than the liberalism of the nineteenth-century free traders and constitutionalists. It includes all socialism that is not totalitarianism, all conservatism that is not authoritarianism or mere defense of some status quo. It is not pledged to any specific economic theory, nor to any particular theory of the "best" form of government. It is derived from the ideal of freedom that underlies the major idealistic theories, thus accepting the age-old ideals that center around terms such as "liberal," "democratic," "humanitarian," "socialist." Negatively it tends to combat all use of power that is not put into the service of the liberal ideal but serves to establish or maintain privilege and oligarchism, exploitation and the infliction of violence; in short, it opposes all the natural forces and trends which are the direct or indirect consequence of the security and power dilemma.

In order to avoid mere eclecticism in the juxtaposition of the "realist" insights and the aims of Idealism it is very necessary to keep this basic difficulty in mind. Liberalism in this sense is, to quote Ortega y Gasset, "paradoxical," "acro-batic," "anti-natural." [44] It partakes of the general antinomy between ethical ideals and natural trends and forces which was already clearly perceived at the heyday of Darwinism (both biological and social):

> The practice of that which is ethically best involves a course of conduct which, in all respects, is opposed to that which leads to success in the cosmic struggle for exist-ence. In place of ruthless self-assertion, it demands self-restraint; in place of thrusting aside, or treading down, all competitors, it requires that the individual shall not merely respect, but shall help his fellows; its influence is directed, not so much to the survival of the fittest, as to the fitting of as many as possible to survive. It repudiates the gladiato-rial theory of existence. . . . The ethical progress of society depends, not on imitating the cosmic process, still less in running away from it, but in combating it. [45]

In following this advice, Realist Liberalism must, above all, be conscious of the limits which the "gladiatorial" facts put to its endeavors. Realist Liberalism is the theory and practice of the *realizable* ideal. As Koestler once put it, "the difference between utopia and a working concern is to know one's limits." Such policy is the most difficult of arts, and to formulate its principles the most difficult of sciences. But if successful, Realist Liberalism will prove to be more lastingly rewarding than utopian idealism or crude power-realism. While less glamorous than Political Idealism, it is also less utopian; while less emotional, it is more sober; while less likely ever to become the battleground of great political movements which stir the imagination of the masses, it has more of a chance to contribute to lasting achievements for human free-dom. Even though it will be attacked from both sides—for it can say, with Ibsen, "I have within me both the Right and the Left"—it may be able to lend to both Realism and Idealism some measure of attenuation, thus rendering the former more humane and the latter less chimerical. A kind of "second

44. Jose Ortega y Gasset, *The Revolt of the Masses* (London, 1932), p. 83.
45. Thomas H. Huxley, *Evolution and Ethics and Other Essays* (New York: Appleton, 1896), pp. 81 ff.

liberalism," it emerges as synthesis from the "thesis" of utopian idealism and the "antithesis" of cynical realism.

While it is impossible here to convey a more precise impression of the great variety of approaches, devices, and institutions which Realist Liberalism would suggest for the realm of internal government and politics, it may be remarked in conclusion that in international relations the mitigation, channeling, balancing, or control of power has prevailed perhaps more often than the inevitability of power politics would lead one to believe. Thus, a conscious balance-of-power policy, despite the opprobrium attached to the term, has in modern times maintained a system of major and smaller nations which, while not able to prevent wars, injustice, or even the independence of *all* units in the system, at least preserved many of them from total subjugation at the hands of one hegemonial power. A system of collective security, as rationalization of the balance principle (automatic formation of the "Grand Alliance" whenever a member turns aggressor), perhaps came closer to practical realization in the interwar period than debunking of the League-of-Nations experiment would have us assume. Concessions, even if made out of "enlightened self-interest" (such as made by the British in respect to the Dominions and now India) may substitute relations of cooperation and comparative equality for those of enforced domination. Today, it is true, any such devices seem to incur even greater difficulties in view of the bipolarity of the present power-system, which, lacking the traditional balancing power or group of powers, renders the maintenance of the balance more precarious and excludes collective security; for, while one may have collective security with ten, or five, or possibly even three units of power, it cannot be achieved with two. The use of a terminology of collective action then becomes mere ideology and subterfuge in order to provide bloc-building with a semblance of legality; thus, collective self-defense becomes a pretext, however understandable and justified such regionalism may be, in East or West, from the standpoint of security. For the security dilemma today is perhaps more clear-cut than it ever was before. It would appear that from the point which concentration of power has now achieved, it can only either proceed to actual global domination by one power-unit or recede into diffusion and disintegration. But the greater the difficulties, the greater is the task of a policy of restraint and the merit of those who, as Realist Liberals, would know how to forego the "easy" solution, the "Gordian knot" solution of force, in favor of a peace that would be neither appeasement and abdication nor the Carthaginian result of a war which might spell the destruction of our civilization.

RISE AND DEMISE OF THE TERRITORIAL STATE

This chapter was first published in *World Politics* 9, no. 4 (July 1957): 473–93. Condensating portions of my *International Politics in the Atomic Age* (New York, 1959), it analyzes the nature of the modern, "territorial" state, whose characteristic "sovereignty" and "impermeability" are found to be based, at least in part, upon the development of the military means of defense. The essay then traces the impact on traditional statehood of more recent weapons, such as the airplane and, in particular, nuclear arms. For further analysis, see pages 12–15 of the *Introduction* and chapter 8 in this volume.

Students and practitioners of international politics are at present in a strange predicament. Complex though their problems have been in the past, there was then at least some certainty about the "givens," the basic structure and the basic phenomena of international relations. Today one is neither here nor there. On the one hand, for instance, one is assured— or at least tempted to accept assurance—that for all practical purposes a nuclear stalemate rules out major war as a major means of policy today and in the foreseeable future. On the other hand, one has an uncanny sense of the practicability of the unabated arms race, and a doubt whether reliance can be placed solely on the deterrent purpose of all this preparation. We are no longer sure about the functions of war and peace, nor do we know how to define the national interest and what its defense requires under present conditions. As a matter of fact, the meaning and function of the basic protective unit, the "sovereign" nation-state itself, have become doubtful. On what, then, can policy and planning be built?

In the author's opinion, many of these uncertainties have their more profound cause in certain fundamental changes which have taken place in the structure of international relations and, specifically, in the nature of the units among which these relations occur. This transformation in the "statehood" of nations will be the subject of this article.

I. BASIC FEATURES OF THE MODERN STATE SYSTEM

Traditionally, the classical system of international relations, or the modern state system, has been considered "anarchic," because it was based on unequally distributed power and was deficient in higher—that is, supranational—authority. Its units, the independent, sovereign nation-states, were forever threatened by stronger power and survived precariously through the balance-of-power system. Customarily, then, the modern state system has been contrasted with the medieval system, on the one hand, where units of international relations were under higher law and higher authority, and with those more recent international trends, on the other, which seemed to point toward a greater, "collective" security of nations and a "rule of law" that would protect them from the indiscriminate use of force characteristic of the age of power politics.

From the vantage point of the atomic age, we can probe deeper into the basic characteristics of the classical system. What is it that ultimately accounted for the peculiar unity, compactness, coherence of the modern nation-state, setting it off from other nation-states as a separate, independent, and sovereign power? It would seem that this underlying factor is to be found neither in the sphere of law nor in that of politics, but rather in that substratum of statehood where the state unit confronts us, as it were, in its physical, corporeal capacity: as an expanse of territory encircled for its identification and its defense by a "hard shell" of fortifications. In this lies what will here be referred to as the "impermeability," or "impenetrability," or simply the "territoriality," of modern state. The fact that it was surrounded by a hard shell rendered it to some extent secure from foreign penetration, and thus made it an ultimate unit of protection for those within its boundaries. Throughout history, that unit which affords protection and security to human beings has tended to become the basic political unit; people, in the long run, will recognize that authority, any authority, which possesses the power of protection.

Some similarity perhaps prevails between an international structure consisting of impenetrable units with an ensuing measurability of power and comparability of power relations, and the system of classical physics with its measurable forces and the (then) impenetrable atom as its basic unit. And as that system has given way to relativity and to what nuclear science has uncovered, the impenetrability of the political atom, the nation-state, is giving way to a permeability which tends to obliterate the very meaning of unit and unity, power and power relations, sovereignty and independence. The possibility of "hydrogenization" merely represents the culmination of a development which has rendered the traditional defense structure of nations obsolete through the power to by-pass the shell protecting a two-dimensional territory and thus to destroy—vertically, as it were—even the most powerful ones. Paradoxically, utmost strength now coincides in the same unit with utmost vulnerability, absolute power with utter impotence.

This development must inevitably affect traditional power concepts. Considering power units as politically independent and legally sovereign made sense when power, measurable, graded, calculable, served as a standard of comparison between units which, in the sense indicated above, could be described as impermeable. Under those conditions, then, power indicated the strategic aspect, independence the political aspect, sovereignty the legal aspect of this selfsame impermeability. With the passing of the age of territoriality, the usefulness of these concepts must now be questioned.

Thus the Great Divide does not separate "international anarchy," or "balance of power," or "power politics," from incipient international interdependence, or from "collective security"; all these remain within the realm of the territorial structure of states and can therefore be considered as trends or stages *within* the classical system of "hard shell" power units. Rather, the Divide occurs where the basis of territorial power and defensibility vanishes. It is here and now. But in order to understand the present, we must study more closely the origin and nature of the classical system itself.

II. THE RISE OF THE TERRITORIAL STATE

The rise of the modern territorial state meant that, within countries, "feudal anarchy" of jurisdictions yielded to the ordered centralism of the absolute monarchy, which ruled over a pacified area with the aid of a bureaucracy, a professional army, and the power to levy taxes, while in foreign relations, in place of the medieval hierarchy of power and authority, there prevailed insecurity, a disorder only slightly attenuated by a power balance that was forever being threatened, disturbed, and then restored. Such has been the customary interpretation.

It is possible to view developments in a somewhat different light. Instead of contrasting the security of groups and individuals within the sovereign territorial state with conditions of insecurity outside, the establishment of territorial independence can be interpreted as an at least partially successful attempt to render the territorial group secure in its outward relations as well. Especially when contrasted with the age of anarchy and insecurity which immediately preceded it, the age of territoriality appears as one of relative order and safety.

Indeed, the transition from medieval hierarchism to modern compartmentalized sovereignties was neither easy, nor straight, nor short. Modern sovereignty arose out of the triangular struggle among emperors and popes, popes and kings, and kings and emperors. When the lawyers of Philip the Fair propounded the dual maxim according to which the king was to be "emperor in his realm" *(rex est imperator in regno suo)* and was no longer to "recognize any superior" *(superiorem non recognoscens)*, it was the beginning of a development in the course of which, in McIlwain's words, "Independence *de facto* was ultimately translated into a sovereignty *de jure*." [1] But centuries of disturbance and real anarchy ensued during which the problems of rulership and security remained unsettled. The relative protection which the sway of moral standards and the absence of highly destructive weapons had afforded groups and individuals in the earlier Middle Ages gave way to total insecurity when gunpowder was invented and common standards broke down. Out of the internal and external turmoil during the age of religious and civil wars, a "neutralist" central power eventually managed to establish itself in and for each of the different territories like so many *rochers de bronze*.

The idea that a territorial coexistence of states, based on the power of the territorial princes, might afford a better guarantee of peace than the Holy Roman Empire was already widespread at the height of the Middle Ages when the emperor proved incapable of enforcing the peace. [2] But territoriality could hardly prevail so long as the knight in his castle (that medieval unit of impermeability) was relatively immune from attack, as was the medieval city within its walls. Only with a developing money economy were overlords able to free themselves from dependence on vassals and lay the foundations of their own power by establishing a professional army. Infantry and artillery now proved superior to old-style cavalry, firearms prevailed over the old weapons.

As in all cases of radically new developments in military technology, the "gunpowder revolution" caused a real revolution in the superstructure of economic, social, and political relationships because of its impact on the units of protection and security. A feeling of insecurity swept all Europe. [3] Though

1. Charles H. McIlwain, *The Growth of Political Thought in the West* (New York, 1932), p. 268.
2. F. A. von der Heydte, *Die Geburtsstunde des souveränen Staates* (Regensburg, 1952), pp. 103 ff., 277, 293 ff.
3. Ariosto expressed the feeling of despair which invaded the "old powers" of chivalry when gunpowder destroyed the foundations of their system, in terms reminding one of present-day despair in the face of the destructive forces loosed upon our own world:
"Oh! curs'd device! base implement of death!
Framed in the black Tartarean realms beneath!

a Machiavelli might establish new rules as to how to gain and maintain power, there still followed more than a century of unregulated, ideological "total" wars inside and among countries until the new units of power were clearly established. Before old or new sovereigns could claim to be recognized as rulers of large areas, it had to be determined how far, on the basis of their new military power, they were able to extend their control geographically.[4]

The large-area state came finally to occupy the place that the castle or fortified town had previously held as a unit of impenetrability. But the new unit could not be considered consolidated until all independent fortifications within it had disappeared and, in their place, fortresses lining the circumference of the country had been built by the new central power and manned by its armed forces.[5] If we contrast our present system of bases and similar outposts surrounding entire world regions with what are today small-scale nation-states, perhaps we can visualize what the hard shell of frontier fortifications consolidating the then large-scale territorial states meant by way of extending power units in the age of absolutism. They became, in the words of Frederick the Great, "mighty nails which hold a ruler's provinces together." There now was peace and protection within. War became a regularized military procedure; only the breaking of the shell permitted interference with what had now become the internal affairs of another country.

In this way was established the basic structure of the territorial state which was to last throughout the classical period of the modern state system. Upon this foundation a new system and new concepts of international relations could arise. And as early as the second half of the seventeenth century a perspicacious observer succeeded in tying up the new concepts with the underlying structure of territorial statehood.

By Beelzebub's malicious art design'd
To ruin all the race of human kind."
Quoted from *Orlando Furioso* by Felix Gilbert, in *Makers of Modern Strategy*, ed. Edward M. Earle (Princeton, N.J., 1943), p. 4.

4. On this, see Garrett Mattingly, *Renaissance Diplomacy* (Boston, 1955), pp. 59 ff., 121 ff., 205 ff.

5. See Friedrich Meinecke, *Die Idee der Staatsraison in der neueren Geschichte* (Munich and Berlin, 1925), pp. 241 ff.

III. THE NATURE OF TERRITORIALITY

It was hardly a coincidence that this connection was established shortly after the end of the Thirty Years' War, when formal sanction had been given to territorial sovereignty in the Westphalian Peace. For here was the turning point, the Great Divide between what were still partially medieval situations reflecting a certain permeability of the rising nation-state (when, for instance, outside powers could still ally themselves with *frondes* within a country against that country's sovereign) and the modern era of closed units no longer brooking such interference.[6]

The clarification of the nature of territoriality to which we referred above is found in a little and little-known essay by Leibniz, written for an entirely pragmatic purpose—namely, to prove the right of legation of the territorial ruler (the Duke of Hanover) in whose service the philosopher then was.[7] Leibniz' problem derived directly from the situation created by the Peace of Westphalia. This settlement, for all practical purposes, had conferred sovereign independence upon those princes who formally were still included in the Empire; yet it had not abolished the long-established, essentially feudal structure of the Empire itself, with its allegiances and jurisdictions, its duties of membership, and even its clumsy and scarcely workable framework of government. Thus some of the factually sovereign territorial rulers in Europe were somehow still under a higher authority. Were they now "sovereign" or not? What accounted for sovereignty?

Leibniz' contemporaries failed to see the problem in this

6. The emergence of "nonintervention" as a legal concept illustrates this transition. A complete change in the meaning of the term occurred in the brief period between the time of Grotius and that of Pufendorf. Grotius, writing during the last phase of the pre-modern era of religious and "international civil" wars and still thinking in terms of "just" and "unjust" wars, considered a ruler entitled to intervene in the affairs of another sovereign if it was necessary to defend oppressed subjects of the latter; Pufendorf, barely fifty years later, rejected such interference in the "domestic affairs" of another sovereign as a violation of the sovereign's exclusive jurisdiction over his territory and all it contained. See Walter Schiffer, *The Legal Community of Mankind* (New York, 1954), pp. 34 f., 56.

7. "Entretiens de Philarète et d'Eugène sur le droit d'Ambassade"; quoted here from *Werke*, 1st series (Hanover, 1864), 3:331 ff.

light. The muddled state of affairs was made to order for those jurists and others who argued fine points perennially with the aid of sterile or obsolete concepts. Leibniz, instead, proceeded to study "what actually happens in the world today," and as a result could boast of being "the first to have found the valid definition of sovereignty." [8]

As he saw it, the first condition for sovereignty was a minimum size of territory. Minuscule principalities, at that time still abundant, could not claim to be on a par with those that recognized each other as equally sovereign in respect to peace and war, alliances, and the general affairs of Europe, because, not possessing sufficient territory, they could at best, with their garrisons, only maintain *internal* order.[9] But there remained the chief problem: how to define the status of those rulers who, because of their membership in the Empire, were subjects of the emperor. Could one be "sovereign" and "subject" at the same time? If not, what was the status of these "subject" rulers as compared with that of their "sovereign" European brethren? If so, what did their subjection to the emperor amount to? These questions were further complicated by the fact that at every European court, and in the Empire as well, there were certain high dignitaries, often called "princes," "dukes," etc., who customarily held the rank of "sovereign." It was through this maze of relationships that Leibniz arrived at his definitions.

He elaborated his concept of sovereignty by distinguishing it from "majesty." Majesty, the authority which the emperor has qua emperor over the Empire's members, consists of a number of jurisdictions that confer the right to demand obedience and involve duties of fealty, but it is not sovereignty. Why not? Simply because, with all its supreme authority, majesty does not involve an "actual and present power to constrain" subjects on their own territories. Their territory, in other words, is impermeable. The subject, on the other hand, if he is a territorial ruler, is sovereign because he has the power to constrain *his* subjects, while not being so constrainable by superior power. The decisive criterion thus is actual control of

8. Ibid., pp. 340, 342.
9. Ibid., p. 349.

one's "estates" by one's military power, which excludes any other power within and without. Contrariwise, the absence of such forces of his own on his subjects' territories accounts for the absence of "sovereignty" in the emperor's "majesty." He can enforce his authority or rights only by applying his own or other sovereigns' forces from the outside, "by means of war." But in doing so, his condition is no different from that of any other sovereign vis-à-vis *his* fellow-rulers, for war is a contest which can be inaugurated not only by majesties but by any sovereign ruler. And force of arms may constrain a sovereign outside the Empire quite as well as one inside; in fact, war constitutes the only way in which even sovereigns can be constrained.[10] By perceiving that the emperor's power to enforce his authority was actually reduced to means of war, Leibniz was in a position to demonstrate that any and all rulers of impermeable territory, whatever their status in regard to imperial authority, were equal in their sovereign status.

This capacity also distinguished them from those dignitaries who were sovereigns in name only. Leibniz, by way of example, referred to the non-sovereign status of certain papal "princes," contrasting it with that of sovereign princes: "Should His Holiness desire to make . . . [the papal princes] obey, he has merely to send out his 'sbirros' [bailiffs], but in order to constrain . . . [the sovereign princes] he would need an army and cannon." [11] Similarly, if the Empire wants to constrain a sovereign member, "what would begin as court procedure in an imperial Tribunal, in execution would amount to a war." [12] In the new age of territoriality, those superior in law no longer could use the machinery of government (courts, etc.) to enforce claims against territorial rulers.[13] In more

10. "La souveraineté est un pouvoir légitime et ordinaire de contraindre les sujets à obéir, sans qu'on puisse être contraint soy même si ce n'est par une guerre" (ibid., p. 352).

11. Ibid., p. 354.

12. Ibid., p. 358.

13. Leibniz' emphasis on constraint as a primary prerequisite of sovereignty might strike later observers as over-materialistic. But one should remember that the *rocher de bronze* of sovereignty was only then being established, not only against outside interference but also against still recalcitrant feudal powers within the territorial ruler's realm, and even in the latter case frequently by force of arms and armed forces which to the defeated may well have appeared as something very much like occupation forces. As a

recent times, this has come to be the relationship between sovereign nation-states as members of international organizations (like the League of Nations or the United Nations) and the organizations as such.

IV. THE TERRITORIAL STATE IN INTERNATIONAL RELATIONS

From territoriality resulted the concepts and institutions which characterized the interrelations of sovereign units, the modern state system. Modern international law, for instance, could now develop. Like the international system that produced it, international law has often been considered inherently contradictory because of its claim to bind sovereign units. But whether or not we deny to it for this reason the name and character of genuine law, it is important to see it in its connection with the territorial nature of the state system that it served. Only then can it be understood as a system of rules not contrary to, but implementing, the sovereign independence of states. Only to the extent that it reflected their territoriality and took into account their sovereignty could international law develop in modern times. For its general rules and principles deal primarily with the delimitation of the jurisdiction of countries. It thus implements the de facto condition of territorial impenetrability by more closely defining unit, area, and conditions of impenetrability. Such a law must reflect, rather than regulate. As one author has rightly remarked, "International law really amounts to laying down the principle of national sovereignty and deducing the consequences." [14] It is not for this reason superfluous, for sovereign units must know in some detail where their jurisdictions end and those of other units begin; without such standards, nations would be involved in constant strife over the implementation of their independence.

---

matter of fact, "garrisoning" is a key word in Leibniz' arguments: "As long as one has the right to be master in one's own house, and no superior has the right to maintain garrisons there and deprive one of the exercise of one's right of peace, war, and alliances, one has that independence which sovereignty presupposes (liberté requise à la Souveraineté)" (ibid., p. 356).

14. François Laurent, as quoted by Schiffer, Legal Community, p. 157.

But it was not only this mutual legal accommodation which rendered possible a relatively peaceful coexistence of nations. War itself, the very phenomenon which reflected, not the strength, but the limitations of impermeability, was of such a nature as to maintain at least the principle of territoriality. War was limited not only in conduct but also in objectives. It was not a process of physical or political annihilation but a contest of power and will in which the interests, but not the existence, of the contestants were at stake. Now that we approach the era of absolute exposure, without walls or moats, where penetration will mean not mere damage or change but utter annihilation of life and way of life, it may dawn on us that what has vanished with the age of sovereignty and "power politics" was not entirely adverse in nature and effects.

Among other "conservative" features of the classical system, we notice one only in passing: the balance of power. It is only recently that emphasis has shifted from a somewhat one-sided concern with the negative aspects of the balance— its uncertainty, its giving rise to unending conflicts and frequent wars, etc.—to its protective effect of preventing the expansionist capacity of power from destroying other power altogether.[15] But at the time of its perfection in statecraft and diplomacy, there were even theories (not lived up to in practice, of course) about the *legal* obligations of nations to form barriers against hegemony power in the common interest.[16]

More fundamental to the conservative structure of the old system was its character as a community. Forming a comparatively pacified whole, Europe was set off sharply against the world outside, a world beyond those lines which, by common agreement, separated a community based on territoriality and common heritage from anarchy, where the law of nature reigned and no standards of civilization applied. Only recently have the existence and role of so-called amity lines been rediscovered, lines which were drawn in the treaties of the

15. See my *Political Realism and Political Idealism* (Chicago, 1951), pp. 206–21.

16. J. von Elbe, "Die Wiederherstellung der Gleichgewichtsordnung in Europa durch den Wiener Kongress," *Zeitschrift für ausländisches öffentliches Recht und Völkerrecht* (1934), 4:226 ff.

early modern period and which separated European territories, where the rules of war and peace were to prevail, from overseas territories and areas.[17] There was to be "no peace beyond the line"; that is, European powers, although possibly at peace in Europe, continued to be *homo homini lupus* abroad. This practice made it easier for the European family of nations to observe self-denying standards at home by providing them with an outlet in the vast realm discovered outside Europe. While the practice of drawing amity lines subsequently disappeared, one chief function of overseas expansion remained: a European balance of power could be maintained or adjusted because it was relatively easy to divert European conflicts into overseas directions and adjust them there. Thus the openness of the world contributed to the consolidation of the territorial system. The end of the "world frontier" and the resulting closedness of an interdependent world inevitably affected this system's effectiveness.

Another characteristic of the old system's protective nature may be seen in the almost complete absence of instances in which countries were wiped out in the course of wars or as a consequence of other power-political events. This, of course, refers to the territorial units at home only, not to the peoples and state units beyond the pale abroad; and to the complete destruction of a state's independent existence, not to mere loss of territory or similar changes, which obviously abounded in the age of power politics.

Evidence of this is to be found not only in a legal and political ideology that denied the permissibility of conquest at home while recognizing it as a title for the acquisition of territorial jurisdiction abroad.[18] For such a doctrine had its non-ideological foundation in the actual difference between European and non-European politics so far as their territorial-

17. See Carl Schmitt, *Der Nomos der Erde* (Cologne, 1950), pp. 60 ff.; also W. Schoenborn, "Über Entdeckung als Rechtstitel völkerrechtlichen Gebietserwerbs," in *Gegenwartsprobleme des internationalen Rechts und der Rechtsphilosophie*, ed. D. S. Constantinopoulos and H. Wehberg (Hamburg, 1953), pp. 239 ff.

18. On this, see M. M. McMahon, *Conquest and Modern International Law* (Washington, D.C., 1940); M. F. Lindlay, *The Acquisition and Government of Backward Territory in International Law* (London, 1926); and Robert Langer, *Seizure of Territory* (Princeton, N.J., 1947).

ity was concerned. European states were impermeable in the sense here outlined, while most of those overseas were easily penetrable by Europeans. In accordance with these circumstances, international politics in Europe knew only rare and exceptional instances of actual annihilation through conquest or similar forceful means.

Prior to the twentieth century, there were indeed the Napoleonic conquests, but I submit that this is a case where the exception confirms the rule. The Napoleonic system, as a hegemonial one, was devised to destroy the established system of territoriality and balanced power as such. Consequently, Napoleon and his policies appeared "demonic" to contemporaries,[19] as well as to a nineteenth century which experienced the restoration of the earlier system. During that century occurred Bismarck's annexations of some German units into Prussia in pursuance of German unification. As in Napoleon's case, they appeared abnormal to many of his contemporaries, although the issue of national unification tended to mitigate this impression.[20] Besides these, there was indeed the partition of Poland, and considering the lamentable and lasting impression and the universal bad conscience it produced even among the ruling nations in a century used to quite a bit of international skulduggery, again one may well claim an exceptional character for that event.[21]

What, in particular, accounts for this remarkable stability? Territoriality—the establishment of defensible units, internally pacified and hard-shell rimmed—may be called its foundation. On this foundation, two phenomena permitted the system to become more stable than might otherwise have been the case: the prevalence of the legitimacy principle and, subsequently, nationalism. Legitimacy implied that the dynasties ruling the

19. As witness the impression made on contemporaries by the destruction of the first ancient European unit to fall victim to these policies—Venice.
20. See Erich Eyck, *Bismarck* (Zurich, 1943), 2:305 ff.
21. Except for these cases, we find only marginal instances of complete obliteration. The annexation of the Free City of Krakow by Russia eliminated a synthetic creation of the Vienna settlement. British conquest of the Boer Republics, if considered as an instance of annihilation of European polities in view of the European origin of the inhabitants, happened at the very rim of the world, as it were, remote from the continent where the practice of non-annihilation prevailed.

territorial states of old Europe mutually recognized each other as rightful sovereigns. Depriving one sovereign of his rights by force could not but appear to destroy the very principle on which the rights of all of them rested.

With the rise of nationalism, we witness the personalization of the units as self-determining, national groups. Nationalism now made it appear as abhorrent to deprive a sovereign nation of its independence as to despoil a legitimate ruler had appeared before. States, of course, had first to become "nation-states," considering themselves as representing specific nationality groups, which explains why in the two regions of Europe where larger numbers of old units stood in the way of national unification their demise encountered little objection. In most instances, however, the rise of nationalism led to the emergence of *new* states, which split away from multinational or colonial empires. This meant the extension of the European principle of "non-obliteration" all over the world. It is perhaps significant that even in our century, and even after the turmoil of attempted world conquest and resulting world wars, a point has been made of restoring the most minute and inconsiderable of sovereignties, down to Luxembourg and Albania.[22]

This hypertrophy of nation-states presented new problems—above all, that of an improved system of protection. For by now it had become clear that the protective function of the old system was only a relative blessing after all. Continued existence of states as such was perhaps more or less guaranteed. But power and influence, status, frontiers, economic interests—in short, everything that constituted the life and interests of nations beyond bare existence—were always at the mercy of what power politics wrought. Furthermore, much of the relative stability and political equilibrium of the territorial states had been due to the extension of Western control over the world. When what could be penetrated had been subjugated, assimilated, or established as fellow "sovereign" states, the old units were thrown back upon themselves. Hence the demand for a new system which would offer more security to old and new nations: collective security.

22. Cf. also the remarkable stability of state units in the Western Hemisphere qua independent units; unstable as some of them are domestically, their sovereign identity as units appears almost sacrosanct.

I propose to view collective security not as the extreme opposite of power politics, but as an attempt to maintain, and render more secure, the impermeability of what were still territorial states. To an age which took territoriality for granted, replacing power politics with collective security would indeed appear to be a radical departure. From the vantage point of the nuclear age, however, a plan to protect individual sovereignties by collective guarantees for continuing sovereignty appears questionable not because of its innovating, but because of its conservative, nature. Its conservatism lies in its basic objective: the protection of the hard-shell territorial structure of its members, or, as the core article of the Covenant of the League of Nations put it, its guarantee of their "territorial integrity and political independence" against external aggression. The beginning of air war and the increasing economic interdependence of nations had indicated by the end of World War I that the old-style military barriers might be by-passed. If territorial units were to be preserved in the future, it would be accomplished less by reliance on individual defense potentials than by marshaling collective power in order to preserve individual powers.

But since the idea of organizing a genuine supranational force—an international police force—was rejected, the League had to cling to classical arrangements insofar as the procedures of protection were concerned. The guarantee to the individual states was to be the formation of the "Grand Coalition" of all against the isolated aggressor, which presupposed the maintenance of a certain level of armed strength by the member states. A member without that minimum of military strength would be a liability rather than an asset to the organization—in Geneva parlance, a "consumer" and not a "producer" of security.[23] Thus classical concepts (the sovereignty and independence of nation-states) as well as classical

---

23. In League practice, therefore, membership applications of countries without this minimum were rejected (for instance, that of Liechtenstein); cf. Walther Schücking and Hans Wehberg, *Die Satzung des Völkerbundes* (2nd ed.; Berlin, 1924), pp. 252 ff. The decline of genuine collective security in our time is apparent from the fact that, in contrast to this practice, the United Nations pays hardly any attention to the question of defensibility, particularly in connection with membership applications.

institutions (in particular, hard-shell defensibility) were to be maintained under the new system.

Whether there ever was a chance for the system to be effective in practice is beside the point here. It is sufficient to realize how closely it was tied to the underlying structure as well as to the prevailing concepts and policies of the territorial age.

V. THE DECLINE OF THE TERRITORIAL STATE

Beginning with the nineteenth century, certain trends became visible which tended to endanger the functioning of the classical system. Directly or indirectly, all of them had a bearing upon that feature of the territorial state which was the strongest guarantee of its independent coexistence with other states of like nature: its hard shell—that is, its defensibility in case of war.

Naturally, many of these trends concerned war itself and the way in which it was conducted. But they were not related to the shift from the limited, duel-type contests of the eighteenth century to the more or less unlimited wars that developed in the nineteenth century with conscription, "nations in arms," and increasing destructiveness of weapons. By themselves, these developments were not inconsistent with the classical function of war. Enhancing a nation's defensive capacity, instituting universal military service, putting the economy on a war footing, and similar measures tended to bolster the territorial state rather than to endanger it.

Total war in a quite different sense is tied up with developments in warfare which enable the belligerents to overleap or by-pass the traditional hard-shell defense of states. When this happens, the traditional relationship between war, on the one hand, and territorial power and sovereignty, on the other, is altered decisively. Arranged in order of increasing effectiveness, these new factors may be listed under the following headings: (a) possibility of economic blockade; (b) ideological-political penetration; (c) air warfare; and (d) atomic warfare.

(a) *Economic warfare.* It should be said from the outset that so far economic blockade has never enabled one belligerent to force another into surrender through starvation alone. Although in World War I Germany and her allies were seriously endangered when the Western allies cut them off from overseas supplies, a very real effort was still required to defeat them on the military fronts. The same thing applies to World War II. Blockade was an important contributing factor, however. Its importance for the present analysis lies in its unconventional nature, permitting belligerents to by-pass the hard shell of the enemy. Its effect is due to the changed economic status of industrialized nations.

Prior to the industrial age, the territorial state was largely self-contained economically. Although one of the customary means of conducting limited war was starving fortresses into surrender, this applied merely to these individual portions of the hard shell, and not to entire nations. Attempts to starve a belligerent nation in order to avoid having to breach the shell proved rather ineffective, as witness the Continental Blockade and its counterpart in the Napoleonic era. The Industrial Revolution made countries like Britain and Germany increasingly dependent on imports. In war, this meant that they could survive only by controlling areas larger than their own territory. In peacetime, economic dependency became one of the causes of a phenomenon which itself contributed to the transformation of the old state system: imperialism. Anticipating war, with its new danger of blockade, countries strove to become more self-sufficient through enlargement of their areas of control. To the extent that the industrialized nations lost self-sufficiency, they were driven into expansion in a (futile) effort to regain it. Today, if at all, only control of entire ccntinents enables major nations to survive economically in major wars. This implies that hard-shell military defense must be a matter of defending more than a single nation; it must extend around half the world.

(b) *Psychological warfare,* the attempt to undermine the morale of an enemy population, or to subvert its loyalty, shares with economic warfare a by-passing effect on old-style territorial defensibility. It was formerly practiced, and practicable, only under quite exceptional circumstances. Short periods of genuine world revolutionary propaganda, such as the early stages of the French Revolution,[24] scarcely affected a general practice under which dynasties, and later governments, fought each other with little ideological involvement on the part of larger masses or classes. Only in rare cases—for instance, where national groups enclosed in and hostile to multinational empires could be appealed to—was there an opening wedge for "fifth column" strategies.

With the emergence of political belief-systems, however, nations became more susceptible to undermining from within. Although wars have not yet been won solely by subversion of loyalties, the threat involved has affected the inner coherence of the territorial state ever since the rise to power of a regime that claims to represent, not the cause of a particular nation, but that of mankind, or at least of its suppressed and exploited portions. Bolshevism from 1917 on has provided the second instance in modern history of world revolutionary propaganda. Communist penetration tactics subsequently were imitated by the Nazi and Fascist regimes and, eventually, by the democracies. In this way, new lines of division, cutting horizontally through state units instead of leaving them separated vertically from each other at their frontiers, have now become possible.

(c) *Air warfare* and (d) *nuclear warfare.* Of all the new developments, air warfare, up to the atomic age, has been the one that affected the territoriality of nations most radically. With its coming, the bottom dropped out—or, rather, the roof blew off—the relative security of the territorial state. True, even this new kind of warfare, up to and including the Second World War, did not by itself account for the defeat of a belligerent, as some of the more enthusiastic prophets of the air age had predicted it would. Undoubtedly, however, it had a massive contributory effect. And this effect was due to strategic action in the *hinterland* rather than to tactical use at the front. It came at least close to defeating one side by direct action against the "soft" interior of the country, by-passing

24. See my article, "Idealist Internationalism and the Security Dilemma," *World Politics* 2, no. 2 (January 1950): 157 ff.; reprinted above, pp. 72–98.

outer defenses and thus foreshadowing the end of the frontier
—that is, the demise of the traditional impermeability of even
the militarily most powerful states. Warfare now changed
"from a fight to a process of devastation." [25]

That air warfare was considered as something entirely
unconventional is seen from the initial reaction to it. Revolutionary transition from an old to a new system has always
affected moral standards. In the classical age of the modern
state system, the "new morality" of shooting at human beings
from a distance had finally come to be accepted, but the
standards of the age clearly distinguished "lawful combatants"
at the front or in fortifications from the civilian remainder of
the population. When air war came, reactions thus differed
significantly in the cases of air fighting at the front and of air
war carried behind the front. City bombing was felt to
constitute "illegitimate" warfare, and populations were inclined to treat airmen engaging in it as "war criminals." [26] This
feeling continued into World War II, with its large-scale area
bombing. Such sentiments reflected the general feeling of
helplessness in the face of a war which threatened to render
obsolete the concept of territorial power, together with its
ancient implication of protection.

The process has now been completed with the advent of
nuclear weapons. For it is more than doubtful that the
processes of scientific invention and technological discovery,

25. B. H. Liddell Hart, *The Revolution in Warfare* (New Haven, Conn.,
1947), p. 36. Suspicion of what would be in the offing, once man gained the
capacity to fly, was abroad as early as the eighteenth century. Thus Samuel
Johnson remarked: "If men were all virtuous, I should with great alacrity
teach them all to fly. But what would be the security of the good, if the bad
could at pleasure invade them from the sky? Against an army sailing through
the clouds, neither walls, nor mountains, nor seas, could afford security"
(quoted in J. U. Nef, *War and Human Progress* [Cambridge, Mass., 1952], p.
198). And Benjamin Franklin, witnessing the first balloon ascension at Paris in
1783, foresaw invasion from the air and wrote: "Convincing Sovereigns of
folly of wars may perhaps be one effect of it, since it will be impracticable for
the most potent of them to guard his dominions. . . . Where is the Prince who
can afford so to cover his country with troops for its defense, as that ten
thousand men descending from the clouds, might not in many places do an
infinite deal of mischief before a force could be brought together to repel
them?" (from a letter to Jan Ingelhouss, reproduced in *Life Magazine*, 9
January 1956).

26. See Julius Stone, *Legal Controls of International Conflicts* (New
York, 1954), pp. 611 ff.

which not only have created and perfected the fission and fusion weapons themselves but have brought in their wake guided missiles with nuclear warheads, jet aircraft with intercontinental range and supersonic speed, and the prospect of nuclear-powered planes or rockets with unlimited range and with automatic guidance to specific targets anywhere in the world, can in any meaningful way be likened to previous new inventions, however revolutionary. These processes add up to an uncanny absoluteness of effect which previous innovations could not achieve. The latter might render power units of a certain type (for instance, castles or cities) obsolete and enlarge the realm of defensible power units from city-state to territorial state or even large-area empire. They might involve destruction, in war, of entire populations. But there still remained the seemingly inexhaustible reservoir of the rest of mankind. Today, when not even two halves of the globe remain impermeable, it can no longer be a question of enlarging an area of protection and of substituting one unit of security for another. Since we are inhabitants of a planet of limited (and, as it now seems, insufficient) size, we have reached the limit within which the effect of the means of destruction has become absolute. Whatever remained of the impermeability of states seems to have gone for good.

What has been lost can be seen from two statements by thinkers separated by thousands of years and half the world; both reflect the condition of territorial security. Mencius, in ancient China, when asked for guidance in matters of defense and foreign policy by the ruler of a small state, is said to have counseled: "Dig deeper your moats; build higher your walls; guard them along with your people." This remained the classical posture up to our age, when a Western sage, Bertrand Russell, in the interwar period could still define power as something radiating from one center and growing less with distance from that center until it finds an equilibrium with that of similar geographically anchored units. Now that power can destroy power from center to center, everything is different.

VI. OUTLOOK AND CONCLUSION

It is beyond the compass of this article to ask what the change in the statehood of nations implies for present and future world relations; whether, indeed, international relations in the traditional sense of the term, dependent as they have been on a number of basic data (existence of the nation-state, measurable power, etc.) and interpreted as they were with the aid of certain concepts (sovereignty, independence, etc.), can survive at all; and, if not, what might take their place.[27] Suffice it to remark that this question is vastly complex. We cannot even be sure that one and only one set of conclusions derives from what has happened or is in the process of happening. For, in J. Robert Oppenheimer's words, one of the characteristics of the present is "the prevalence of newness, the changing scale and scope of change itself. . . ."[28] In the field of military policy, this means that since World War II half a dozen military innovations "have followed each other so rapidly that efforts at adaptation are hardly begun before they must be scrapped."[29] The scientific revolution has been "so fast-moving as to make almost impossible the task of military men whose responsibility it is to anticipate the future. Military planning cannot make the facts of this future stay long enough to analyze them."[30]

If this applies to military planning, it must apply equally to foreign policy planning, and, indeed, the newness of the new is perhaps the most significant and the most exasperating aspect of present world relations. Hardly has a bipolar world replaced the multipower world of classical territoriality than there loom new and unpredictable multipower constellations on the international horizon. However, the possible rise of new powers does not seem to affect bipolarity in the sense of a mere return to traditional multipower relations; since rising powers are

27. Some of the pertinent questions are discussed in more detail in my book *International Politics in the Atomic Age* (New York, 1959).

28. *The Open Mind* (New York, 1955), p. 141.

29. Roger Hilsman, "Strategic Doctrines for Nuclear War," in *Military Policy and National Security*, ed. William W. Kaufmann (Princeton, N.J., 1956), p. 42.

30. Thomas K. Finletter, *Power and Politics: US Foreign Policy and Military Power in the Hydrogen Age* (New York, 1954), p. 256.

likely to be nuclear powers, their effect must be an entirely novel one. What international relations would (or will) look like, once nuclear power is possessed by a larger number of power units, is not only extremely unpleasant to contemplate but almost impossible to anticipate, using any familiar concepts. Or, to use another example: We have hardly drawn the military and political conclusions from the new weapons developments, which at one point seemed to indicate the necessity of basing defense on the formation and maintenance of pacts like NATO and the establishment of a network of bases on allied territory from which to launch nuclear weapons "in case" (or whose existence was to deter the opponent from doing so on his part), and already further scientific and technological developments seem to render entire defense blocs, with all their new "hard shells" of bases and similar installations, obsolete.

To complicate matters even more, the change-over is not even uniform and unilinear. On the contrary, in concepts as well as in policies, we witness the juxtaposition of old and new (or several new) factors, a coexistence in theory and practice of conventional and new concepts, of traditional and new policies. Part of a nation's (or a bloc's) defense policy, then, may proceed on pre-atomic assumptions, while another part is based on the assumption of a preponderantly nuclear contest. And a compounding trouble is that the future depends on what the present anticipates, on what powers now think and how they intend to act on the basis of their present thinking; and on the fact that each of the actors on the scene must take into consideration the assumptions of the others.[31]

31. The expectations connected with the situation of nuclear deterrence may serve as an illustration. Each side, so we may assume, wants to act "rationally"—that is, avoid resort to a war which it knows would be suicidal; in this, in fact, is grounded the widespread present belief in the obsoleteness of major—i.e., nuclear—war. However, not knowing for sure that the other side can be trusted to behave rationally, each feels that the possibility of irrational behavior by the opponent must be included in its own calculations. For instance, assuming that rationally the United States would not permit itself to be provoked into nuclear action, can it rely on Soviet abstention from nuclear attack for similarly rational reasons? Or can the Soviets, who may actually believe that the "imperialist" powers are ready to inflict the worst on them, rely on Western rationality? And if, knowing that the other side may be swayed by considerations like these, one side takes these amended calcula-

There then evolves the necessity of multilevel concepts and of multilevel policies in the new era. In this we have, perhaps, the chief cause of the confusion and bewilderment of countries and publics. A good deal in recent foreign policies, with their violent swings from one extreme to another, from appeasement or apathy to truculence and threats of war, and also much in internal policies, with their suspicions and hysterias, may be reflections of world-political uncertainties. Confusion, despair, or easy optimism have been rampant; desire to give in, keep out, or get it over with underlies advocacy of appeasement, neutralism, or preventive war; mutually exclusive attitudes follow each other in rapid succession.

One radical conclusion to be drawn from the new condition of permeability would seem to be that nothing short of global rule can ultimately satisfy the security interest of any one power, and particularly any superpower. For only through elimination of the single competitor who really counts can one feel safe from the threat of annihilation. And since elimination without war is hardly imaginable, destruction of the other power by preventive war would therefore seem to be the logical objective of each superpower. But—and here the security dilemma encounters the other great dilemma of our time—such an aim is no longer practical. Since thermonuclear war would in all likelihood involve one's own destruction together with the opponent's, the means through which the end would have to be attained defeats the end itself. Pursuance of the "logical" security objective would result in mutual annihilation rather than in one unit's global control of a pacified world.

If this is so, the short-term objective must surely be mutual

---

tions as yardsticks for its own, what rational considerations remain? Policies then become so dependent on considerations of what you believe the other side believes, etc., ad infinitum, that no sane calculations are any longer feasible. One is caught here in the vicious circle inherent in the problem of the effects of assumptions (in behaviorist parlance, the problem of "anticipated reactions"), of what David Easton has called the possibility of an "infinite regress of effects" (*The Political System* [New York, 1953], p. 27). It may be doubted that even the theory of games as applied to international relations can cope with this one. And suppose that, sometime in the future, more than two major units "play"? In the face of this prospect, as Herbert Butterfield says, "The mind winces and turns to look elsewhere" (*History and Human Relations* [New York, 1952], p. 23).

accommodation, a drawing of demarcation lines, geographical and otherwise, between East and West which would at least serve as a stopgap policy, a holding operation pending the creation of an atmosphere in which, perhaps in consequence of a prolonged period of "cold peace," tensions may abate and the impact of the ideologies presently dividing the world diminish. May we then expect, or hope, that radically new attitudes, in accordance with a radically transformed structure of nationhood and international relations, may ultimately gain the upper hand over the inherited ones based on familiar concepts of old-style national security, power, and power competition? Until recently, advocacy of policies based on internationalism instead of power politics, on substituting the observance of universal interests for the prevalence of national interests, was considered utopian, and correctly so. National interests were still tied up with nation-states as units of power and with their security as impermeable units; internationalist ideals, while possibly recognized as ethically valid, ran counter to what nations were able to afford if they wanted to survive and prosper. But the dichotomy between "national self-interest" and "internationalist ideals" no longer fits a situation in which sovereignty and ever so absolute power cannot protect nations from annihilation.

What used to be a dichotomy of interests and ideals now emerges as a dichotomy between two sets of interests. For the former ideal has become a compelling interest itself. In former times, the lives of people, their goods and possessions, their hopes and their happiness, were tied up with the affairs of the country in which they lived, and interests thus centered around nation and national issues. Now that destruction threatens everybody, in every one of his most intimate, personal interests, national interests are bound to recede behind—or at least compete with—the common interest of all mankind in sheer survival. And if we add to this the universal interest in the common solution of other great world problems, such as those posed by the population-resources dilemma (exhaustion of vital resources coupled with the "population explosion" throughout the world), or, indeed, that of "peace-time" planetary pollution through radio-active fallout, it is perhaps not entirely utopian to expect the ultimate spread of an attitude of "universalism" through which a rational approach to world problems would at last become possible.

It may be fitting to conclude this article by quoting two men, one a contemporary scientist whose words on nuclear problems may well apply to other problems of world relations, the second a philosopher whose statement on the revolutionary impact of attitude changes seems as valid today as when it was first made: "It is a practical thing to recognize as a common responsibility, wholly incapable of unilateral solution, the complete common peril that atomic weapons constitute for the world, to recognize that only by a community of responsibility is there any hope of meeting the peril. It would seem to me visionary in the extreme, and not practical, to hope that methods which have so sadly failed in the past to avert war will succeed in the face of this far greater peril. It would in my opinion be most dangerous to regard, in these shattering times, a radical solution less practical than a conventional one" (J. Robert Oppenheimer).[32] And: "Thought achieves more in the world than practice; for, once the realm of imagination has been revolutionized, reality cannot resist" (Hegel).

32. "Atomic Weapons," *Proceedings of the American Philosophical Society* 90 (29 January 1946): 9f.

4

INTERNATIONAL POLITICS AND THE NUCLEAR DILEMMA

This essay formed the first chapter of a volume written by seven authors from such varied fields as physics, psychology, theology, and political science: John C. Bennett, ed., *Nuclear Weapons and the Conflict of Conscience* (New York, 1962), pp. 15–38. Continuing the discussions of chapter 3, it is chiefly concerned with the international system to which the advent of the nuclear weapon gave rise. It criticizes the then widespread reliance on "mutual deterrence" as a guarantor of peace and suggests policies of a "holding operation" as well as, eventually, an attitude of "universalism" for saving mankind from nuclear extinction. For further analysis, see pages 15–17 of the *Introduction*.

Reprinted by permission of Charles Scribner's Sons, Publishers, New York.

One day, in the spring of 1961, people all over the world could read that a man had for the first time circled the globe in outer space; it happened to be the same day the papers reported the beginning of the trial of another "human" being chàrged with the murder of six million fellow humans. The coincidence pointed up the extreme contrast between the heights of man's achievements in the material sphere and the depth of his moral failure.

The moral predicament of which the Nazi extermination camp was a symbol is now duplicated by the potentialities of thermonuclear warfare. Exactly as technology enabled the Nazis to dispose neatly, efficiently, and expeditiously of such masses of people as even a Tamerlane and other mass killers of the past had been unable to cope with, the new weapon enables us to destroy at one blow millions of lives in similarly streamlined fashion. And the moral implications of the situation are all the more vexing because the preparation is no longer based on irrational hatred or emotional ideology but on seemingly cool and rational calculation of "defense," "security," and "national interest." A decision, arrived at and implemented in bureaucratic fashion, a few minutes later and halfway around the world, "effectuates" the destruction of that part of the world; and, by way of counteraction, results in the annihilation of the "initiating" part of the world. The "transaction" as a whole produces mutual annihilation, neatly and according to plan.

This goes to show that there is not only a moral but also another, a so-to-speak physical dimension to the nuclear dilemma. Since seemingly rational action is bound to result in something utterly irrational (*mutual* annihilation, and possibly even race-suicide), the dilemma pertains to the survival of the human race in the physical sense, and therewith to all that which used to be concerned with existence, coexistence, and survival of human groups: policy. Again, contrasting the new with an older condition may serve to point up the radical novelty of our predicament. Some time ago, the newspapers reported what they referred to as "a bizarre incident": "Jet Shot Down By Its Own Gunfire As It Speeds Faster Than Shells." [1] Substituting "mankind" for "jet," and "nuclear weapon" for "gunfire," could one have a more apt description of the potentiality inherent in our situation? Compare this with even the more pessimistic interpretations of the human condition in the past. Hobbes, for instance, saw nations, as nations, in that condition of "war of everybody against everybody" which he called the "state of nature": "In all times, Kings, and Persons of Soveraigne authority, because of their Independency, are in continuall jealousies, and in the state and posture of Gladiators; having their weapons pointing, and their eyes fixed on one another; that is, their Forts, Garrisons, and Guns, upon the Frontiers of their Kingdoms; and continuall Spyes upon their neighbors; which is a posture of War." [2] Yet he

1. *New York Times,* 10 October 1956.
2. Leviathan, I, chapter 13.

continued: "But because they uphold thereby, the Industry of their Subjects; there does not follow from it, that misery, which accompanies the Liberty of particular men." [3] Leviathan was still a protector. Hobbes understood that protection, such as there was, could only be afforded "particular men" through a "posture of war," an institution whose function it was to preserve states as units of defense and security and in this way to protect the elementary interests of their inhabitants.

This protective function of the state and its defenses seems to be in jeopardy today. The weapon has outgrown its capacity to defend. Its all-out use would not leave anything worth defending. There have been previous revolutions in weapons and arts of war that also played great havoc with traditional concepts and existing institutions (such as the gun-powder revolution). But the present revolution is unlike any earlier one in that its effects are absolute: absolute destructiveness of weapons and war; absolute penetrability of political entities; and the globe now absolutely too small for new, larger units of genuine protection. . . .

FOREIGN RELATIONS IN THE PREATOMIC AGE

What accounts for political entities—tribes, city-states, nations—their emergence and identity, their actions and their policies? There are two chief answers from opposite sides: Economic determinism, emphasizing the economic needs of people, interprets everything in the nature and the emergence of political entities in the light of economic developments; this contrasts with an interpretation which considers irrational factors like human "pride," or the aggressiveness of individuals and groups and their ensuing expansionism, as the prime causes of what happens in history.

These theories neglect the impact of weapons and defense systems. I do not propose to substitute for an economic determinism a "strategic determinism" which, in equally one-sided fashion, might consider all historical developments as

3. Ibid.

superstructure on the means of destruction. But whoever studies how weapons developments and military technique have affected the structure of states and governments cannot help recognizing in how large a degree identity, structure, and interrelations of political units *are* determined by their capacity to defend themselves. This is hardly surprising. Besides the satisfaction of basic economic wants, the other most basic human need is that of protection of lives and goods; thus, the preserving of internal and external security has been a second essential function of political units. Means of defense and weapons systems determine, at least in part, what are the entities that can perform the protective function. People in the long run recognize that authority which possesses the power of protection. . . .

The now worldwide system of "territorial" or "nation"-states originated in Europe in the sixteenth and seventeenth centuries. Under the more primitive military conditions of the European Middle Ages units of protection could only be small: manors, castles, walled cities. Larger ones—kingdoms or similar principalities—were generally too large for effective control. Politically this caused a muddle of overlapping, ill-defined jurisdictions into which the public power disintegrated under feudalism. But with the invention of gun-powder the small medieval units became indefensible, while rulers of larger territorial units, with the aid of standing armies, infantry, and artillery, and backed by a rising middle class interested in a developing money economy, were now able to free themselves from dependence on vassals, eliminate feudal power, pacify large-scale areas, and surround them with walls of fortifications to protect them from similarly armed and fortified units outside. In this way, after an extended period of transition and turmoil, the large-area, territorial state emerged as the new unit of protection. Its nature and characteristics have largely determined internal and international politics of the last couple of centuries.

So much have we become used to the modern nation-state system that we are inclined to consider its characteristics and the concepts which relate to it as so-to-speak eternal ones, valid for all times. Closer analysis reveals that categories like "sovereignty" and "independence," national interest and national power, and even "nation" itself, have all been closely tied to the specific conditions of a particular period, emerging with these conditions and now becoming inapplicable with the change of times and conditions. Thus, the "sovereign independence" of the modern state simply reflected a relatively high degree of "impenetrability" of large-area territorial entities surrounded by hard shells of military defenses that necessitated frontal attack for breaching. Power, likewise, was based on the self-contained, impermeable nature of the unit. As the sum-total of the strength of one unit relative to others, power in the modern state-system became measurable and calculable, and thus enabled each nation to maintain itself vis-à-vis similar units: national power became the chief instrument of so-called power politics. The main features of international politics throughout the classical period of the modern state-system were alliances, balance of power, and limited war; and, as these terms indicate, the emerging system, despite the absence of overruling authority, was not entirely anarchic; in some measure, it was stable and even "conservative," in the sense of lending itself to the preservation of the units which composed it. . . .

Small powers, which despite their "hard shells" were more easily penetrable than big ones, could join larger ones in alliances which made them, for all practical purposes, parts of larger defense systems. All could and most did see in the maintenance of a balance among all a means to prevent any one from attaining hegemony. There were indeed always those nations which were intent on destroying the system by establishing themselves as hegemony powers, from Spain in the beginning, through France, to Germany. But the system functioned in such a way that, under the leadership of a "balancer" (in modern times, England), the other major European powers would rally in time to defeat them.

War itself had a partially stabilizing function. It is true that even in this period war frequently was a force for change, too. But though it often served the aggrandizement of nations, or national unification, at other times it served as ultimate means for restoring a lost equilibrium. Indeed, major wars, or whole series of wars, can be characterized as "wars for the restoration of the balance," from the coalition wars against Louis

XIV, through the "wars of liberation" against Napoleon, to World War II against Axis hegemony in the world. Without war as the ultimate means to preserve a system of self-contained, defensible entities the mitigation of power politics which the balance system implied, would not have been possible. By the twentieth century, of course, with the emergence of territorial units on the European pattern outside Europe, the European balance had become a world balance, a system in which, beginning with World War I, the United States had to relieve England in its role of the "balancer" whose intervention shifted the scales. . . .

At a time when some degree of national security was still attainable, "national interest," that somewhat elusive indicator of foreign-policy objectives, could likewise be defined in reasonably concrete terms. Whatever more far-reaching and ambitious goals of foreign policy would from time to time be couched in terms of the national interest, it was understood to comprise at least those minimum requirements of safety which at that time could still be specified in usually concrete geographical terms: maintenance and defense of one's present territorial status and possibly, beyond the status quo, certain modest acquisitions, such as a "better" river frontier or a similar "natural" boundary. Such minimal definability of the national interest rendered even the problem of international morality manageable. True, the ancient dichotomy of individual and group ethical standards remained. Nations could not afford pacifism. Certain wars were under certain conditions meaningful and even necessary. In a way, the development of the military art, which led from the medieval feud to the territorial fortress, even meant extending the range of *raison d'Etat*. Killing human beings from a distance—abhorrent to the Middle Ages—became part of international morality, and standards of such morality, or amorality, expanded subsequently with each extension of units and range of weapons (long-range artillery, machine gun, submarine, and so forth). But as long as it was possible to distinguish minimum aims of security from more ambitious objectives of national foreign policy and as long as one could alleviate the power struggle through systems and policies like the balance of power, one could draw the line between the "moral" and the "immoral" by distinguishing between the more and the less moderate, the more and the less peaceful, the more and the less egocentered policy of nations and their rulers. International morality could be defined in the meaningful sense of giving preference to the more moderate objective and the more peaceful means if and when there was a choice. In this way, diplomacy was part not only of the rational but also of the ethical universe.

FOREIGN POLICY IN THE NUCLEAR AGE

Looking backward from our age of nuclear predicament toward the classical system of international relations, these might now appear to us as an almost idyllic interlude of protection and stability rather than the Hobbesian nightmare of war of all against all. But like every human creation it carried in itself the seeds of destruction. As early as the nineteenth century certain developments tended to inhibit the functioning of the system through their impact on that feature of the territorial state which constituted the strongest guarantee of its "sovereign independence," its hard shell of defensibility in case of war. . . . The decisive change was in the means and conduct of war itself. Air warfare already indicated the new possibility of a nation's defeat through penetration from above. And if even in World War II large-area conventional bombing did not prove quite enough to defeat a nation (breaking the fronts in East and West Europe being required in the case of Germany, and atomic weapons in that of Japan), atomic and nuclear weapons now do not seem to allow any protection against the most radical penetration. Utter permeability now negates the traditional territoriality of units, and it is exactly the most powerful nuclear powers which as targets of other nuclear powers become the most vulnerable. Utmost power coincides with utmost impotence, and the most powerful and elaborate machinery ever devised for defense and protection presages universal destruction.

Even bipolar block formation could not stay this development. The emergence, after World War II, of two huge defense systems, each comprising a large part of the globe under the leadership of one "superpower," constituted an effort to extend the principle of territoriality, now no longer applicable to the nation-state. The hard shell surrounding one single nation was simply expanded into a wall surrounding entire halves of the globe. Integrated defense systems like NATO, with troops of different block powers stationed along the rim of the block and with bases dotting its outer boundaries, are a clear expression of this purpose. Discounting the factor of nuclear exposure, a new system of large-scale area protection, defensibility, and even balance might have emerged at the end of World War II. But since the nuclear factor cannot be discounted, bipolarity merely adds to the confusion by pulling additional units into the area of permeability and possible holocaust.

Can any "sane" nuclear policy, indeed, any rational foreign policy, be developed under these circumstances? Among the numerous proponents of solutions we can distinguish those who are confident regarding what can be done without much change in the present situation from others who are pessimistic in respect to the existing condition and optimistic regarding the changes they advocate; the former want, in the main, to stabilize a status quo, the latter advocate radical change. In between are those who, realizing that change is necessary, propose to proceed gradually and by way of relatively moderate steps.

Policies of Deterrence

The attitude primarily tied up with advocacy of the maintenance of the nuclear status quo is based on the emergence of what is referred to as the system of "mutual deterrence" (or "nuclear stalemate," or "balance of terror"). Since two power blocks have risen, both equipped with almost equal nuclear weapons, they can be relied upon—so this theory goes—to refrain from attacking each other for fear of retaliation. Indeed, so much reliance was placed initially upon the functioning of this system that the idea of a utopia of permanent peace was developed out of a situation of utmost peril. Churchill, at that time, believed it possible that "we would by a process of sublime irony have reached a stage in this story where safety will be the sturdy child of terror, and survival the twin-brother of annihilation." [4]

Undoubtedly, fear of nuclear retaliation has had much to do with the fact that the nuclear weapon has so far not been used. Certainly, reliance on retaliation accounts for the feeling of safety which still exists among people in many parts of the world, including the nuclear countries. But there is now much less confidence that the system will always function in this dependable way. Closer investigation of what is involved in deterrence—and the study of deterrence has by now developed into something like a special branch of the social sciences somewhere between strategy and international politics—has impressed even adherents of the status-quo attitude with the incredible complexity of the problem and thus raised serious doubts concerning too much reliance on it. Out of a welter of conflicting and often confusing views on things like "first strike" and "second strike strategy," "preventive and preemptive attack," "stable and unstable," or "symmetrical and asymmetrical deterrent situations," "counter-forces strategy," or "finite," or "graduated" deterrence, and so forth, a kind of consensus seems to emerge at least concerning what is problematical in deterrence.

Thus, there is the possibility of "war by accident," either because of somebody's "irrational" action (including the case of "nuclear war of desperation" when one side, in conventional or limited nuclear war, is about to be defeated) or, more likely, because of technical error (misinterpretation of some event, some signal, or some similarly ambiguous evidence of impending or beginning attack) or human malfunction (e.g., misinterpretation of orders, either by design or unintentionally, on the part of subordinates). Ever shorter time available between discovery of a suspicious phenomenon and decision, and ever greater spread of retaliatory installations and weapons must obviously add to these dangers.

Even besides accidental war there remains enough uncertainty in mutual deterrence. Stable deterrence means absence of decisive technological "breakthroughs"; how can they be prevented without strict supervision? And even under condi-

4. Speech in the House of Commons, 1 March 1955.

tions of stability where each side has about what the opponent has, a temptation may well develop to strike first and destroy the opponent by "surprise attack"; it depends on one's calculation of the risks involved. If one side believes that, by striking first, it can destroy so much of the opponent's retaliatory force that the damage to be expected in retaliation is not unacceptable, it will sooner or later justify such a policy by claiming that it owes it to history or its "cause" once and for all to wipe capitalist imperialism from the face of the earth; or, conversely, that it cannot afford to miss the chance to rid the world once and for all of the scourge of Communism. The security dilemma itself, which reaches its pinnacle in the nuclear situation, reinforces such temptations. Not knowing whether the opponent is not calculating exactly as outlined above, one may be driven to forestall his presumed "preventive" blow by one's own "preventive" blow—a first strike to avert a first strike. Somebody will always be able to prove that "this is the last chance" either because of one's present margin of superiority (which may vanish) or because of one's inferiority (which may tempt the opponent to strike first).

A further serious hazard in mutual deterrence is misunderstanding concerning the *casus belli nuclearis;* that is, "war by miscalculation" may break out because the circumstances are left undefined or unclear in which "aggression" or a similarly provocative step on the part of one side will cause the other side to react by nuclear force; for instance, where "massive" nuclear retaliation is being threatened in case of "serious" aggression. While the uncertainty inherent in such a threat may well cause the other side to abstain from aggressive or expansionist moves in 99 out of 100 cases, it may be misled into action in the 100th instance where it mistakenly believes that no nuclear retaliation will be forthcoming. True, a policy of spelling out exactly when "massive retaliation" may be expected has its disadvantages too; it would by implication define cases and areas to which the retaliatory threat would not apply, this way encouraging attack there. It has been suggested that a mutual commitment not under any circumstances to use all-out nuclear weapons first would eliminate such uncertainties; it would further eliminate the use of "nuclear blackmail" to attain one's ends. But while this would pretty well eliminate the danger of war by miscalculation, it would put that side at a disadvantage which is inferior in conventional armaments, which at this point means the West. Such a commitment on the part of the West would therefore have to be coupled with an effort to achieve a better balance of conventional forces, which, in the absence of arms control reducing the East to some equilibrium level, implies Western rearmament, e.g., of NATO forces in Europe. Conventional rearmament has become necessary in any event—even apart from a "no first strike" commitment—since the threat of American nuclear retaliation in case of Soviet attack with conventional weapons on allies has become less plausible now that American cities are within reach of Soviet missiles. *Si vis pacem, para bellum non-atomicum.* Only in this way can an ultimate situation where one might be faced with the agonizing choice between starting the holocaust and surrendering be avoided or, at least, be made less likely.

In the face of these difficulties it has been suggested that both sides aim at making the deterrence system more stable by rendering the deterrent force invulnerable. Instead of chasing after nuclear "superiority" through developing ever more weapons of ever more destructive force—something nonsensical in an age of nuclear plenty where an opponent, even though inferior in absolute number of weapons, has in any event enough for saturation—the existing weapons system should be protected in such a way that no attack can wipe it out; that is, it should be rendered invulnerable through "hardening" missile bases or through dispersal, mobility, or concealment of weapons and delivery systems. Thus, ability to survive any first strike and come back with devastating effect would seem to provide an absolute guarantee that a first strike will never be undertaken.

Apart from the question whether absolute invulnerability is obtainable, doubts arise even here. The risk of war by accident is not diminished (perhaps, through dispersal, etc., even increased). Temptation to stage preventive or surprise attack may be reduced. But an attack, conventional or even nuclear, on *non*nuclear powers may even be encouraged where there is no longer any assurance of retaliation by invulnerable nuclear powers on their behalf. This lack of protection may drive more and more powers to develop their own nuclear deterrent, as in the case of France. Ironically, then, increased stability between two powers might give rise to complete instability in a system of plural nuclear powers. The world may become one of an indefinite, growing number of independent nuclear power centers.

Such an extension of the "nuclear club" (the so-called nth power problem) represents a grave danger to the system of mutual deterrence. While the acquisition of nuclear weapons might give the new nuclear powers some amount of protection against nuclear blackmail, it also means that, where today some measure of rational calculation is still possible among what in essence amounts to two, and only two, clear-cut opponents, an indefinite number of nonaligned powers would bring about an indefinite and infinite extension of risks of error, of action in madness, or in despair, or out of spite, or for reasons of domestic policy, or—especially in the case of conflicts between smaller powers—for the sake of local or regional policy. Such nuclear polycentrism imaginably even renders the attacker unidentifiable, giving an anonymous aggressor a chance to instigate nuclear contest among others ("catalytic war," as it has been called).

Even now, with only two power centers, the complex nature of the considerations and calculations involved in the deterrent situation constitutes perhaps the most unstabilizing factor of all. Deterrence becomes dependent on a "complicated process of mutual mind-reading," upon the credibility of threats and similar policies.[5] Where policy previously was based on the relatively simple assessment of military capabilities, it now becomes the result of assessment and counter-assessment of attitudes and intentions.[6] And where previously, if the worst came to the worst, malassessment might mean outbreak of and defeat in war, its consequence now may be an infinitely greater disaster: mutual annihilation. For, it is the

5. Robert E. Osgood, "Stabilizing the Military Environment," *American Political Science Review* 55, no. 1 (March 1961): 25.
6. One is reminded of a Jewish story from old Russia. Shmule meets Moshe on the road and asks him, "Where do you go?" Moshe: "To Minsk." Shmule: "When you say 'I go to Minsk,' you want me to believe that you go to Pinsk, but I know that you go to Minsk, so why do you lie?"

most paradoxical effect of nuclear penetrability that the weapon is successful only as long as it remains an unused threat; used, it means deadly failure. . . .

Advocacy of Radical Change

In the face of the doubts and difficulties involved in policies of deterrence, must we then despair, or resign ourselves to a fate from which there is no escape? It is understandable that some of the solutions advocated by those favoring a radical change in present policies are based on a feeling of despair. Confronting the alternative of "rather dead than Red," or "rather Red than dead," it might, under nuclear conditions, not be mere cowardice to opt for the latter and give up liberty so that mankind can at least continue to exist. While in times past the heroic self-sacrifice of individuals or groups for the sake of their ideals was meaningful, it is questionable whether the present generation would have the right, by sacrificing itself, to doom perhaps all future generations as well. Capitulation, so one might feel, would at least leave the hope that the victorious system, like all systems and regimes before, would in time be transformed or pass away.

It is this alternative and this choice which is implied in the propositions of the "unilateralists," those who propose either nuclear or total unilateral disarmament. An expectation, sometimes voiced, that this would shame the other side into following one's own example seems illusory. Communist leaders who, on the basis of their doctrine, might well be convinced that the abdication merely proved Western degeneracy, are not likely to be so influenced even by "world opinion." True, the idea, sometimes proferred by those who object to unilateralism, that the Soviets would then drop the "Bomb" right away or force immediate surrender by threatening to do so, is oversimplified. More likely they would use the next international crisis to extend their power.

The radicalism of unilateralism supposes that there is no choice. If there really were no alternative to launching the nuclear holocaust or capitulation, we would indeed confront an agonizing situation. But it seems that, if some advocates of deterrence have sinned through overoptimism, this approach sins through overpessimism. At least today, other choices are still open. Even among the advocates of radical change some put their hopes in such possibilities. There are the world federalists who believe that nothing short of world government can and will solve the nuclear dilemma. It is certainly in the logic of weapons developments that only global authority could henceforth provide the protection which no partial power or block, however large and "powerful," can convey any longer. But to infer that what "ought to be" or "must be" "will happen" is pseudo-logic. How to get from a situation of extreme power-concentration in separate power units to world authority in one jump is not apparent. Could it perhaps be done by disarmament (general, not unilateral), as proposed by other "radicals"?

The story of the efforts to achieve universal disarmament, now again on the agenda through Khrushchev's proposal, is the long and sad saga of failure—failure not only in regard to practical, diplomatic attempts to arrive at agreement—which would not be conclusive in view of the urgency, under nuclear conditions, to try again and again—but more seriously because of theoretical objections. No plausible plan can disregard the need for internal "police" forces and armament to cope with domestic disorder. Even if these could be fixed in such a way as not to give anybody international advantage, the status of external defenselessness which would ensue would seem to put too high a premium on deception. Suppose that an agreement on controlled armament allows each side a maximum of 500 nuclear weapons; if one side hides 50 more, the balance would not thereby be fatally disturbed. But in an environment of supposedly complete disarmament such cheating would convey overwhelming superiority on the evader. Under "complete disarmament," therefore, it is likely that nobody would be able to resist the urge to evade and conceal, if merely for reasons of security, and the ensuing uncertainties and suspicions might render conditions more unstable than they would be at higher armament levels. These considerations also apply to mere nuclear disarmament. In either case, safe controls through "ironclad inspection" would be necessary to overcome evasion, and such controls are impossible, even for nuclear stockpiles. Ironically enough, both the believers in mutual deterrence and the believers in disarmament are in a sense eighteenth-century optimists: the former because they put all stock in rational behavior, the latter because they must make everything dependent on "fair play."

The picture we derive from an analysis of both the "status quo" and the "radical" schools is grim. There are, however, proposals of a third group of analysts envisaging less radical, more moderate and gradual changes. It is probably somewhere in-between the "standpat" attitudes of the preparedness crowd and the visionary utopianism of the radicals that progress toward heightened security and lessened tension can realistically be expected.

What Can Be Done?

Many limited proposals have been made in the field of armaments proper. Whatever their nature, one should begin where *some* control, *some* regulation seems possible. Since the dawn of the atomic age opportunities have tragically been missed time and again simply by allowing that moment to pass when certain steps were still technically feasible. Thus control of production or stockpiling of atomic bombs, at first possible, became impossible with the passing of time. If today the use of outer space for military purposes can still be prevented by agreements on inspection and similar control measures, this may no longer be possible tomorrow or next year. If it is still possible to halt the spread of nuclear armaments to nonnuclear countries, it may soon be too late. Agreement on cessation of nuclear tests has long been deferred; what is clearly controllable there should be controlled. But there are pitfalls even in matters of moderate arms control. There is not only the general difficulty of preventing evasion but also the little discussed problem of enforcement. What should be the penalty for discovered evasion? If all that can be done is to permit the "cheated" to do what the cheater clandestinely has begun before, he may be at a great disadvantage, and such an "asymmetry" might itself encourage evasion. And there is irony as well as danger in the fact that inspection systems, surveillance measures, etc., may themselves create those suspicions and increase those tensions they were supposed to alleviate; thus, conflict over discovery of some slight or alleged evasion may conceivably lead to a crisis where nondiscovery might have produced less dangerous consequences.

Therefore, that which can be done unilaterally or by tacit agreement may occasionally be less risky than formal control systems. Nuclear powers intent on not misleading the opponent into precipitate action should plan their policies carefully so as to avoid anything which could be provocative, even though intended defensively, like "fail-safe" test flights toward "enemy" territory. They should make sure that communication remains possible and open with the opponent during periods of tension, and even after hostilities have occurred. They might disperse their industries and emphasize and strengthen meaningful civil defense, not only in the interest of actual protection of the population but also in order to make their defensive nuclear policy more plausible. These are ways to render deterrence more stable, wars less likely, perhaps even hostilities more limited.

One of the main suggestions in this area concerns "limited war," and in particular limited nuclear war. There is certainly great merit in trying to devise policies under which even nuclear war would be "tamed." The more enthusiastic supporters of the idea assert that, through use of smaller and "cleaner" weapons and dispersal of task forces, such a war would turn out to be even less destructive than was conventional war just prior to the atomic age. But this seems doubtful, especially since limited nuclear war is least likely to occur in sparsely populated jungle regions and similar out-of-the-way parts of the world; it is most likely to occur in populous industrial regions such as Western Europe where it would be so devastating as to become indistinguishable from all-out war to the peoples affected. Besides, there is always the danger of "escalation," of limited war gradually but irresistibly snowballing into all-out war. Indeed, this problem also presents itself in the case of conventional war; for, once general hostilities involve major powers, the use of first limited and ultimately unlimited nuclear weapons will tempt belligerents as long as they possess them as "deterrents."

The impact of the new weapon is most directly noticeable in the field of military strategy, but it is no less decisive in foreign policy where weapons and war used to be the *ultima ratio.* Where "mere" conventional war now involves a threat of ultimate catastrophe, war seems to be available to policy only as bluff; even then it is tremendously dangerous, since the bluffing game may fail when nobody knows who's bluffing whom. On the other hand, what means of policy exist where force is no longer available? How can powers then pursue their objectives?

It is clear that in the field of policy, as in that of strategy, more "radical" proposals become increasingly doubtful. It is in a way understandable that the threat which Communism poses to a "free world" induces some to advocate "getting it over with" at one blow, either in the world at large or in specific regions where Communism installs itself; or to emphasize "preparedness" to the exclusion of any kind of negotiation or accommodation. But the seriousness of this threat to the West is matched by the threat of the weapon to all mankind. Not only can we no longer indulge in "wars of liberation"; even the traditional "war for the restoration of the balance of power" is now implausible. Not only must we ourselves refrain from force, we must do all we can to prevent the opponent from resorting to something which would be suicidal to all. The nuclear predicament challenges statesmen to act in a dual capacity: not only in defense of "national" interest but as agents and caretakers of what Reinhold Niebuhr calls the developing "community of the fate of the common threat of nuclear annihilation." A new realism of universalism must put the common weal—in the elementary sense of a common interest in survival—before the traditional interest in having one's opponent commit mistakes. The great religions and moral systems of the world have exalted an altruistic behavior-pattern, according to which consideration was given to the interests of others, whether individuals or nations. Under the standards of a new humanism which places the preservation of the human race above any and all partial interests, the same behavior-pattern now emerges as indispensable to national policy if the entire race is not to perish.

Most important among the emerging more moderate foreign policy attitudes are therefore those which stress the necessity of maintaining a balance between the two major blocks and systems. This seems to involve a policy of mutual accommodation, of delimitation of spheres, by and large on the basis of the bipolar status quo. Such an approach could not fail to reduce suspicions and relax tensions; nuclear war, except accidental war, will hardly break out without "war crises." It might also create an environment where those moderate and realizable arms agreements which we have mentioned would have a better chance of success, for armaments problems cannot be separated from the general political climate. It is true that acceptance of the present status would involve renunciations and sacrifices of broader aims on either side. But the recognitions involved would not have to sanction regimes or territorial acquisitions in any moral sense; they would merely constitute the practical acknowledgement of what exists de facto, and the renunciation of claims to what, being under the opponent's control, could in any event be gotten only by force. It could, on the other hand, eliminate dangerous trouble spots. If a firmer guarantee of West Berlin and the access routes could be obtained through Western recognition of the Oder-Neisse line and the East German regime, or if a confirmation of the present status of Taiwan was obtainable in return for recognition of the Peiping regime as de facto government of the Chinese mainland, this might appear worth the price. And so around the world. This delimitation of spheres would not, by itself, solve the problem of indirect penetration into the other side's sphere, through economic means, political infiltration, or "subversion." Here, and especially in the intermediate world of "uncommitted" and under-developed nations, the West must accept the Communist challenge to "peaceful competition," and it can do so if it trusts its economic means and the power and impact of its political and general ideals, provided it is ready to make the necessary sacrifices, financial and otherwise. Force has always been a poor response to the challenge of revolutionary or even pseudo-revolutionary movements anyway. There certainly is great risk for the West in Communist dynamism. Still, the danger to us and all would be immeasurably greater if the Chinese doctrine of the "inevitable war" would prevail over present Soviet realization of war's suicidal nature. A Chinese leader is said to have suggested that such a war might spare 10 million Americans, 20 million Russians, and 300 million Chinese. The implications of such an attitude are terrifying. As in the field of armaments proper, it would be tragic if the chances of negotiating a political rapprochement with a relatively moderate opponent were allowed to pass. Ever so slight actual successes (the neutralization of Austria, the agreement to keep Antarctica demilitarized) point out the direction in which to go.

Paradoxes in the Nuclear Situation

Nothing will be easy or easily gained in an approach of this nature. It is much easier to continue habitual policies of the national interest narrowly conceived. But in that case a catastrophic blowup will become an almost mathematical certainty. On the other hand, we must be aware of the paradoxes which confront the attitudes here considered. The paradoxes are in the things themselves, and it is therefore not surprising that they are reflected in attitudes and policies. How shall one act consistently and rationally in a world where utmost power coincides with impotence, where power of protection, based on armaments of unimaginable potency, vanishes because the weapons are not to be used, where, in other words, the familiar unit of security no longer fulfils its function of affording security? In such a situation, everything is driven to its ultimate: What is most urgently needed is also the most hazardous and dangerous. If we try to develop an "absolute" weapon (such as missiles fired from undiscoverable submarines) in order to have an "absolutely" stable deterrent, we also run the danger that should it ever fail in its deterrent effect it would prove to be the most absolutely destructive. If in the present nuclear situation a show of absolute determination to resist and retaliate is necessary to avoid giving the impression of bluffing, this will, if it fails to deter, lead to all-out war or else a loss of face equalling surrender. The element of uncertainty in leaving the *casus belli* indefinite may successfully deter, but if it ever causes one side to misinterpret the other's intentions, it means war by miscalculation; this was the case in Korea, and today the chances of general blowup would be much larger. . . .

These paradoxes are reflected in language itself, which here, as often, betrays underlying traits and trends. The new language of the nuclear age indicates that weapons (machines) take the place of humans; human relations are "reified," machine relations "humanized." We speak of "second genera-tions" of weapons, not people; of their "overkill capacity"; of the "survivability" of weapons systems; of "invulnerability" again of armaments, not men.

The paradoxes recur in the contradictory advice of experts, where both sides seem often equally convincing. Thus, the arguments of the erudite for or against limited nuclear war are about equally strong on either side; or consider a more recent debate on the merits of making NATO a separate, fourth nuclear power.[7] Little wonder, then, that policies get confused again and again, even where serious efforts are being made to solve previously mixed-up issues. Thus, in the all-important area of the "first or second strike" problem, President Ken-nedy, in one and the same message on defense problems, managed to straddle the issue by advocating both mutually exclusive policies. The message began with an emphasis on America's second-strike policy: United States strategic de-fenses must make it clear to the potential aggressor "that sufficient retaliatory forces will be able to revive after a first strike. . . . *We will not strike first in any conflict.* But what we must have is the ability to survive a first blow and respond with devastating power." Later, it asserted the necessity of striking first in certain circumstances: "In the event of a major aggression that could not be repulsed by conventional forces we must be prepared to take *whatever action with whatever weapons are appropriate.*" "Major aggression" obviously re-fers to non-nuclear aggressions too, and thus first-strike policy is envisaged here. In the end, the President reverted to his initial, second-strike posture: "As a power which will never

7. Pro: Henry A. Kissinger, *The Necessity for Choice* (New York, 1960), pp. 121ff., and "For an Atlantic Confederacy," *The Reporter*, 2 February 1961, pp. 16ff.; contra: Albert Wohlstetter, "Nuclear Sharing: NATO and the N + I Country," *Foreign Affairs* 39, no. 3 (April 1961): 355ff. (especially 372ff.).

strike first, our hopes for anything close to an absolute deterrent must rest on weapons which rest on hidden, movable, or invulnerable bases. . . ." [8]

Perhaps this reflects the travails of a still inexperienced administration. Somewhat the same kind of confusion has been noticeable in the more "political" sector of American foreign policy, where attempts at preparing the ground for an apparently broad and comprehensive effort at accommodation are hampered by a kind of "nineteenth century"-type approach to more specific problems, like Cuba. Neither East nor West, nor anyone else, can any longer afford policies of "going it alone," of national security in the old-fashioned sense. The necessity of a long-range, consistent policy line, indeed, of a new philosophy of foreign policy, imposes itself when one considers world trends and world problems not only in the area of nuclear strategy and bipolar block policy but also in other fields. This is not the place to discuss in any detail the other world revolutions of our time and the problems they raise. But it is important to realize that there, too, we encounter similar difficulties and even paradoxes. There is the sweep toward "One World"; for the first time in the history of civilizations one of them, the Western, has become worldwide, rendering the world "one" at least in a technical sense. At the same time, with the awakening of the colored races, with their very entrance into a technologically unified world, "one world" is breaking apart into ever more national entities; and while nationalism and national entities can no longer fulfil their once basic function, nationalist sentiment seems to be the mainstay of the emerging peoples of the world. Somehow their increasing number must be fitted into a world of "peaceful coexistence."

Another paradox concerns the "population explosion," not of nations but of human beings. While technological developments for the first time in history indicate a chance that mankind may live in plenty as far as its material wants are concerned, the increase in the world's population is such that it threatens to cancel out all benefit of increased production, so

8. From President Kennedy's message on defense spending, quoted from *New York Times*, 29 March 1961 (emphasis supplied).

that the very subsistence of mankind in the material sense seems now threatened.

And in the field of belief-systems, where ideologies and their propagation poison the international atmosphere like fall-out poisoning the air, people and nations still feel that they are committed to certain values which they cannot sacrifice without giving up their "way of life." At the same time, the two most important systems with contrasting ideologies tend to become more similar to each other in many respects, and especially in their organization and structure as large-scale industrial mass societies. While to some, in particular to the intellectuals, it still makes all the difference in the world whether they live on this or the other side of the Iron Curtain, to the New York, London, or Moscow straphanger it seems to make less of a difference. At a time when the development of personality, or "the dignity of man," appears as the highest goal, trends in the organization of the economy, of culture and entertainment, and even in government and politics, threaten to render the individual a cog in the machine, while strategic developments leave him an even more insignificant, tiny unit of protection, or destruction; that is, unless he belongs to those few who have today more actual control over the fate of billions than leaders ever possessed before.

The Ethics of Universalism

In all this confusion one can yet discern trends and directions which policy might follow. The world has become surveyable, and worldwide planning of policy has become possible. If we take the population problem, for instance, a consistent, long-range policy based upon world-consciousness can pay attention to the effect policies of foreign aid and development have in this area; it might therefore establish priorities, under which preference would be given to nations that promise to tackle not only such problems as that of their land tenure, but also that of their population pressures, since without the solution of the latter problem everything else seems to be futile. So also in regard to problems of exhaustion of soil and other resources. Such truly conservative and preservative policy would in the long run even pay political and security dividends to the policy-inaugurating countries, since it would lead to the establishment of sounder, more viable national entities less likely to fall victims to Communist infection.

In the field of ideologies, a policy of the common interest might well identify and take into consideration those fundamental value-standards of the respective opponent which in the process of accommodation and "give and take" he cannot be supposed to sacrifice, exactly as one would oneself refuse concessions in matters of principle. Thus, while the West could not permit populations now free and to whose freedom it has committed itself to pass under Communist control (West Berlin comes to mind), Communists might find it similarly impossible to yield to "capitalism" what to them constitutes "socialist achievements" (East Germany, perhaps, is a case in point). Such distinction between the negotiable and the non-negotiable would by itself serve to clear the air and reduce tensions created by unfulfillable claim, threat, and recrimination. It is in between such opposite value-standards that policy, in our age, will have to find its tortuous way.

It is at this point, perhaps, that the difference between the traditional policy of the "national interest" and the new, world-conscious approach reveals itself most clearly. As we have seen, so long as weapons were less destructive and wars limited, the basic security interests of nations could be spelled out in concrete terms, and one could even establish minimum precepts of "international morality" on this basis. Today, distinguishing between more or less "moderate" policies in regard to the security of individual nations hardly makes sense anymore. Absolute permeability renders even the more powerful nations insecure unless they control the world. Geographic proximity of "enemy" territory or bases makes less and less of a difference where the delivery time of missiles is measured in minutes. Where distance no longer matters and a nation's security may be threatened from anywhere on the globe, it no longer makes sense to judge the "morality" of a foreign policy on the basis of whether its objectives and concerns are more or less limited, or more or less ambitious geographically.

If distinguishing between policies by ethical yardsticks is

to make sense, it must henceforth be founded on different grounds. These grounds are found in what can be established as "common interests of mankind": Its interest in physical survival, that is, avoidance of all-out war; its interest in rational planning of populations, resources, development of the underdeveloped; its emerging new common domain in outer space, and so forth. As pointed out before, this approach implies that the statesman now act in the dual capacity of caretaker of his own unit's as well as the larger community's interests. If such a policy of taking into consideration, together with one's own, the interest of the world at large and even the opponent's, should lead to an extended period of relaxation of tension, one might then perhaps envisage a future where more radically new attitudes would gradually replace concern with national interests. This then would constitute the international ethics of the nuclear age. I have called this approach a "universalist" one and defined universalism as "that comprehension of mankind as one group which imposes itself on those aware of the absolute peril in which the new weapons have placed mankind. . . ." [9]

Now that destruction threatens everybody in every single one of his most intimate, personal interests, national interests are bound to compete with and eventually to recede behind the common interest in sheer survival. If we add to this the general interest in the solution of the other great world problems, it is perhaps permissible to concede at least some chance to the ultimate spread of an attitude through which rational foreign policies would at last become possible.

9. *International Politics in the Atomic Age* (New York, 1959), p. 309.

5

THE RELEVANCY AND IRRELEVANCY OF APPEASEMENT

Originally published in *Social Research* 31, no. 3 (Autumn 1964): 296–320, this chapter places the concept of appeasement into its historical context and traces its use in ideological and actual political contests from its origin in the 1930s to the postwar period. The charge of appeasement is found to be justified in certain circumstances, unjustified in others, depending on the prevailing international system and the threats to its maintenance. For further discussion, see pages 19–22 in the *Introduction* and chapter 10 in this volume.

Reprinted by permission of the New School for Social Research, New York.

Appeasement is an emotive term referring to a highly emotional issue. The issue underlies much in recent and current foreign policy debate, not only in this country and the West but also on the other side of the Iron Curtain. In the West it has long divided the participants in the cold war debate over the problem of what to do about the world split, what to do about Communism. It goes back to the traumatic experience of the 1930s, which made appeasement appear as the great sin, or fallacy. It caused the appeasement policy of the prewar era to be considered the prototype of what to avoid in the face of the Communist menace.[1] One believes that one has learned from

1. The failure of appeasement in the 1930s "made a deep impression on the American consciousness, and its rejection is a basic tenet in the American

history. Santayana's statement that "those who do not learn from history are condemned to repeat it" has deeply impressed the minds of modern statesmen. President Truman has told us time and again how forcefully the lesson of appeasement imposed itself at times of decision.[2] And if we hear the most realistic statesman of the 1930s, Winston Churchill, who was the earliest to warn us at that time, warn us again in the late 1940s,[3] the parallel seems to be amply justified.

But the question is: What lesson must be learned? There is always the possibility of drawing the wrong parallels. Like those generals who "fight the last war," statesmen are inclined to cope with "the last crisis." [4] Parallels are justified only when situations are essentially alike. They were not, for instance, when those who believed that they had learned a lesson from the impotence of the League of Nations tried to set up the United Nations as an "improved" collective security organization with "teeth" in it; the bipolar distribution of power, which in the meantime had replaced the multipower system of the interwar period, had rendered the idea obsolete. There are those who feel that a similar incongruity applies to the comparison between the Nazi and the Communist threat; in other words, that the parallel does not really stick. Those who

ideological position today." Charles O. Lerche: *Principles of International Politics* (New York, 1956), p. 375.

2. Thus, at the outbreak of the Korean war: "I recalled some earlier instances: Manchuria, Ethiopia, Austria. I remembered how each time that the democracies failed to act it had encouraged the aggressors to go ahead. Communism was acting in Korea just as Hitler, Mussolini, and the Japanese had acted ten, fifteen, and twenty years earlier. . . . If this was to go unchallenged it would mean a third world war, just as similar incidents had brought on the second world war." Harry S Truman, *Memoirs* (New York, 1958), 2:333. That Truman, in turn, was subsequently accused of appeasement by the adherents of General MacArthur for having limited his objectives to the restoration of the status quo in Korea, is one of the ironies in the situation.

3. "If we add the United States to Britain and France: if we change the name of the potential aggressor; if we substitute the United Nations Organization for the League of Nations, the Atlantic Ocean for the English Channel, and the world for Europe, the argument is not necessarily without its application today." *The Second World War*, vol. 1, *The Gathering Storm* (Boston, 1948), p. 211.

4. See also Kenneth Waltz's warning not to apply the lesson in an uncritical way: "Seeming aggressiveness of one state may invite a war of prevention that a more pacific pose might have avoided." *Man, the State, and War* (New York, 1959), p. 222.

hold this view are, in turn, accused of being latter-day "appeasers," "soft" on Communism, etc. He who would deny the charge must ask, and ask thoughtfully and with the utmost sincerity, why he refuses to take the same attitude toward Communism he once took toward the Nazi-Fascist threat. This applies above all to those whose personal fate was involved with the issue in the 1930s. Belonging to that group, I shall try to approach the problem in this spirit.

I

"Appeasement" is not only an emotive, but also an extremely imprecise and ambiguous term, and we must start with an attempt at definition. In so doing we meet with problems of semantics, of conflict theory, of value theory, of political philosophy, of empirical history, and of international politics. While I shall emphasize the meaning and role of appeasement in international politics, we cannot entirely escape consideration of the other areas in which it is significant.

As far as semantics is concerned, we may here observe what is perhaps the most significant development: during the 1930s appeasement changed from a traditionally neutral term into a word with a "bad" connotation. Prior to this period appeasement meant pacification or conciliation in the genuine sense; that is, in the sphere of international politics it denoted a policy aiming at and conducive to peace. Thus, according to a historian of the period of the 1920s, in 1924 the French, after a time during which hostile and even aggressive attitudes toward Germany were dominant, inaugurated a *politique d'apaisement,* a policy of reconciliation and genuine appeasement.[5] The "appeasers" of the 1930s, as we shall see, still had this connotation in mind, but the failure of their policy gave the word, and the policy, its second, current meaning of futility, if not immorality. Webster's Dictionary, 1944 edition, still mentioned only the first connotation: "To pacify (often by satisfy-

5. Erich Eyck, *A History of the Weimar Republic* (Cambridge, Mass., 1962), p. 324.

ing), to quiet, calm, soothe, allay." The 1956 edition adds: "To conciliate by political, economic, or other considerations; now usually signifying a sacrifice of moral principle in order to avert aggression; as, 'an attempt to *appease* the Nazi rulers was made at Munich in 1938'." Consequently, Webster's *Third New International Dictionary* of 1961 distinguishes, first, appeasement as "pacification," "conciliation," "to bring to a state of peace," and second, appeasement as "a policy of appeasing a potential aggressor."

While this clearly indicates the emergence of the "fighting term" out of the experience with, and opposition too, a certain type of policy, it still leaves the term, even in its new significance, rather short of clarity. Was its essence immorality, i.e., the sacrifice of democratic, or other principle, in order to satisfy the aggressor? Or should we emphasize cowardice, the attempt to avoid a test of strength by a policy of peace at any price? Or was it characteristic of an effort, dominated by pro-fascist elements, to join up with the Nazi-fascist "wave of the future?" On the other hand, it may have involved an attempt through power politics to save oneself from immediate attack by deflecting the dictators in another direction, e.g., east, or to delay the attack in order to gain time and rearm. Finally, it may have been primarily what the first definition implies, a genuine though unsuccessful attempt to establish more harmonious, peaceful conditions in Europe by satisfying allegedly justified grievances.

Historians will find—indeed, have found already—elements of all of these in the policies of the "appeasers" from 1933 to 1939. It is not our task here to assess their efforts but rather to point out that, to be a meaningful term in international politics, appeasement proper should be distinguished from related attitudes and policies. Thus, as the term itself indicates, the appeaser must stand in a certain opposition at least to the aggressiveness of the aggressor, whom, through concessions, etc., he tries to make change his ways. If the policy is one of joining the aggressor in order to be on the stronger side—as A. L. Rowse says some of the appeasers were inclined to do[6]—this would be, from the viewpoint of the

6. A. L. Rowse, *Appeasement: A Study in Political Decline* (New York,

anti-appeasers, even "worse than appeasement" but should not be given the same designation. Also, seen from the appeaser's point of view, the policy must not be one of appeasement in the pejorative sense, i.e., in the sense of trying to appease one whom one knows to be "unappeasable." The appeaser hopes actually to be able to satisfy (that is, appease in the original sense) through concessions and similar means which are assumed to bring about "peace in our time," that is, a stable settlement of issues. Deflection elsewhere, winning time to become stronger, all these may be part and parcel of a given policy but, in the absence of that hope or expectation, should not be subsumed under appeasement. In a general conflict theory appeasement might thus be placed in a larger continuum of attitudes and policies ranging all the way from aggression to surrender-readiness.[7] Study of significant statements by the most prominent of appeasers of the 1930s, Neville Chamberlain, would indicate that the suggested definition, a policy of unilateral concession with the view of arriving at a genuine and long-range settlement, does apply here. This can be seen despite attempts by his defenders to show that he was also motivated by the objective of gaining time for rearming, and despite attempts by his detractors to prove that there was an element of anti-Soviet bias, and of pro-facism, in his actions.

Chamberlain believed—as A. J. P. Taylor still does—that Hitler would have been satisfied with a revision of the Versailles settlement. And thus he became the Great Appeaser. Both Churchill and Taylor attest that he was not, like Baldwin, acting from mere drift or from fear, but from a sense of mission: "He was driven on by hope, not fear";[8] "his all-pervading hope was to go down in history as the Great

---

1961), e.g., on page 28, where he refers to a remark of Geoffrey Dawson of the London *Times*: "If the Germans are so powerful as you say, oughtn't we to go in with them?"

7. Along this continuum lies a spectrum of attitudes and policies, of which the following may be noted: active aggressiveness: stand-pattism; readiness to compromise; unilateral concessions for reasons of appeasement; joining the stronger to share in the spoils; unconditional surrender.

8. A. J. P. Taylor, *The Origins of the Second World War* (London, 1961), p. 136.

Peacemaker; and for this he was prepared to strive continually in the teeth of facts." [9] The degree to which he suffered from illusion may be seen from a few statements culled from the work of his first biographer.[10]

With the Nazi documents now available, one can read these statements like a kind of fugue, with the appeasers' interpretations, hopes, and expectations counterpointed by Hitler's then secret comments concerning his intentions and plans for attack. Occasionally a third voice, Churchill's generally correct surmises and interpretations, appears in the fugue.

After the Austrian invasion, when Churchill had characterized appeasement as a "policy to come to terms with the totalitarian powers in the hope that by great and far-reaching acts of submission, not merely in sentiment and pride, but in material factors, peace may be preserved," [11] Chamberlain momentarily seemed to have doubted the wisdom of appeasement, only to discard the doubt immediately thereafter: "Heaven knows I don't want to go back to alliances but if Germany continues to behave as she has done lately, she may drive us to it. . . . If we can avoid another violent coup, it may be possible for Europe to settle down again, and some day for us to start peace talks again with the Germans." [12] After Berchtesgaden: "I got the impression that here was a man who could be relied upon when he had given his word," while on the other hand stating: "I must confess to the most profound distrust of Russia." [13] After Munich: "I sincerely believe that we have at last opened the way to that general appeasement which alone can save the world from chaos." [14] Note his use of the word "appeasement" in the sense of genuine pacification, not in the opprobrious sense it was acquiring at that time. In the spring of 1939, when pacification was still not in the offing, he continued to trust in a development "towards a more wholesome era, when reason will take the place of force." [15] Sir Lewis Namier's remarks to this point seem apropos: "They (the appeasers) had been tripped, had reeled and rolled down a

9. Churchill, *Gathering Storm*, p. 222.
10. Keith Feiling, *The Life of Neville Chamberlain* (London, 1946).
11. Churchill, *Gathering Storm*, p. 266.
12. Feiling, *Chamberlain*, p. 342.
13. Ibid., pp. 367, 403.
14. Ibid., p. 375.
15. Ibid., p. 404.

pit; muddy and dazed, and uncertain how to emerge, they declared themselves well satisfied with the progress they had achieved. . . . Self-condemned to argue the justice of Hitler's conquests and to profess trust in his promises, they burdened their policies with make-belief and disabled themselves from striking out in a new and clear line." [16]

Even after Prague, at the end of July 1939, Chamberlain held that Germany must be convinced "that she has a chance of getting fair and reasonable consideration and treatment from us and others," [17] while about the same time his man in Berlin, Nevile Henderson, asserted: "The Corridor and Danzig were a real German national grievance, and some equitable settlement had to be found if there was ever to be genuine peace." [18] The outbreak of the war seemed to have finally disabused Chamberlain of these illusions: "As long as that government exists and pursues the methods it has so persistently followed during the last two years, there will be no peace in Europe." [19] But now there are new illusions: "What I hope for is not a military victory—I very much doubt the feasibility of that—but a collapse of the German home front." [20] This of course, did not occur in six years of war. Yet even close to his death he would not admit to past mistakes: "Never for one single instant have I doubted the rightness of what I did at Munich. . . . I do not feel that I have anything to reproach myself for in my attempts to avoid the present war, which might well have succeeded if they had not come up against the insatiate and inhuman ambitions of a fanatic." [21] Perhaps this last statement is the most revealing: His was the picture of a normal, peaceful world in which statesmen behaved like gentlemen, and one ought not to be blamed for discounting the abnormal. That insatiable ambition and fanaticism bent on war had become a part of that world—something obvious to all those without blinkers—could not enter closed minds.

16. Lewis B. Namier, *Diplomatic Prelude—1938–1939* (London, 1948), p. xi.

17. Feiling, *Chamberlain*, p. 409.

18. Quoted in Namier, *Diplomatic Prelude*, p. 219.

19. Feiling, *Chamberlain*, p. 415.

20. Ibid., p. 418.

21. Ibid., pp. 452, 456.

II

We have already remarked upon the tremendous impact of the disastrous results of prewar appeasement upon the minds of decision-makers and publics in the postwar era. As one observer puts it: "Even with a sophisticated public, when (the government) is negotiating with a potential enemy, the cry of 'appeasement' is sooner or later heard." [22] This not only reflects a weakness of democracy, with its oftentimes hampering influence of public opinion on policy-making, but a degeneration in the use of the concept itself. Its meaning has become so all-inclusive as to comprise any foreign policy one desires to brand as weak, vacillating, or indeterminate. These new-style appeasement charges range all the way from almost paranoid accusations of engaging in Communist conspiracy, launched against presidents, ex-presidents, other political leaders, to indicting policies of negotiation, or attempts to negotiate, as soft, "no-win" policies. A prominent and influential nuclear physicist states: "The drift toward appeasement, toward making some accommodation with the Soviet Union (note the identification of appeasement with accommodation!) on the part of both the American people and American officials made me more uneasy with each passing month." [23] A prominent United States Senator complains: "The U.S. government has been trying for thirty years to appease the Latin American countries by whittling down its traditional legal rights to protect the persons and property of its citizens in Latin America." [24] On the other side of the Curtain, Tass calls the recent Franco-German friendship treaty "a step toward a new Munich," opening a path for renewed aggression to German "revanchists." Closer to crisis policy, the unidentified admiral referred to in a notorious *Saturday Evening Post* article by Alsop and Barlett charged that "Adlai wanted a Munich" when, allegedly, proposing to trade missile bases in Turkey for Soviet bases in Cuba. Other critics of the Administration's

22. Frederick H. Hartmann, *The Relations of Nations* (2nd ed.; New York, 1962), p. 107.
23. Edward Teller, *The Legacy of Hiroshima* (Garden City, N.Y., 1962), p. 35.
24. Barry M. Goldwater, *Why Not Victory?* (New York, 1962), p. 93.

policy during the Cuban crisis based a similar charge on the alleged United States commitment, or promise, of non-invasion of Cuba. The Chinese, on the other hand, accused Khrushchev of "surrender," a policy of "adventurism" leading to "capitulationism." His alleged sacrifice of Cuban sovereignty could "only be called a hundred-percent appeasement, a pure Munich"; Khrushchev's reliance on Kennedy's promise of noninvasion is compared to Chamberlain's belief in Hitler's promises, but, like Hitler's, the imperialist leaders' appetite will merely be stimulated.

To this almost symmetrical pattern of accusation corresponds a symmetrical pattern of defense. The official United States attitude, of course, sees the result of the Cuban crisis as constituting an unmitigated and clear victory for the West, the Soviets having been forced to withdraw their missiles and thus to retreat abjectly. This, then, would confirm the Chinese interpretation. Khrushchev, on the other hand, has defended his retreat by calling it "a concession we made for a concession by the other side; it was a mutual concession. . . . The aggressive forces in the U.S. had to retreat and publicly declare that they renounced an invasion." *His* interpretation, then, tends to confirm the charges leveled against Kennedy by *his* domestic critics.

What can we make of these charges and counter-charges, these defenses and counter-defenses? The very fact of their symmetry seems to indicate that in a situation of bipolar and nuclear stalemate anything and everything, or nothing, can be called appeasement. What appears aggressive to one side is defensive to the other, and vice versa. What, in such situations, constitutes "concessions," in particular, concessions without counter-concessions? Is it possible to elaborate, in this respect, objective criteria without taking into consideration intentions and over-all policies? Supposing that Khrushchev's retreat was a one-sided concession, was it not a step toward restoring a strategic balance which had been disturbed by the introduction of missiles in an area that, according to American claims, by tacit agreement was to remain outside the Soviet sphere? On the other hand, can such a clear-cut and unambiguous balancing and drawing of lines persist in the face of technological changes? How does one balance an increase in armament and military strength of the opponent? Do new bases, or new political or strategic alignments, constitute equivalents, and if so, under what conditions? To make the assessment dependent on whether or not there is exact balance in each quid pro quo seems unfeasible, especially where even inaction might be interpreted as appeasement. Is appeasement in evidence when the United States does *not* take further action against Cuba? Are Robert Oppenheimer's famous "two scorpions in the bottle" appeasing each other when abstaining from exchanging deadly stings? Extremists have always been inclined to call for the strongest imaginable kind of action in the face of what they consider aggression, and such critics can interpret almost any kind of policy which falls short of their extreme standard as appeasement.[25] From such a viewpoint, all sides emerge as appeasers mutually appeasing one another. This is absurd. If one desires more meaningful and more generally valid standards, one must distinguish between strategy and tactics, that is, between long-range principles and policies, on the one hand, and their specific implementation, on the other. The question is whether it is possible to distinguish that which is "objectively" required for the defense of national interests or the maintenance of international systems (such as balance of power), and also possible, from that which is not. Neglect of what is necessary and possible would, then, constitute appeasement. A

25. The issue of inaction, or mere verbal protest, raises interesting problems even in regard to the 1930s, when appeasement was most conspicuous. Was inaction, e.g., in the face of *internal* events (such as the persecution of Jews within Germany), the beginning of external appeasement? One author has recently suggested that a distinction be made between two kinds of appeasement: "active" and "passive," the first involving negotiations and satisfaction of demands, the second, letting things happen while merely protesting. See George A. Lanyi, "The Problem of Appeasement," *World Politics* (January 1963): 216ff., especially p. 319. This distinction is perhaps less significant than another one, which I shall discuss below, namely that between policies where there is clear intent of appeasement, and policies where the intent of appeasement is absent. Once intent exists, even mere recognition of a given state of affairs without trying to do something about it can amount to appeasement (e.g., recognition of, that is, continuing normal relations with, the Nazi regime, or the Soviet government or satellite regimes); where intent does not exist, e.g., under an overall policy of containment, even active steps benefiting the other side may escape the opprobrium of being defined as appeasement.

brief glance at the history of international relations and of international systems in this connection may clarify what I have in mind.

III

Looking backward at the history of international constellations, one finds situations which lend themselves, tailor-made, as it were, to the possibility of appeasement. There are multiple units or "powers," in a more or less balanced system. One unit, clearly and unmistakably aspiring to hegemony, emerges. This confronts the others with the problem of how to react: whether to try to resist and obstruct its expansionist, "aggressive" policies; to join it and share in the spoils; to deflect it; or, finally, to appease it by concessions. We encounter all of these attitudes long before we find them in the face of Hitlerite Germany. We can go as far back as antiquity and discover similar constellations and similar policies in a Greek city-state system confronting Philip of Macedonia's expansionism. The undecided, vacillating attitude of many a polis came close to appeasement: "We look on while the man grows greater, because every one has made up his mind . . . to profit by the time during which his neighbor is being ruined, and no one cares or acts for the safety of the Hellenes."[26] Some thought of organizing a defensive alliance with the old, no longer expansionist opponent, Persia, but only halfheartedly, since this ran counter to all traditional policy.[27] This reminds one of the equally halfhearted efforts on the part of the Western powers to negotiate with Stalin in 1939. And the attitude of the Persians was likewise one of indecision. According to Werner Jaeger, it seemed from their point of view "better to let them (the Greeks and Macedonians) wear each other down than to attempt any further intervention in these affairs."[28] The parallel with Stalin's calculations when concluding his pact with Hitler is only too obvious. The entire *Third Philippic* reads like Churchill in 1938, with its anxiety to

26. From the *Third Philippic*.
27. See A. W. Pickard-Cambridge, *Demosthenes* (1914), pp. 340ff.
28. Werner Jaeger, *Demosthenes* (1938), p. 181.

convince fellow Athenians that what they considered peace was no peace: "But if any man supposes this to be peace, which will enable Philip to master all else and attack you last, he is a madman."

Whether or not one can speak of a genuine balance-of-power system in antiquity, it is most obviously present in the modern state system, and the potentialities of appeasement appear most clearly in the modern balance-of-power situation. A balance-of-power policy, that is, a policy of preserving an existing equilibrium of power, requires quite specific attitudes toward that unit which threatens to overthrow the balance; attitudes and policies of resistance, alignment with others, containment. Opposing policies, if conducted in the hope of seeing the power that is reaching for hegemony satiated or similarly tranquilized, then constitute appeasement. In view of the unlimited ambitions and objectives of the expansionist power, they are liable to fail and eventually to place the system they endeavor to maintain in jeopardy. Such "wrong" policies are interspersed throughout the entire history of the modern state system, which, for centuries, has been one of balances neglected, defended, destroyed, restored. Appeasement, under these conditions, may be defined as a policy ignoring (or ignorant of) what balance policy requires. What is required, and what must be avoided, has always been most forcefully expressed by leaders of the nation which for so long was the "holder of the balance," from Bolingbroke to Crowe, and again by Winston Churchill: "For hundreds of years the foreign policy of England has been to oppose the strongest, most aggressive, most dominating power on the Continent. . . . It would have been easy and must have been tempting to join with the stronger and share the fruits of his conquest. However, we always took the hardest course, joined with the less strong powers, made a combination among them, and thus defeated and frustrated the Continental military tyrant whoever he was, whatever nations he led. . . . Our national salvation depends upon our gathering once again all the forces of Europe to contain, to restrain, and if necessary to frustrate, German domination." [29]

29. Churchill, *Gathering Storm*, pp. 207 ff. (From an address to Conservatives, March 1936.)

Similar to a balance of power, a genuine collective security system requires for its functioning certain well-defined policies, the opposite of which may constitute appeasement. Collective security being the institutionalization of the balance system, the requirement of opposing hegemony trends here assumes the form of legal and organizational commitment, and appeasement—through concessions or mere inaction—appears in the form of disregard of one's commitment to defend a victim of aggression. Appeasement in the 1930s took this turn whenever the League of Nations took up cases of aggression, that is, as long as it was still functioning. This lasted through the period of the Ethopian war. After that time (when appeasement had killed the League) balance of power became again the directing principle in international affairs.[30]

IV

What can we say about appeasement under nuclear-age conditions, in particular as they affect the relations of two, and only two, major power centers? Can we still distinguish, as we did in the case of the classical balance-of-power system, what, in reference to the maintenance of the international system, is contra-systemic from what is required for safeguarding the system? I submit that three factors fundamentally differentiate present conditions from those in the 1930s: (a) the nature of

30. The above interpretation of appeasement as a contra-system policy in balance systems or systems of genuine collective security raises the question of its more general application to any and all policies of expansion under all international systems. As far as I can see, there has been only one attempt to place appeasement in such a generalized framework, viz., that of Hans Morgenthau in applying his well-known division of all foreign policy into status quo policy and "imperialism"—the latter in the sense of "expansionism" —in showing that appeasement is a policy of compromise misapplied in order to counter imperialism rather than status quo policy. ("Appeasement tries to deal with imperialism as though it were a policy of the status quo. . . . Appeasement is a corrupted policy of compromise, made erroneous by mistaking a policy of imperialism for a policy of the status quo." *Politics Among Nations*, 3rd edition, p. 64.) This leads to the question, did the "appeasers" of the 1930s mistake the policies of Hitler, of Mussolini, or of the Japanese for status quo policies? What about "revisionism," which can, perhaps, be "appeased" (in the earlier sense of genuine *apaisement*) by concession and "satiation"? Morgenthau, to be sure, goes on to state that the

war and the function of violence; (b) the balance of power qua international system; and (c) the nature of the West's totalitarian opponent. These, I believe, account for the difference in the assessment and relevance of appeasement today.

In the classical balance system, and into the 1930s, force threatened, or actively used, was the chief and sometimes only available means to deter, restrain, or destroy a hegemony power; in the face of a Hitler hell-bent on war preventive war should have been waged, or at least threatened. Today, all-out use of force is no longer a rational, and therefore no longer a credible means of policy. Without risking the destruction of everything and everybody, including oneself, one cannot wage nuclear war to restrain or destroy an expansionist power; and because of the danger of "escalation," conventional force likewise has become of doubtful utility. By the same token, a minimally rational expansionist country or regime will not try to attain its objectives by violence, at least not by that kind of violence which may provoke warlike retaliation. A policy of avoiding war with such a power, therefore, does not necessarily constitute appeasement, since peace need not be bought that way any more.[31] True, renouncing all use of force, or use of a particular kind of force, such as nuclear weapons, from the outset and unilaterally, might encourage the opponent to advance under the threat of nuclear war, and would in this way render a policy of "peace at any price" a policy of appeasement, if pursued in hopes of assuaging the opponent. Although policies of this kind are occasionally advocated by radical pacifists, unilateralists, etc., this certainly has not constituted general Western policy. Even policies which looked like unilateral yielding, like those of Yalta or the early postwar period, were hardly based on expectations of satisfying or satiating an expansionist Stalin—wrong as some of the assumptions about Communism may have been at this period —but rather on (partly incorrect) strategic calculations and

distinction between a policy of status quo and a policy of imperialism depends on whether or not a nation seeks "a fundamental change in the existing distribution of power" (ibid., p. 65.) Is moderate revisionism, then, a status quo policy? These distinctions need further clarification.

31. "I speak of peace because of the new face of war" (President Kennedy, commencement address at American University, 10 June 1963).

considerations.[32] The overall Western intention and policy have consisted of balancing, containment and deterrence. The threat of retaliation with weapons one expects never to use has become the counterpart of what in earlier times was the correct way to oppose expansionism, that is, active nonappeasement, including, possibly and ultimately, war.

On the other side of the picture, while Communism, as a cause, a creed, a movement, is expansionist, at least in its Soviet version it is no longer bent on waging a war deemed inevitable.[33] Under nuclear conditions both sides are vitally interested in avoiding war, and negotiations for mutual accommodation are therefore meaningful in order to avoid running into it. Armament, during the 1930s necessary in order to counter military aggression, today makes sense only inasmuch as the balance of deterrence has to be maintained, and arrangements for its control or reduction, far from constituting appeasement, constitute insurance against race suicide. Preventive war, which in the 1930s might actually have prevented the subsequent worldwide war, today would be truly suicidal. Attacking the opponents of preventive war on the ground that they are appeasers no longer makes sense. Indeed, it can be argued with some plausibility that greater than the danger of genuine appeasement today is that of *charges* of appeasement driving one or the other side, or both, in the opposite direction, that of risking the nuclear holocaust.

Turning now to the impact of the second factor, that of bipolarity as the characteristic structure of major power relations today, we may recall the striking symmetry in charges and counter-charges on the part of both sides in their interpretations of postwar events and policies. This is only natural in a bipolar situation, a system in which the security

32. Appeasement presupposes at least the consciousness, or intention of making unilateral concessions; if what turns out to be a concession was caused by misjudgment of the situation—e.g., because one forecast developments incorrectly—one should not speak of appeasement. See, for instance, the Yalta "concessions" in the Far East, which were based on wrong assumptions by United States naval strategists concerning the final stage of war against Japan; or similarly incorrect Western forecasts concerning the final stages of the war against Germany at the time of the drawing of zonal occupation lines for Germany.

33. See Frederic S. Burin, "The Communist Doctrine of the Inevitability of War," *American Political Science Review* (June 1963): 334 ff.

dilemma, the apprehension of being "buried" if one does not forestall one's burial by burying the other fellow, reaches its highest point. Every defensive move meant to counter aggression or expansion will then be interpreted by the other side as offensive, and failure to make such a move—or not moving quite as quickly as some expect—will be indicted as appeasement. Under conditions of bipolar balance both interpretations—that of aggression and that of appeasement—are mistaken, provided that maintenance of the balance, that is, defense of what one has and containment of the opponent to what he possesses, remains the overall policy. This, in my opinion, has been true of both Soviet and Western policies in the postwar period, at least insofar as traditional political-military means and traditional objectives of territorial control are concerned. (I do not include here a different type of expansionism, characteristic of Communist totalitarianism, to which I shall refer below.) It follows that "peaceful coexistence" in the political-territorial field, and "peaceful competition" in the ideological sphere are meaningful, indeed prerequisites for the preservation of a bipolar system of ideologically opposed major actors. Mutual accommodation through delimitation of spheres, mutual recognition of what each side possesses de facto, and similar policies emerge in such circumstances as the opposite of appeasement in the pejorative sense of the word; rather can they turn out to be means toward *apaisement* in the earlier sense of the term—attempts to create stabler conditions of more durable peace.

One could not "do business with Hitler" by trying to establish lines of demarcation or spheres of influence. One can, with proper precautions, do business of this sort with Khrushchev, as the cases of Austria, Finland, and even Germany and Berlin, have shown. In this connection, it is revealing to compare the fate of smaller nations facing the Axis powers (and Stalin) in the 1930s with these more recent cases: no "Finnish solution" was possible for any of them, not even Poland. Upon the face of it, it seemed that appeasement made sense in the instance of a weaker country confronting an aggressive stronger one. A policy of "going along," of agreeing to certain demands, etc., as Poland attempted to do in 1934 and the years following, then appeared as the only way to survive.

There was some hope that the strong power would turn elsewhere and leave the weak one alone. In the end, of course, it meant only postponement of the inevitable, temporary relief which ultimately led to disaster. Whether some of the present Communist countries in their relations with weaker countries will have to be judged, and countered, by similar tests of territorial-military aggression remains to be seen. China, of course, poses the greatest problem. But it must be said that, appearances and verbal outbursts notwithstanding, in its relation to its major opponent China so far has evinced caution, as witness its criticism of Soviet Cuban policy as "adventurism" involving the danger of subsequent "capitulationism," [34] Its greater aggressiveness has been displayed, on the one hand toward neighboring countries, and on the other hand in the sphere of social-political-ideological penetration from within. On the larger plane it is, perhaps, deterred by its own doctrinal belief in imperialism's inherent recklessness and aggressiveness.

From what has been said it should be apparent how important it is to measure appeasement or nonappeasement against the *overall* attitudes and policies of powers. Specific day-to-day steps and short-range decisions, in contrast, should be viewed as tactical matters of trying to attain the strategic goal, matters that depend on the situation of the moment and that should not be judged separately from overall objectives. Thus, in a relatively well-balanced bipolar situation a specific step looking like appeasement may find its justification in a total policy of nonappeasing accommodation (e.g., Kennedy's decision not to conduct underground nuclear testing during test-ban negotiations, a measure which promptly provoked charges of appeasement on the part of Governor Rockefeller), while in a multipower balance threatened by an aggressive would-be hegemony power even the mildest concession, such as a merely verbal expression of "friendship" (like French Foreign Minister Georges Bonnet's declaration after Munich)[35]

34. And as witness its cautious attitude and reaction during the "Tonkin crisis" of Summer 1964.
35. See Bonnet's own statement, betraying the typical appeaser's illusion, in Georges Bonnet, *Fin d'une Europe, de Munich à la Guerre* (Geneva, 1948), p. 50.

or of hope for some kind of settlement (such as Under-Secretary of State Sumner Welles' statement in the same period, backing up "the efforts of Great Britain, supported by France, to reach the basis for a practical understanding with Germany both on colonies and on security")[36] may be as illusory as any major appeasement policy. On the other hand, once an overall strategy of containment has been adopted, the issue of "hardline" versus a "softer" policy toward the opponent—which so frequently underlies charges of appeasement today—resolves itself likewise into a matter of tactics rather than principle.

We confront a paradox: In the West, right-wingers still call for a fight against an allegedly militant Communism bent on "world conquest," and accuse of appeasement those who doubt its militancy and world-conquering aggressiveness. In the East, left-wingers still consider the West aggressively imperialist, or neo-colonialist, and level the appeasement charge against those in their camp who, in their view, fail to combat this opponent actively. Again symmetrical attitudes! But is there not something which is genuinely expansionist in our world? In particular, in Communism? It would be foolish to overlook the latter's dynamism, and it is here, I submit, that the problem of appeasement assumes entirely novel significance.

V

To cope with this third factor—the character of Communist totalitarianism—it is necessary to know where the real conflict situation lies, and it is exactly here that both Western and Eastern extremists make their mistakes. At the latest since Korea there has been no attempt on the part of Soviet Communism to extend its control through open violence or military aggression across frontiers. And at the latest since Prague[37] there has been no attempt to take over, through conquest of power "from within," in the area of the "stable

36. See the document quoted in William L. Langer and S. E. Gleason, *The Challenge to Isolation, 1937–1940* (New York, 1952), p. 25.

37. This, of course, refers to the takeover of 1948, not the action of 1968 (JHH, 1975).

world." For, viewed from Moscow, the Communist world is faced with two worlds. One is the relatively stable one of Europe, North America, etc., where, despite doctrines on the "ultimate" maturity of society for class struggle and proletarian revolution, attempts to achieve "socialism" now seem nugatory. The other sector consists of the more or less "promising" unstable units of the former colonial or semicolonial, so-called underdeveloped world. It is in the latter that Communism seeks to "conquer" through what the West considers subversion and propaganda, that is, through political-ideological penetration rather than by military force. If there is success, it arises from "within," sometimes even without much assistance from "Big Brother." China was a surprise to Stalin, Cuba even more so to Khrushchev. The decisive fact is that conditions favoring Communism are worldwide and indigenous, while very little abroad favored Nazi, Fascist or Japanese expansionism, which were basically nationalistic (or racialist) and therefore had to rely primarily on military force. As for the conditions in the underdeveloped world which are favorable to the assumption of Communist control—whether they take the form of Castroism in Latin America, of Maoism in the Far East, or any other form—it is hardly necessary to describe them here in detail. It is to these conditions, however, that we must adapt the uses of the terms appeasement and nonappeasement.

To begin with, one can even agree with our more radical antiappeasers and "forward strategists" when they emphasize that the West is involved in more than the traditional military and power conflict, indeed in an all-pervasive conflict with Communist totalitarianism. And yet, these critics fail to understand the true nature and the real threat of present-day Communism, namely, nonviolent expansion. *Terribles simplificateurs*, they usually recommend as counter-action more stepped-up anti-Communism at home coupled with a more determined posture vis-à-vis the Soviet Union, or the Communist bloc, including a continued or even accelerated armament race and attempts to reconquer or otherwise "liberate" lost areas. This way, quixotically, they fight either windmills or, at best, the battles of the 1930s and '40s. What is at stake is not the reconquest of Cuba, or of other Cubas, but the forestalment of additional Cubas, or Chinas, and this through a whole range of difficult, intricate, costly, long-range policies of a nature and dimension from which the self-styled bold anti-appeasers shrink in horror. Rather than fight a largely imaginary Communist enemy within our gates[38] we must try to present an image of liberal democracy to the outer world which would render it less easy for Communist propaganda to picture us as racists. Rather than vie with the Soviet Union for ever more over-kill capacity in the armament field, we must engage in bona fide arms control negotiations which would make it impossible for the Soviets to present themselves as the only "peace-lovers." And in the decisive "third" realm of the world, vastly more vital than fighting Communism where civil war has already broken out, or replacing leftist or "popular front" types of regimes by more reliable ones,[39] is the positive policy of creating conditions under which the Western version of social and political life has a chance to survive or to be established. To oppose Communist policies in this arena effectively one has to know exactly the ideological premises and expectations, and the economic-political strategies and tactics on which they proceed. In regard to the problem of appeasement and nonappeasement what follows is simple: To devise and implement policies suitable to counter this Communist offensive cannot be appeasement in the pejorative sense; rather, it may result in appeasement in the original sense, at least for some area and for some period of time. How, in this

38. It is amazing, in view of existing conditions, that Communism has not made inroads among American Negroes. It is to our great good fortune—which I doubt we have deserved—that this has not been the case.

39. The question of whether permitting a totalitarian party to participate in government may constitute appeasement is an interesting and complicated one. In a way, the appointment of the Hitler cabinet in 1933 was the prototype, domestically, of all subsequent appeasement on the international level. Hitler's coalition partners, who had thought to make Hitler their "prisoner," were faced with the disastrous results of their illusions mere months later; and subsequent efforts by still autonomous forces, such as the Catholic Church (both the German Church and the Vatican itself) and army leaders, to keep Nazism within certain limits proved equally unsuccessful. The entire problem of the connection between "internal" and "foreign-political" appeasement deserves further study. See, in this connection, remarks by the foremost German historian of the Nazi era, Karl Dietrich Bracher (in reference to the Center Party's voting for the Enabling Act of March 1933) in his still untranslated book, *Die nationalsozialistische Machtergreifung* (2nd ed., 1962),

respect, to devise the right mixture of military backing (of the "right" kind of regime), of democratization (of still "wrong" systems), and, above all, of general and economic development should form a large part of Western statesmanship. For it will be in this genuinely "proletarian" sector of the world that the issue of world "class warfare" (with, possibly, Communist worldwide victory) versus the issue of creating economic plenty combined with liberty for all will be decided. "Appeasement," here, would lie in withdrawing from this task in the forlorn hope that thus Communism may be repelled from one's own little bailiwick. True nonappeasement and "forward strategy" lie in an active policy of internationalism and foreign aid.

VI

Finally, we come to value theory. Here we run into particularly intricate problems. They are indicated by that definition of appeasement which ties appeasement policy to moral insufficiency, to disregard or betrayal of moral principle. It may well happen that appeasement, in some particular instance, has nothing to do with such principles; that it has resulted from policy based on considerations—whether correct or incorrect does not matter here—of national interest and assessment of power relations. Even so, the issue cannot be separated from value considerations. In the field of diplomacy

---

p. 160: "This was a domestic prelude to that tactic of assuagement, that policy of appeasement which was used subsequently by foreign governments in order to appease Hitler by concessions. . . ." He goes on to state that, although Hitler probably would have attained what he aimed at even without this backing, the latter was a valuable aid in achieving total power in that it increased his "moral authority" and appearance of "legitimacy" in the eyes of Germans as well as abroad.

Evidence in reference to Communism is less conclusive: Formation of "popular front" governments, *qua* efforts to contain a participating Communist Party, were unsuccessful where, as in postwar Eastern Europe, the Communist Party was either stronger than the non-Communist forces, or shrewder, or both. On the other hand, there have been instances of successful containment, for instance (so far) in Indonesia, where the PKI has been "domesticated" by Sukarno and serves rather his purposes than vice versa. See Donald Hindley, "President Sukarno and the Communists: the Politics of Domestication," *American Political Science Review* 56 (1962): 915 ff. It seems to be a matter of (a) the respective power constellation, (b) the purpose and policy of the non-Communist parties. In addition, success will ultimately

this correlation is indicated by the distinction between the "negotiable" and the "nonnegotiable," a distinction which plays such a powerful role in international negotiation, and which becomes particularly acute in a contest of ideologies and systems. The appeasers of the 1930s appeared as "immoral" not so much because they were too easily inclined to risk national interests, and not even because they placed the entire balance of power system in jeopardy, but rather because they were ready to put the freedom from fascist control of individuals, groups and entire nations on the bargaining counter; or, ultimately, even to make it a matter of unilateral concession. Today we would be equally guilty of violating basic principle if we should make the freedom from Communist totalitarianism a matter of bargaining (not to mention unilateral concession) even though it might occur in the process of negotiation and mutual accommodation. There are limits to bargaining which both sides ignore at the risk of disregarding basic values. Thus the West could not sacrifice to Communist control populations to whose protection it has committed itself (such as those of West Berlin or Taiwan.) By this I do not refer to land or material possessions but rather to people and their basic rights and freedoms. By the same token, however, we must recognize that Communists, too, have basic values: thus, once "socialism" has become established in an area, the Communists could hardly be expected to surrender it to "capitalism." [40] Any bona fide attempt to arrive at genuine *apaisement* through bargaining, delimitation of spheres, etc., must keep in mind the respective value systems of the parties, and the limitations they impose; awareness of these limits on each side might then even help in the process.

---

depend on whether those opposing the totalitarian group are ready to perform the tasks which would withhold from the "movement" its chief appeal. Even assuming that Chinese Communism had not been strong enough to prevail by military means, it could have been contained only by forces which would have been what appeasers thought the Chinese Communists were—agrarian reformers.

40. In view of these antithetical values, each side, in order to "coexist" with the other, must be careful not to commit itself in respect to something which is "nonnegotiable" to the opponent (e.g., the West to the "liberation" of the satellite nations, the East to that of, let us say, the Italian "proletariat.") Such overcommitment would involve inevitable conflict and ultimately lead into the dilemma of having to choose between surrender or all-out war.

Actually, owing to greater doctrinal consistency, there is more agreement on values on the Eastern side than in the West. The latter, all too often, gives the impression of not knowing what to defend against whom. The dichotomy of "free world" versus "totalitarianism," for instance, is marred by disagreement about what one means by "freedom." Is it "free enterprise" as opposed to regulation or nationalization of private property, or is it human rights and political liberties versus total control of life? Those who are honestly (although probably mistakenly) convinced that these values and liberties cannot flourish except under free enterprise are entitled to identify the two pairs of contrasts, but one must object to an attitude which under the guise of defending freedom is merely interested in preserving private property rights. The prevalence of such an attitude in the end would confirm China's interpretation of imperialism and its indictment of "peaceful coexistence" as appeasement of the unappeasable. . . . On the other hand, if liberal democratic values are to be the controlling ones in the "free world," this world should realize that they are slighted not only by Communist totalitarianism but—sometimes in even more flagrant manner—by fascist, semifascist, racist, or other "extreme rightist" forms of police-state suppression. The leading Western democracies here confront the well-known dilemma of what to do in case such regimes are needed in the anti-Communist struggle. Where their cooperation is of real moment (e.g., in regard to military bases) the decision must probably be in favor of using them to assist against the politically greater danger. Too frequently, however, their anti-Communism has been the ground for considering them "allies" or even friends. Instead, they hamper not only the job of the West in the underdeveloped world (which can hardly be supposed to believe in our good intentions so long as we regard an ever more Nazi-like "apartheid" regime as "friendly") but lay open to doubt the West's entire moral position and moral credibility. How greatly moral blindness in the face of oppressive regimes has undermined our effort in Latin America has lately become apparent. A shift of emphasis on what here, too, is "nonnegotiable" would render issues meaningful once more in a world which, in terms of power and power relations, must resign itself to protracted coexistence of all kinds of systems.

To summarize briefly: Charges of appeasement levelled against a policy that aims at avoiding war are no longer relevant in an age when major war, because of its nature, has ceased to be an instrument of policy even on the part of expansionist regimes. Stigmatizing as appeasement policies of balancing and adjustment misses the point in a world where such policies are the only means to assure peaceful coexistence of, or peaceful competition among, antagonistic blocs and systems. Appeasement—if we want to use the term at all—lies in abandoning people and nations to the ideological conquest by totalitarian movements or regimes through failure to engage in the policies and to take the measures, and even to make the sacrifices, which are suitable and necessary in order to preserve the values of a liberal and humanitarian democracy.

THE IMPACT OF THE
TECHNOLOGICAL-SCIENTIFIC
PROCESS ON THE
INTERNATIONAL SYSTEM

This essay was first published as chapter 7 of a volume
edited by Abdul A. Said, *Theory of International Relations—
The Crisis of Relevance* (Englewood Cliffs, N.J., 1968), pp.
107–26. It reflects my developing insights into the impact of
the technological acceleration process upon the most diverse areas of human life and societies (see chapter 7),
applying them here to the field of international systems and
policies. Findings: a side-by-side of growing uniformity and
stability with brittleness and underlying instability. For further analysis, see pages 24–25 in the *Introduction*.

Reprinted by permission of Prentice-Hall, Inc., Publishers, Englewood Cliffs, N.J.

It is not my intention to deal in this essay with the influence
any particular technological invention or innovation has upon
international relations. One might, for instance, study the
impact of the discovery of gunpowder on the arts of warfare
and, this way, on units of international relations and relations
among such units. Or, looking forward rather than backward,
one could ask what likely consequences the substitution of
nuclear energy for petroleum as chief source of energy will
have on the oil countries of the Middle East and on industrial
nations dependent on their oil.

My intention is more general. I am interested here in an
overall historical process which I first shall have to identify
before describing its relation to international affairs. This

process is perhaps best defined by referring to the theory of great historical processes developed by Alfred Weber.[1] Weber distinguished the three most basic processes of historical development: the cultural, the sociopolitical, and the one he referred to as the "civilizational process" *(Zivilisationsprozess)*, by which he meant the process in the area of science and technology. While, according to Weber, two of these, the cultural and the sociopolitical, have in the main been either cyclical (with "cultures," e.g., enfolding, flourishing, declining) or else indeterminate (with political structures, e.g., following upon each other at one point in this and at that point in another fashion and sequence), the process of science and science-based technology has been characterized by its unilinear "progress" through the entire history of whatever civilizations. Based as it is upon the rational faculties common to man as man, it remained unaffected by culture cycles, transformations in social structures, and so forth. It advances through history as a one-directional, uniform process.

Weber thus viewed the scientific-technological process as essentially separate, as one leaving the other processes pretty much alone. Despite its uniformity, there was still diversity in the spheres of civilizations and their cultural and sociopolitical structures. This, I submit, is changing now. The great new factor is acceleration. The basic underlying feature of our world is the rate of change, the speed with which scientific discoveries and technological inventions follow upon each other. Acceleration in science and technology accounts for acceleration in almost everything else, whether in the area of population increase, of use and exhaustion of resources, of strategy and weapons, or the spread of ideas and ideologies.[2]

1. See above all, his fundamental essay "Prinzipielles zur Kultursoziologie: Sozialprozess, Zivilisationsprozess und Kulturbewegung," in *Archiv für Sozialwissenschaft und Sozialpolitik* 47 (1920–21): 1–49. Similar distinctions are found in Robert MacIver's theory of society, see his *Society: An Introductory Analysis* (New York: Holt, Rinehart & Winston, 1949).

2. The general phenomenon of acceleration was first seen, or at least first emphasized, by Henry Adams, cf. his famous theory of ever shorter "phases" of ever steeper advance, which he developed already toward the turn of this century (*The Rule of Phase Applied in History*, written in 1909, published posthumously in *The Degradation of the Democratic Dogma*, 1919). By now the "exponential" Adams curve is found wherever the respective phenomena are described. However, in regard to the relation between acceleration and

What does this mean in terms of the theory of history I have referred to? It means something revolutionarily new. For the first time in history, the three basic historical processes no longer proceed independently from each other. One of them, the technological process, becomes overpowering. In its one-directional sweep and onrush it tends to determine the other processes and this way to create an overall and uniform technological cosmos. A novel, synthetic environment replaces the natural habitat of man. Previous diversity of cultures, systems, values, ways of life is in the process of being wiped out or transformed. It is a process of ever speedier and ever more radical change and transformation; while it is destabilizing in the extreme, at the same time it leads us paradoxically toward uniformity: we rush into uniformity.

As one wit has put it: "Even the future nowadays is no longer what it used to be." That is, it is no longer an open, indeterminate horizon of possibilities. Today, everything seems predetermined; we anticipate even the most radical change; we can forecast what science and technology can and will do, and plan for it; we even plan the direction in which science, invention, etc., are to go. Thus the future seems fatalistically closed, no longer a universe of diverse possibilities. In the conclusion of this essay I will have to say a few words about this alleged closedness and inevitability. In the main part, I shall deal with the question, What are the consequences for international relations?

I

We can observe the impact of this explosive acceleration of things and developments in the international arena on attitudes and policies, processes and systems, on actors, units, organizations. The most elementary observation, perhaps, refers to the effects of the speed-up in communications, transportation, etc., on processes in the conduct of foreign

international affairs, I have discovered very little attention and analysis so far. A brief but emphatic call for such attention is found in Ernst B. Haas, "Toward Controlling International Change," *World Politics* 17, no. 1 (October 1964): 1–12.

affairs. These effects are radical: For the first time in history we can speak meaningfully of "world politics," based on *universality of information and discourse, universalization of concern, and ubiquitousness of power and weapons.*

In a way, of course, we had "world politics" long before the end of World War II. Indeed, what was more global than two world wars? But in two important respects international politics, as system and process, was still less than global. In the first respect, world relations had been carried on by Western-type powers only and were shaped by their particular approach and institutions, with the majority of mankind not admitted on an equal footing to the business at hand; the international system, in this sense, had remained parochial. Now, with modernization in the form of independent statehood granted to almost all people of the world, the affairs of the world are in the hands and the responsibility of all. Obviously, this does not imply actual equality of all in regard to power, etc., but that the presence of the new countries makes an actual and not merely formal difference is clear from a comparison in composition, role, and impact of the League of Nations and the United Nations, the so-called world organization of before World War II, and the genuine world organization of the present.

The second respect in which international relations formerly lacked true universality is perhaps more elusive. It becomes apparent when one contrasts how events in widely separated parts of the globe affected others, and how they interact now. Then, a revolution in Latin America might greatly affect the United States but little, or not at all, Germany or even Britain; an event in Southeast Asia might greatly interest Britain but not much the United States. Although peace was declared "indivisible" already in the interwar period, it was not quite as indivisible as it is now when even remote danger of hostilities, whether near the coast of China, or Cuba, or at the autobahn to Berlin, make the world shudder with fears of global conflagration. Indeed, in case of a "central" nuclear war, the physical impact would be such as no longer to allow of much geographical differentiation.

Foreign policy, in anticipation or attempted prevention, must therefore be truly global, true world politics. All this clearly is the effect of the technological factor of annihilation of time and distance through speed: speed in information and communication, enabling, in principle, everybody to know about everything and be in touch with everybody about it; speed in transportation, enabling leaders to be almost instantaneously wherever needed; speed in marshalling military forces, in particular the capability of nuclear powers to be present at every point of the globe within hours or fractions of hours. It is above all this destructive aspect of immediacy that accounts for integration of systems and processes. *Admission of all mankind to participation in world politics has rendered process universal; fear of annihilation has rendered the system global.*

This does not imply that the world is in the stage of being unified. The discrepancy between what is possible technically and the actualities of antagonisms of power, ideology, and so forth, constitutes a basic characteristic of our world. Indeed, what I have called the security dilemma of international units—their concern with survival in a world of competing powers and their ensuing urge to accumulate power, if only to be able to face others doing the same on an equal footing—has never been more painfully experienced than in an age where the least neglect in security arrangements and policies may spell doom.

The discrepancy between the possible and the actual is no less potent than paradoxical. It means such paradoxes as the instantaneousness of communication through the "hot line" between Washington and Moscow, on the one hand, and the absence of communication between members of one and the same family living in Berlin but separated by the wall (or of corresponding authorities); or, the discoverability of almost everything occurring on the surface of the planet through the supermodern means of intelligence, such as aerial photography and space reconnaissance. This implies that secret services and secret gathering of information are losing much of their legitimate function and, on the other hand, anxious insistence on national privacy, sovereignty of airspace, exclusion of foreigners from specified areas and installations, and so forth.

Let us return to processes, that is, to the question of how the technological process has affected them by way of acceleration. Processes—the more formal, procedural arrangements for transaction of business—may seem secondary to substantive policy and action but they clearly affect them materially. For instance, if nation-states had not developed the procedural system of constantly being in touch with each other—the system known as "permanent diplomacy"—the modern state system might have turned out differently; policies of balance of power, for instance, might well have proved impracticable. But the system based on permanent diplomacy still was restricted to a limited number of sovereign nations. And while it gradually spread from Europe to other continents, it remained a system of leisurely processes, for the most part with bilateral contacts, little overall planning and adjustment, and haphazard solution of problems. It was based on more or less intermittent, spotty, oftentimes vague information. One proceeded on the basis of what became known by and by.

Universality of information has led to great innovations. The transformation of dependent areas into independent states receiving and sending diplomatic agents meant *universalization of permanent diplomacy;* their increasing penetration by other agents (for instance, for economic, cultural, educational aid and development) has opened them in other respects to the new universe of global intercourse; the new techniques of communication and transportation have consummated the process of establishing a universe of discourse.

Ideally, at least, everybody can react to everything immediately. This has become the basis of a new type of diplomacy, which, to a large degree, proceeds through international organization and agencies, approaching what has been called "parliamentary" diplomacy. There has come into existence a kind of central market exchange of information, a universal clearing system, which, again ideally, should render action and reaction more calculable and better adjustable.

How immediacy of communication has affected the conduct of foreign affairs within each unit is well known: it means immediacy of contacting one's agents abroad, with lessened discretion for missions and more centralized decision making, even in detail, at home; in short, consolidation of foreign affairs controls at one central point.[3]

It means something more: when information and communication are instantaneous, this by itself tends to accelerate events and policies. In particular, it may accelerate crises—as well as, hopefully, their peaceful solution. Where formerly more leisurely but also cooler and more thoroughly thought-out action was possible, one now must act or react immediately; indeed, the almost instantaneous presence of the nuclear weapon may render decision making a process of hours—or minutes. There is a vicious circle in the necessity for fast decision in turn leading to the invention of ever faster-working technological devices to speed up decision making; more perfect computer systems, for example, to enable leaders to calculate and decide in almost no time. Exchanges of steps, decision, and, ultimately, weapons tend to escalate into instantaneousness. Actual nuclear war, of course, is likely to be compressed into days, if not hours.

A trend toward concentration of decision making in fewer units of power, and within them, in fewer agents (besides other, chiefly domestic factors), thus is related to the necessity of speed in decision making. Where there remains little or no time to contact, and confer with, numbers of other nations and leaders, and even less time to convene the councils of international organizations, the process must revert to the few. It is true that the lone actors may be tempted to exploit difficulties of consulting domestic leaders and organs or of contacting allies or international agencies in order to strengthen their positions, but the technical difficulties are no less real for that. Thus, in the Cuban missile crisis it was actually only two powers that were involved, and within each, presumably, a mere handful of top agents. In the case of the United States, one went through the formalities of informing allies but could not (or would not) consult with them; it amounted merely to getting additional policy backing. On the other side, Castro probably was no more delighted to have decisions vital for him made in Moscow.

3. This is the one, and almost only, area in which the impact of the technological process on foreign affairs has been noticed more generally.

Thus, acceleration of decision making cannot but affect strategy and security policies of alliances. Both the North Atlantic and the Warsaw Pact alliances are essentially systems of nuclear deterrence, and in neither case has the leading power been ready to share weapon or ultimate decision about its use with allies. Necessity to act swiftly and decisively can, indeed, be invoked in favor of such monopolization. It has been one reason why it has been so hard, if not impossible, to devise a practical system under NATO for jointly running a multilateral force; a dozen "fingers on the trigger" would either inhibit procedures and devaluate the entire setup, or else—in case each finger, without veto by the others, could launch the weapon—mar or destroy common policies, substituting individual adventurism for them. On the one hand, concentration of controls in the superpowers, by way of countereffect, has led to the attempts of some others to build up their own retaliatory forces. The result has been instability of alliances, if not, indeed, disintegration of the entire bipolar world structure.

Conduct of foreign affairs is rendered more difficult by another technology-produced problem, namely, how to deal with the explosively accelerating increase in the mere amount of inflowing information: of sifting and digesting it, of channeling it to the policy makers. The age-old problem of "access to the power holder" assumes vital importance under modern crisis conditions. Who is listened to by the top man, or top group, whose information and interpretation of facts are considered in preference to others? All of these, although largely *arcana imperii* even in democracies, are potentially more vital than formal rules and procedures relating to participation of parliaments in foreign policy and similar traditional factors. What communication experts call the problem of "noise": the problem of how to hear particular pieces of communication in the welter of incoming information, enters the picture and complicates matters. Some authors, referring to the increasing number of independent centers of policy and communication in the world, have argued that increase of number of units in a system increases stability by making their "noise" imperceptible.[4] I would argue to the

4. See Karl W. Deutsch and J. David Singer, "Multipolar Power Systems and International Stability," *World Politics* 17 (1964): 390 ff.

contrary that, if communication actually gets lost this way, ensuing lack of awareness of problems on the part of those for whom the information was meant may increase instability. However this may be, the problem of mere quantity of information, the paradox of availability of everything to a decreasing number of decision makers, persists.

Universality of information leads to universalization of concern. Where there exists universal awareness of situations and happenings, events anywhere become not only of interest but of political concern to everybody. A famine or similar catastrophe, a revolution, a persecution anywhere in the world becomes a matter of concern and responsibility in the sense of "something to be done about"; this is particularly true for those richer and more powerful countries whose action or inaction determines or influences what happens after the event in question. They no longer can withdraw into an attitude of indifference, declaring that the situation, event, or region in question were outside the sphere of their national interests or solely within the "domestic jurisdiction" of the respective country. The mere fact of being in a position to intervene renders the matter one of concern and responsibility, at least in the eyes of the world public or a large portion of it. "Foreign aid," for instance—the problem of the modernized North of the world assisting the underdeveloped South—is no longer a matter of mere charity or moral concern, but in view of the revolution of rising expectations, and of impending disillusionments, one of national and international *political* concern.[5]

Owing to the worldwide impact of nuclear weapons and the threat nuclear war poses to all, power-political issues turn into matters of global concern. People and nations at large no longer assess big-power policies merely under viewpoints of power and power shifts, of triumph and success of this power and defeat and humiliation of another, but also, and increasingly more so, under aspects of preserving the peace and living

5. This is not to deny that such situations cannot be exploited by the "aiding" nations for their own, individual advantage; what, indeed, is more exploitable than distress or starvation? Here we encounter again the conflict of power politics and "universalism" in a technologically more and more integrated world.

up to one's "universalist" responsibilities.[6] This, in turn, can influence attitudes and policies of the big themselves; enable a Khrushchev, for instance, to yield more gracefully on Cuba at the price of what, under the old standards, constituted humiliation but which now permitted him to claim before the world the role and merit of the peace maker. American policy makers might ponder this when weighing an alleged "loss of face" in withdrawal from Vietnam against a universal feeling of relief and appreciation of a big power's moderation.

Hegel once said, "Consciousness of the situation creates the situation." The fact that we know what is technically possible, what we can plan, and what are the consequences of our action or of failure to act, by itself makes mankind's condition today radically different from the traditional foreign-policy environment. Such things as overuse of resources in that common domain of mankind, the interconnected oceans of the world, had already given rise to concern and ensuing international cooperation in attempts to prevent it—international treaties, in particular, served as a chief instrument in solving the problems. This is no longer enough in view of more serious situations. The technological process itself, with its acceleration, is making an increasing number of problems truly global, especially the ones connected with the human environment. The threats to all inherent in such phenomena as exhaustion of vital resources, or pollution of air, atmosphere, and water are now second in importance only to the threat to survival itself, and to the population explosion. There is here the rational basis of demands for, and trends toward, global authority to set enforceable rules, or, at least, global planning. Modernization is as much required here as in the area of economic backwardness.

II

In turning now from processes to systems, I would like first to clarify certain terms. It may be advisable to discuss the

6. On the concept of "universalism" and the issue of "universalist" vs. "particularist" policy see my *International Politics in the Atomic Age* (New York: Columbia University Press, 1959), pp. 300 ff.

impact of the technological process on international systems and structures by using the terms "stability" and "instability." I would like to use these terms in their simplest connotations: internationally, a system is (relatively) stable where changes are relatively slow, gradual, and peaceful; unstable, where they tend to be sudden, far-reaching in impact, and frequently violent. The incidence of violence, in particular, is an important indicator of the relative degree of stability or instability. However, surface stability may actually conceal rigidity and petrification where there are underlying tensions, imbalances, and so on, which temporarily are prevented from surfacing by the overwhelming weight of controlling power factors. I shall, therefore, distinguish not only between stabilizing and destabilizing factors but also between genuinely stabilizing factors and others that make for rigidity and brittleness.

The overriding factor in emerging patterns is that of accelerating technology channeling diversity and multiformity into one and the same stream of uniform development. Hence the apparent paradox of rapid change and transformation coinciding with growing uniformity of patterns of life and institutions and, frequently, even with rigidity and petrification. A great current of developing new patterns, new ways of life, new institutions, based on the technological revolution, affects in its sweep a growing number of existing societies and their traditional ways of life. In that part of the world where modernization has already transformed most of the traditional patterns, we find, in the main, adaptation to the emerging machine-world of the future. There the technological process promises to be a factor of stability. In the as yet unmodernized portion of the world, on the other hand, change and transformation override trends toward stabilization. There, traditional states of mind and forms of society must first be destroyed, or radically changed and adapted to the new, before modernization can impart to them the stabilizing effects it now has on the other parts of the world.

Modernization may be considered *the* common most basic ideology of the present-day world, more basic than what, by way of attitudes and ideas, divides it—such as religious creeds or political belief systems. Indeed, it has become the universal creed, shared by such opponents as the capitalist West and the

Communist East, both believing in the liberating effect of technological progress. Modernity is, above all, the fervently held aim of the emerging, developing nations which now define themselves wholly in terms of the sweep toward high standards of technical proficiency and material results. A touching, almost religious faith in the desirability, inevitability, and superiority of modernity lies behind their efforts; the major ideal of the developing nations can be summed up as independence plus industrialization.

The universalization of this ideology would not have been possible without the creation of a world audience for ideas, which, in turn, has resulted from the accelerating advance in communication and means of spreading ideas—in other words, propaganda. While in former periods belief-systems such as a new religion or a new sociopolitical creed would originate in a particular area and usually reach other particular areas and people only, through mass media even the remotest countries, civilizations, or races are now reached. And it has been egalitarian nationalism that has been the most radically successful among them.

It is important for my argument to realize that egalitarianism, more than any other ideology, is in line with the very nature of the scientific-technological process. Indeed, the egalitarian sweep in the world reflects again the latter's acceleration curve. Since the age of rationalism and enlightenment, the assumption that inequality and differentiation are naturals has shifted to the assumption of the basic equality of humans. This resulted in accelerated emancipation of groups, castes, classes through the abolition of distinction and privileges; throughout most of history the chief grounds for inequality and domination were race, religion, sex, property ownership and wealth, culture and civilization, and citizenship.

It is easy to see why egalitarianism is so completely in line with that foundation of modernity, the spirit of science and technology. Cultural phenomena (such as styles of art), social and political processes, ideas and systems of government, used to be tied to man's differing civilizations; they were expressive of the differences rather than of the common features of man. But rational science and a technology based on scientific principles express his common approach and an experience that can be shared by all. It makes little difference whether a scientific problem is researched in America, India, or Japan, and the technical rules for establishing an up-to-date atomic pile or system of pest control or linear programming are the same, whether applied by experts of white, Negro, or oriental extraction, by people living under Communism, fascism, or liberal democracy. Indeed, the character-type of "technological man," the cool, detached, "no-nonsense" product of what in Communist areas is known as "polytechnical" education, in short, the expert in modernization, has become increasingly predominant not only in the conduct of international affairs—where the "generalist" diplomat of the traditional type yields to the aide with special know-how, the economic, labor, or area specialist—but also, and partly through foreign missions and international agencies, within the domestic realm of the developing countries. This way the spirit of science and technology, of experimentation and modernization, is being carried to the remotest parts of the world.

Egalitarianism, plus the spread of knowledge—of *this* knowledge—has led to universal demand for abolition of racial and similar discrimination, color-bars, and above all, the substitution of a world system of independent nationhood for the colonial system. The global sweep of nationalism can be traced back to the scientific-technological process as one of the latter's most prominent outgrowths; the demand for national self-determination is nothing else but the application of the egalitarian principle to the human units that define themselves as nations or nationalities. But with the accelerating spread of nationalism from Europe to the world, the intricate problems of defining nations (or "nationalities") and of their viability have likewise spread. By now the destabilizing effect of a growing multiplicity of new, often synthetic and nonviable units and of the inexperience of their agents, has come to beset present world relations and world politics.

This "population explosion of nations" creates instability of units as well as of relations among them and between them and the preexisting world. The paradox of legal and diplomatic equality of big and small coinciding with growing actual inequalities in power and responsibility has reached fantastic proportions. It tends to substitute mass meeting for deliberating assembly in international agencies where blocs of the emancipated new members outvote those on whose measures depends the effectiveness of policies voted upon. Balancing power against power, that former basis of diplomatic stabilization of international affairs, becomes ever more difficult in an age of hundreds of sovereignties whose internal and external stability itself is in doubt. Strategically and economically, the splintering of the world runs counter to interdependencies that are promoted by technological developments. In this respect, federation, integrated markets, etc., offer themselves as solutions, but recent experiments (with the exception of part of the developed world where the problems are less urgent) do not give reason for optimism.

Moreover, the weakness of the newly emancipated appears to be made to order for a new kind of interventionism on the part of the big. Whether intentional or not, assisting the underdeveloped financially and economically (not to mention military and strategic assistance) amounts to maintaining or reestablishing influence and thus brings up the problem of true independence or, as the Communists would put it, that of neocolonialism. Add to this the internal brittleness and instability of those units—in particular, those whose boundaries include different, oftentimes hostile tribes or else cut through one and the same ethnic group—and the constant danger of dissension or disintegration is created. Chaos lurks close to the surface and provides power-empty space for the intervention, competition, and possible clash of outside powers and ideologies.

The difficulty is compounded by the radically destabilizing effect of the real population explosion that has hit those areas hardest which can least afford it. The population explosion, of course, itself is in part a product of the accelerating technological process, especially where it is the result, chiefly, of steep and rapid decline in the mortality rate. It is the main cause of that extremely serious world problem, the widening gap between the world's developed and affluent North and its underdeveloped, impoverished South. In the latter, the desperate race between food and numbers not only turns rising expectations into growing disillusionment but brings about competition for land and territory, instability of regimes and radicalization of populations. Unchecked, it may eventually rally the South against the North on a more or less racialist basis of colored vs. white, or it may rally a South allied with part of the North against the remainder. It accentuates conflict even between such nations as China and the Soviet Union. Within the South itself, it lends territory and boundaries increased importance where populations press against the confines of the units they inhabit. Some of these nations have recently offered the pathetic spectacle of fighting over a piece of desert containing maybe one miserable oasis. What conflicts must we expect with a doubled or tripled world population? Hence, the urgency of radical change in demographic habits and policies, and the responsibility of the North to develop aid policies with the right priorities.

Since it has been so widely discussed, brief reference only need to be made to that other great destabilizer, weapons technology.[7] A contrasting element in the nuclear situation is stability, or rather petrification, resulting from the stalemate of the nuclear monopolists. But nuclear monopolies themselves cause attempts at establishing new centers of nuclear power, that is, proliferation, especially where, under conditions of second-strike capacity, the initial nuclear umbrella becomes doubtful—i.e., where the promise of nuclear defense of nonnuclear units against aggression becomes less credible. With proliferation, the chance of unpredictable use of such power increases. In addition, there is a good deal of instability already in the present nuclear situation. I refer not only to the well-known possibilities of nuclear war breaking out because of "accident," technical errors, misinterpretation of signals, or human failure, but rather to the less well-perceived chances of war through misinterpretation of political intentions, misunderstanding of the seemingly agreed upon *casus belli,* etc. What kind of attack, threat, policy is to meet with retaliation? As long as there does not exist a "no first use of nuclear arms" kind of agreement, the situation remains inherently fuzzy.

7. For more detailed discussion, see my chapter "International Politics and the Nuclear Dilemma," in *Nuclear Weapons and the Conflict of Conscience,* ed. John C. Bennett (New York: Charles Scribner's Sons, 1961), reprinted as chapter 4 of this volume.

What is meant, for instance, where one side threatens massive retaliation in case of a "major attack" by the opponent on not clearly defined allies or others?

Add to this the confusion of strategic doctrine, underlying strategic planning and policies. Where major technological breakthroughs may occur any time, where even lesser developments follow upon each other so rapidly that weapons and delivery systems tend to be outmoded before they move from design to the production stage, thought also tends to become unstable. The incredible complexity of problems leads to a confusing and dismaying welter of views not only among opponents or allies but within one and the same national setup. The esoteric nature of strategic doctrine itself creates incertitude, and deterrence this way threatens to become dependent on mutual mindreading. Policy becomes the result of assessment and counter-assessment of more or less vague attitudes and intentions. At the hour of crisis and decision, therefore, simpler if not simplistic considerations may prevail. All this undermines stability of deterrence.

III

In the face of factors that make for instability, we shall now search for countertrends in the direction of greater stability. Here, a trend of very general nature may first be singled out which, although it is most noticeable in the internal affairs of nations, also has its effect on international relations as well. I refer to the phenomenon of increasing similarity of civilizations and regimes in modernized societies, even where they reflect different ideologies and present correspondingly differing formal structures, for example, Western liberal democracies and the communism of the Soviet Union. The common rush into technological uniformity tends to diminish the differences in traditions and attitudes, ways of life and institutions. In the place of great conflicts and great transformations, we have gradual change or even stability, the opposite of the diversity and turmoil that characterized European and related societies until recently. What strikes the observer of the social and political scene is the absence of those revolutionary or reform movements that characterized their previous history; the disappearance in the main, of the radical movements for change that punctuated the eighteenth and nineteenth centuries.

The great revolutionary pathos is absent, and in the place of utopia one accepts the relative affluence and comfort of the machine age. With modernization victorious, no basic reforms of economic, social, or political structure are needed to achieve plenty. There is a general consensus that modernization *has* achieved plenty for all. This leads to deemphasis of doctrines and ideologies and greater stability of political structures, with political parties less doctrinaire and more pragmatic and with parliamentary oppositions less radically opposed to governments; the function of government then becomes the management of a broad consensus rather than the proving of the superiority of one policy over alternatives. More and more technical planning in more and more areas of public affairs tends to substitute common standards of scientific truth for oftentimes irrational wrangling over how best to manage public affairs.

These developments have, perhaps, progressed fastest in the two leading societies of "East" and "West." Although each had its origin in revolution, their ideals have now become the basis of conservative rigidity; celebrations of the October Revolution as well as the Fourth of July partake of the nature of ritual. In their international relations, this means the possibility of rapprochement or, at least, détente. As a regulated welfare capitalism tends to meet a "libermanized" socialism somewhere in the middle, the revisionist version of communism makes for more peaceful coexistence with a West whose anti-Communist, or at least, anti-Soviet fervor abates. Intransigent doctrinairism of the "communism remains communism" variety, with its conspiracy doctrine, the mirror image of communism's fear of capitalist-imperialist plotting, yields to more sophisticated distinctions of variations and conflicts in the opponents' world or worlds; only in the United States, with its monomaniac fixation on one area and one war, has there been a revival of the more extreme anti-Communist ideology of late. It endangers the overall trend toward détente.

A more long-range threat to stability in the advanced world

lies in an inclination to be satisfied too soon. Progress can be characterized by lopsided developments. There may emerge minorities not participating in modernization and in the affluence it means for the majority of the population. The majority, satisfied with the technological process and what it has wrought for them, may then neglect the interests of still dissatisfied minorities, this way freezing the political, social, and economic status quo. As long as the masses are still underprivileged, democracy has a revolutionary or, at least, change-provoking impact; it tends to become the political instrumentality for the maintenance of the economic and social status quo where these masses, now enjoying a comfortable living standard, are ready to defeat the demands of neglected minority groups with the weapon of the majority vote.

Certain technological factors contribute to the plight of the latter. They form Gunnar Myrdal's new "under-class," characterized by Michael Harrington by their fragmentation and invisibility.[8] Who, living in the sealed-off suburb, meets a beggar? The affluent may pass the dwelling places of the poor but hardly notice the slums from the superhighways. To the nonpoor, the world appears clean of the poor. And even where a more compact and better organized minority stages what is referred to as a revolution, it lacks the chances of revolutionary masses of yore that represented suppressed majorities; now the majority in control reacts through the backlash. There emerges the picture of modernized society rigidly divided into two portions: the ones, participants in the technological-economic process of modernity and, whether workers, employees, or employers, approaching each other more and more closely as members of one huge new middle class; the others are the fragmented out-groups of the poor, out-of-luck, out-of-status, frequently inheriting their poverty and lack of opportunity. The egalitarian progress tends to stop short of them, due, paradoxically, to the workings of the institutions and processes of democracy. Such stalling of social and economic progress within nations finds its international parallel in the

8. See Gunnar Myrdal, *Challenge to Affluence* (New York: Pantheon, 1962); and Michael Harrington, *The Other America* (New York: Macmillan, 1962).

relations between the affluent nations on the one hand, and the underdeveloped that are being omitted from economic growth partly through the refusal of the wealthy to grant favorable terms of trade. Clearly, this latter development, the emergence of Toynbee's "external proletariat," entails vastly greater international dangers, since it comprises the vast majority of mankind.

However, the most conspicuous example of stability, or rather, rigidity, is found where we would expect, and actually have, utmost instability, namely the nuclear race. If we remember the dizzying speed with which weapons and weapons systems have been developed by two powers to such perfection that their all-out use threatens the entire world with extinction, it is no wonder that many at the beginning of the nuclear age thought the holocaust inevitable unless the powers agreed to radical measures of disarmament or arms control. They did not, and yet, in over twenty years of nuclear age the world has escaped not only nuclear destruction but even general war. Obviously, this surprising stability has been due in large measure to the nuclear stalemate, or nuclear balance, among the powers, again revealing the paradox of utmost dynamics and change coexisting with rigidity and petrification. The world is curiously suspended between two extremes: danger of extreme change through actual nuclear war, and petrification of status quo inhibiting even moderate change as long as deterrence works.

The stabilizing effect of nuclear deterrence derives from the annihilative nature of the weapon. Technological progress here has rendered nugatory exactly that which throughout history had been the *ultima ratio* of international politics; the means of force and violence in their actual use for the defense of national interests. Nuclear weapons retain meaning only inasmuch as they are *not* being used, that is, in their capacity as deterrents.

Realizing this, the two major nuclear powers have so far refrained from their use. Under bipolarity, this has meant that they have established the boundaries of their respective blocs, or zones of influence, as spheres of tacitly agreed-upon nonintervention. Nuclear war—or any war which might escalate into one—is not to be risked over issues located in the sphere of the other side. Thus the United States and the Soviet Union have emerged as the two great "conservatives" also on the international plane, both intent on stabilizing the status quo of the post-World War II period in regard to units, boundaries, and actors. This way, Hungary was kept within the Soviet orbit and West Berlin within the West, notwithstanding the sometimes abstruse and seemingly unmanageable arrangements on boundaries and access this implied. But, although caution in the use of these arrangements has characterized the policy of the superpowers, the underlying situation is brittle rather than genuinely stable, as recurring crises, such as those over Berlin, have shown. Instability threatens not only because bipolarity is giving way to multipolarity with its ensuing uncertainty about the policies and actions of rising additional powers, but also because even bipolar deterrence depends on credibility of the mutual threats and definition of *casus belli*. Whenever one side, through the bluffing inevitable in this game, gets itself into a situation from which it cannot extricate itself without surrender or serious loss of face, the actual use of the weapon does threaten. One has only to recall how near catastrophe was at the height of the Cuban missile crisis.

Stability, or rather petrification, of boundaries, territorial arrangements, and of respective governmental setups and regimes can even be observed in regions remote from the two major blocs and their boundaries as, for instance, in regard to the new countries in Africa and Asia. The very fact that many of these are founded on coincidental arrangements dating from the colonial age, and thus are of doubtful ethnical and political coherence, makes for a feeling that it would be hopeless to look for better criteria of statehood in these instances; tribal lines would mean complete chaos in most cases. Thus, what one has appears as a minor evil. Also, vested interests are never long in growing from questionable foundations, tending to consolidate what initially is centrifugal and incongruous. Added stabilizing influence may be exercised through the medium of the United Nations, as in the case of the Congo, reflecting a minimum interest of the leading powers in avoiding conflict over power-empty areas. On the other hand, a power not so interested, such as China, may well be tempted to fish in troubled waters.

In a more general way, we may speak of the stabilizing impact of what can be called the "unavailability of force" in the nuclear age. As we have already seen, nuclear force is considered unavailable in the sense that the effects of nuclear action appear unacceptable to either side. Although this implies that one has to bank on conventional armaments instead, realization that any kind of hostilities directly involving the major powers or their bloc partners may escalate into nuclear war has tended to make them discount even the use of conventional force, for instance, along the Iron Curtain in Europe. It is kept up for balance and held in readiness for defense. But its actual use has become unlikely.

We can go a step further and ask whether the use of force in the traditional military sense has not declined even when not directly involving antagonistic blocs or powers—for instance, in relations of leading powers to smaller countries. Although force has not disappeared from such relationships, one notices hesitation to resort to it, and this, ironically, above all on the part of the big ones toward those who would appear to be at their mercy. Compared with previous practices, American forbearance toward, let us say, Panama, or that of the Soviets toward Albania, has been quite astonishing.

Some of the reasons are nuclear. Less U.S. tolerance toward Cuba might have led not only to the actual "confrontation" but to worse things. The nuclear balance does protect the small, but there are additional reasons. One is the "overcapacity" or unwieldiness of the arms of the big, which renders it so difficult to bring them to bear in situations where the opponent applies the "fish-in-water" theory in guerrilla "wars of liberation." [9] Hence the American frustration in Vietnam. Further-

9. See Stanley Hoffmann's remarks on the "impertinence" of the small: "The very change in the nature of the mobilizable potential has made its actual use . . . self-defeating. As a result, nations endowed with infinitely less can behave as if the difference in power did not matter. The very lightness of their rucksack facilitates their roaming on the world scene, whereas the superpowers are often immobilized by their unwieldy baggage." *Daedalus* 93 (1964): 1279.

more, hostile reaction on the part of what is loosely called "world opinion" was easily disregarded by the powerful in former times, but it cannot be so easily discounted today; the big powers, with force less available, must look for substitute means of conducting foreign policy and safeguarding their interests. They find them in areas of diplomacy, economic relations, etc., where the good will of the smaller ones may become essential; they may want their backing and their votes—for instance, in the United Nations—and this way a hostile reaction to warlike policies of the mighty can be brought to bear on the international plane. A growing conviction that force used for national purposes is "outlawed," whatever the legal nature of this principle, reinforces this impact of opinion, as does, in a particular region, the belief that old-style interventionism is outlawed in inter-American relations. Exceptions, such as American intervention in the Dominican Republic, and, above all, the Vietnamese case, which has led to tragic isolation of the United States in opinion all over the world, merely prove the rule. . . .

It results from the above that unavailability of force to the big in bipolar relationships and relations to the small has stabilized bipolar boundaries and arrangements, intrabloc relationships and regimes, and the units and boundaries of the new states. However, availability of force to an increasing number of small nations carries an element of instability into a system that suffers from brittleness anyway because of unsettled internal conditions and nonviability, economic and otherwise, of many of these units.

In conclusion: The onrush of technology creates, nationally and internationally, instabilities and/or rigidities, with underlying instability that spell possible doom for mankind. Avoidance of catastrophe presupposes a variety of major controls. Control of weapons (in turn involving a measure of control by world authority over national sovereignty in this area); control of population trends as basis for everything else in the modernization and development of nations and their internal stability and external viability; and above all, control of the technological process itself. I am far from implying that one can, or should, redress a process that has brought doubtless

blessings of decent living conditions and higher living standards to masses of human beings for the first time in history.
The danger rather lies in an unthinking technological conformism that is inclined to follow technological progress wherever it may lead regardless of social and general consequences.
There is a further danger that the unparalleled power which
technology conveys on human beings—a select and limited
number of humans, that is—may render them power mad and
imbue them with the simplistic belief that everything can be
achieved, any problem solved, through sheer application of
technological means.

In the fact of such technological barbarism, there is urgent
need of resistance. As one needs, from time to time, civil
disobedience against political and social tyrannies, I would call
for a campaign of "technological disobedience." It is still man
who guides the machine. Nothing commands that, because
supersonic speeds are possible, one must have supersonic
airliners, shattering and destroying what underlies below, and
possibly not even economical; nobody forces us to reach the
moon and the planets before we cope with the slums of Harlem
and the shantytowns. It is a matter of priorities, of planning
according to basic human needs and values. Someone has said
recently, "Man rushes first to be saved *by* technology, and then
to be saved *from* it." [10] But in a deeper sense, man *can* as little
be saved by mere technology as he *should* be saved from it. If
he is worthy to survive, he must learn how to master a process
that threatens to overwhelm him. Mastery of things has
distinguished man from other living species throughout his
history; but so far it was always in the interest of smaller
groups and of separate international units. From now on it has
to be in the interest of *one* world and to the benefit of all.

10. See Gerald Sykes, in *Technology and Human Values* (Santa Barbara,
Calif.: Center for the Study of Democratic Institutions, 1966), p. 6. The head of
the largest advertising agency in the world has said: "In the next decade
Americans must escalate their standard of living on top of the present high
level of consumption by the equivalent of more than the entire growth in
consumption in the 320 years from the landing of the Mayflower to the best
prewar year of 1940." Quoted in James C. Charlesworth, ed., *Leisure in
America* (Philadelphia: American Academy of Political and Social Science,
1964), pp. 61f. Note the word "must"; who commands?

7

THE CIVILIZATIONAL PROCESS AND ITS REVERSAL

This essay forms the concluding chapter of an unpublished manuscript written in the early 1960s. The title of the manuscript, "International Politics in the Technological Age, An Analysis of the Role of Acceleration and Petrification in World Affairs," indicates its broad range. On the basis of a kind of philosophy of history and a general cultural criticism, the manuscript (as well as its conclusion here printed) marks my turn of interest and concern from the area of the strictly political (strategy, etc.) to economic, demographic, and ecological problems and developments. For further observations, see pages 22–24 of the *Introduction* and chapter 6 in this volume.

1. THE UNIFORMITY OF
THE CIVILIZATIONAL WORLD

The civilizational world is a world in which the "process of civilization," with its primacy of scientific approach and technical control of nature, tends to overwhelm the traditional sociopolitical and cultural processes, directing them into the one accelerating, upward-sweeping uniformity of a man-made, machine-controlled universe. In this world a new type of man and of man's life in society is bound to emerge, according to that "law of civilizational conformity," which compels "technological man," or *homo faber*, to follow the technological process, or "progress," to whatever results it will bring about, and regardless of its impact upon the traditions handed down from human history.

The tremendous technological achievements of the age,

following ever more closely and more rapidly upon one another, could hardly fail to create a feeling of euphoria, if not triumph, among most. Man in control of the world—of its secrets in every realm, of space and distance, of production for ever more comfort and for every need imaginable, soon perhaps of the human lifespan itself, of death! How can all this fail to create the impression that the past has indeed been mere prologue to a new, *the* new, perfect life of man, who only now is coming into his own? In the past he was beset with the inflictions of an uncontrolled nature, with misery and want, with the terror and the anxieties caused by unending competition for scarce goods, with group conflicts and wars. In contrast, the blessings of more and more affluence, of longer life lived in easier comfort, of control of environment and, possibly and hopefully, of freedom from the scourge of war, are so obvious that qualifications seem almost ludicrous. Yet the trend is accompanied by an obverse process. It is a process which leads from quality to quantity (e.g., in the field of man-made things, from hand-produced, original, and beautiful pieces for use to mass-produced, nonindividualized, and un-original ones); from "aristocracy" to "democracy" (in the sense of equal distribution of everything, including cultural goods, among people often not qualified to appreciate their values); from individuality to sameness; from producing novel things to merely consuming that which is handed down from ages of creativity (e.g., earlier creations of music and arts); from living in small, "organic" groups to functioning in vast organization; from living for something or somebody to living longer; in short, from diversity to uniformity.

The origins of the development toward the new man, his attitudes and values, his life and society, lie deep in the recesses of ages in which the process of civilization with its discovery of rational laws and rational-scientific approach to life began to accompany, and eventually displace, prerational attitudes and approaches. This emergence of a new spirit, this displacement, can be observed in every area of human life and thought. For example, throughout history, languages show a trend from complexity to simplicity, or paucity, in regard to cases, tenses, etc. Words and concepts exhibit a development from concreteness to generality and rationalization (compare, e.g., the many quality-laden terms for geographical directions in animistic periods and their replacement by four, and only four, mathematically defined terms, usually applied without nondirectional meaning). Or take numbers and number systems. Here, too, the development goes from "meaningful" numbers (i.e., numbers connected with some nonmathematical area—"lucky" and "unlucky" numbers, the role of numbers three and seven, etc.) to pure quantitative rationality, and even there from more complex to more simple systems in practical use and application. Language, script, words, concepts, ideas are characteristic of and in turn shape people. There, too, the trend inexorably goes from individuality and distinctive, unique character to the stressing (and in the future, quite conceivably, the breeding) of common, interchangable, usable, and useful traits and characteristics. This is what the machine, automation, the big organizations need. Numbers are increasingly attached to any conceivable kind of human activity and interest. Educational and job selections, formerly made through person-to-person contact and assessment, proceed according to "testing" that, since it is done by computer, can measure only simple contrasts ("true and false" questions, for instance). It cannot measure, or evaluate, the nonrational "inside," that is, feelings, sentiment, "character." But since those measured, tested, and selected are the ones who, in turn, test and select the next generations, it is a self-perpetuating process: survival of the fittest through "unnatural" selection.

Let us briefly trace the trend in three areas of civilizational development: man's alienation from his natural, traditional environment; his integration into the gigantism of the machine world; and the emergence of a new, "futuristic" mentality.

Control of nature tends to replace the natural habitat of man and other living beings by a new, man-made environment. The original, given habitat yields to an artificial environment in which the entire globe is transformed into one vast utilitarian enterprise. This implies loss of touch with, or destruction of, that which originally existed, including remnants of previous human activity and creativity; the wasteland of the industrial landscape moves across the continents. There is some yearning for the lost world,[1] but it is satisfied with increasing

1. In general, however, resistance is considered "unnatural." To quote a letter received by Brooks Atkinson from an oil corporation executive: "You

difficulty. Vacationing or weekend crowds drive on superhighways through a nature they never touch, in a vain search of a goal, finding (at best) parking space in sanitized "picnic areas" populated by like crowds. Tourism—in part touching testimony to the continual yearning for legacies of the past and meaningful values of the present, in part a commercially or politically exploited attempt to fill a cultural and spiritual void—contributes to destroying what it embraces. There is growing danger anyway that the relics of the past, the cities, the monuments, the landscapes, are being destroyed by the flood-tide of the onrushing future (Strasbourg Cathedral is disintegrating under the impact of poisonous fumes emitted by factories and automobiles; medieval Oxford crumbles under the shattering of motor traffic; Venice is sinking under the lashes of waves stirred up by motorboats). To this, tourism adds the traffic systems, parking spaces, hotel or motel facilities needed for its hordes, which cannot help chewing up the organic configuration of city or landscape. Technology has seen to it that mountains no longer must be "conquered"; they turn into mere tracts or sites for sight-seeing, exercise, or sport. Even the resistance of man to loss of contact with nature and culture contributes to their deterioration.[2]

Alienation from natural and cultural environment is advanced by man's integration into ever bigger and more complex organizations, from state and government to business corporations, educational institutions, professional organizations, and so forth. Population explosion and crowding in urban centers compel even the youngest to be integrated at an early age into the large setup. We are not concerned here with the economic, political, and similar effects of bigness, but rather with its impact on human life and attitudes.

In the preindustrial age man was tied to an environment of

have a lot of undeveloped land up there that's just sitting around being scenery. What are you going to do—sit around supporting a bunch of bluebirds for the rest of your life?" See Atkinson's column "Critic at Large" in *New York Times*, 16 June 1964.

2. It might be rewarding to study tourism as a sociological phenomenon, arising, as it did, with industrialization in the "drab" countries, England at first, subsequently the United States, now *all* modernized countries. Before that, landscape was enjoyed as natural, everyday environment and part of life "at home."

relatively small compass. There was human closeness in the village, town, city, and even city-state. Organization of units was small-scale; there were generally personal relations, although usually authoritarian ones, among its members. Everything was colored by the spirit, the character of the unit or area, but knowledge of and interest in outlying areas and foreign units were limited, if not nonexistent. Few would travel widely or migrate, and fewer still would be influenced by the less parochial, more "enlightened" approach of the "cosmopolitan." In contrast, the "ideal type" of the future, now emerging, is that of man not tied to particular area or unit; fast moving and easibly movable from place to place; exchangeable for like persons in large-scale agencies such as far-flung corporations, whose officers and employees are shifted from branch to branch, with not only the person employed but also the members of his family ("corporation wives") adaptable and adapting to the new environment.

Little intimate relationship and personal contact with others can be and is expected in this shifting environment, but whatever utilitarian contact there is can easily be established in surroundings of increasingly alike character: the vast, colorless suburbia which eats up the "organic" town or city, on the one hand, and on the other hand the village and the rural life-form of the past; no close, lasting friendships, but, in principle, contact with everybody regardless of distance and location. Sense of intimacy, of touch, is lost in and through the organizational machine—but at least those in leading positions must gain a feeling of overwhelming power and control, not merely in respect of persons but of things as well. On the other hand, everything is enmeshed with everything else; there is an ever-growing interdependence of persons, processes, and events; and the effects of error or malfunction extend to everything and all. Increasing complexity of the administrative and technological functioning of the machine renders it more and more unsurveyable even to the ones on top; and a feeling is shaping up that, one day, nobody will be in control anymore. This will then open up the possibility of a breakdown more encompassing and more catastrophic than anything in the past.[3]

3. Forebodings of what the growing dependency of all of us on factors outside our control implies most frequently have been voiced in regard to

The emergence of a new mentality derives logically from man's alienation from his previous environment and his integration into the man-made machine. It is a mentality interested almost exclusively in the technological, utilitarian future, in how mankind can advance farther and farther along the upward path of an unending technical-scientific progress. This progress being based on rationality, that is, on principles and techniques understandable to and shared by all humans qua rational beings, it moves necessarily toward uniformity; diversity and uniqueness, that is, all that has so far distinguished humans and human groups from each other, must appear as outmoded remnants of the past, obstacles in the way of progress. This mentality often involves a strange inability to preserve even that which, in a utilitarian or aesthetic sense, has proved perfectly appropriate to the occasion (e.g., in the utilitarian realm, a perfectly comfortable car or chair). There seems to be an almost metaphysical unrest demanding change for change's sake, feeling uneasy or unhappy whenever something—an object, a situation—remains the same for any length of time. The feeling, to be sure, is aided and abetted by the hordes of people in sales promotion and advertisement who must prove their right of existence by constantly inventing new things, patterns, processes that are frequently less practical and less aesthetically satisfying than what came before (also, because of "built-in obsolescence," more shoddy and less durable). It will be interesting to watch whether the impact of the adman is something restricted to a competitive

"civil defense" against nuclear attack. But even in more peaceful conditions one merely needs to figure out what one element, the failure of electric power, means to the life of people living in the conditions of the average middle class in the developed countries—to lighting, heating, preparation or preservation of food, etc. Nowhere, perhaps, has this dependency been anticipated more harrowingly than in an "anti-utopia" far antedating the famous "negative utopias" of Aldous Huxley and George Orwell—E. M. Forster's little story "The Machine Stops" (in The Eternal Moment and Other Stories [New York, 1928]); written before World War I, it forecast in astonishing detail the alienation of man through entanglement in the machine, and the final breakdown. "Year by year (the Machine) was served with increased efficiency and decreased intelligence. The better a man knew his own duties upon it, the less he understood the duties of his neighbor, and in all the world there was not one who understood the monster as a whole. . . . The Machine develops—but not on our lines. The Machine proceeds—but not to our goal."

system of economy or whether, in one form or another, it will also invade systems such as the Communist ones.

The loss of a sense of the unique is intimately connected with a loss of the historical sense, which, in turn, is caused by much in modern education. There used to exist a branch of psychology called characterology, which dealt with the unique traits of human personality, the sum-total of traits distinguishing one individual from all others. This seems now to be lost,[4] or neglected in favor of experimental psychology. History is the characterology of mankind. It traces the distinguishing characteristics of human groups like tribes or nations, of civilizations, of periods, of styles. There seems to be something like a phobia against tracing things historically in respect to their uniqueness. There is an almost instinctive resistance against placing anything, even historical phenomena, into their historical context. "New Criticism" analyzes literary works "immanently"; works of art, music, etc., are contemplated outside their social, spiritual, cultural connectedness with their times. "History is bunk" was an appropriate statement by the begetter of the machine that now, literally, "overruns" and crushes the products of the past; it is a strangely paradoxical fact that, exactly at a time when archaeology and related sciences uncover the last hidden remnants of man's past, progress threatens to destroy them under the bulldozer that paves the way for the ephemeral new that replaces the most durable old.

Loss of sense for differentiation and the unique, coupled with the acceleration of new scientific findings and technological data, accounts for the fact that education tends more and more to become mere storing of factual information. The increasing importance of testing, which measures factual knowledge and, at best, simple logical performance, adds to this tendency. The "polytechnical" schools of the "East," with their emphasis on building the "new" technical and practical man, point in the same direction. In this process distinction between the significant and the irrelevant in the vast ocean of utilitarian knowledge is lost. There no longer is an effort to provide a coordinated view of things and problems. In the face

4. With graphology—as applied characterology—a lost art.

of accelerating growth of knowledge, all that real education can provide is teaching the way to cope with that accumulation by teaching *how* to know—in old-fashioned parlance, by teaching how to think—and this way to learn how to penetrate and understand the jungle of facts. To learn how to think, however, is possible only through individualized instruction, not through mass instruction which inhibits direct contact between teacher and student and even tends to replace it altogether by television, radio, correspondence course, and the teaching machine. But this tendency too, of course, is the outgrowth of man's increase in numbers and his ensuing atomization in the big organizational machine.

Something else also causes education to become mere part and parcel of the process of civilization: the growing awareness, among the competing modernized countries, that trained manpower is an even more essential "production factor" than material resources. As science and technology permit "planning" future inventions, discoveries, and, consequently, technical-industrial advance, and with automation throwing unskilled and semiskilled labor upon the ash heap of industrial history, "know-how" turns into a genuine power factor of societies and nations, and the value of education becomes measured almost entirely by its utility for the GNP of an economic system.

This trend is reflected in rising international competition for trained people, particularly scientists and engineers. Formerly, the importance of migration was more a quantitative one: the shift of "surplus populations"—usually untrained and unskilled—to underpopulated areas and countries. Now, under the impact of the population explosion, we find restrictions against this kind of migration almost everywhere, but at the same time intense competition for highly trained talent (the "brain drain"), with underdeveloped countries facing refusal by their young elite, sent at great expense to be trained abroad, to return home after completion of their studies.

The formation of the utilitarian, future-oriented mass mind also involves a growing "consumer" mentally. We find it in the emphasis, in economic production, on serving the consumer, the great dictator of fashion and change, in turn fawned upon and dictated to by the giant machine of advertising and distribution. There is what one may call output-worship, amounting to a veritable fetishism of "economic growth" for its own sake, regardless of quality, type of commodity, or need. But in the apparent comfort thus created we find a paradox or two. Thus, while there seems to be more and more to consume and more and more time (leisure) to do so, the young—with the exception of those dropping out of education altogether and, in an age of automation, becoming unemployable—become increasingly enslaved by overwork, the new "exploited class," as it were, taking the place of the proletariat of yore. Our young are forever driven, test- and exam-ridden, burdened with an overwhelming load of facts and figures to be remembered, competing desperately for places in the institutions of higher learning, the only access road to a degree and a more desirable occupation. This contrasts strangely with the tendency to reduced hours of work once one has "arrived," and with the "leisure" one has to cope with once one is retired from work (which tends to happen at an ever earlier age).

The second paradox lies in a doubt whether technology actually has meant as much progress in terms of living standards as is commonly assumed. Does the consumer get his "money's worth" when buying his car or home? Measure the seemingly so-impressive gains made in means and speed of transportation—to and from work, for instance—against the lesser time (because of lesser distance) needed previously for getting to one's place of work.[5] Time spent on what surrounds work (getting there, standing in line for meals, etc.) tends to cancel out gains in reduction of hours. Compare housing conditions for the modern masses, even with the tenements or hovels of yore. Are the chicken-coops offered as "homes" or the paper-thin-walled, low-ceilinged, "modern" apartments with their tiny rooms superior in comfort to higher-ceilinged,

5. See, in this connection, the deliciously ironical treatment of the problem in Louis J. Halle's little utopia, *Sedge* (New York, 1963): "An American philosopher had explained this sort of thing to Pluvis in terms of 'progress.' He explained that the growth of cities stimulated the invention of means of rapid transportation. 'The distance I cover in only two hours on my way to work,' the philosopher had said, 'could not have been covered in less than two days by my grandfather. This shows how the growth of cities has reduced the hardship of getting to work since my grandfather's day.' Pluvis asked whether it had taken his grandfather two days to get to work" (p. 16).

thick-walled older lodgings? Is education superior, with little learned in overcrowded lower-grade schools and with its burden of unnecessary material—no leisure left to chew and digest—in high school and college?

As a matter of fact, there is so large a number of areas where efficiency becomes questionable or tends to stop or even decline at a certain point of development that one is tempted to draw a kind of efficiency (or inefficiency) curve on this basis, looking somewhat like this:

One might apply this to the average time needed to drive from one place to another on an average crowded highway; to the delivery time of mail; to the actual time of flight transportation, including the time spent on getting to and returning from the airport; to goods with "built-in obsolescence"; and to many similar instances. The decline of the above curve, of course, has some connection with the phenomenon of irrationally continuing a technological process wherever it technically leads, regardless of its economic and utilitarian consequences and uses. It likewise is a consequence of population increase and, even more, of population concentration. If these instances should be allowed to multiply and extend to other vital areas, this would eventually lead ad absurdum the technological-civilizational process as such. We might then find that, despite the tremendous acceleration of production, "economic growth" (not, of course, in the backward but in the advanced countries) has been a fetish; that the civilizational process ultimately impoverishes instead of enriching; that, with its shoddy, nondurable, exchangeable products man will eventually call nothing his own (regardless of property system): no home, no solid piece of furniture, no books which would not be eliminated right after use. Thus he no longer would inherit, nor would he care to. He might then lose all sense of tradition, and with it a sense of his own lived-through life as a unique experience.

With this, spiritual and attitudinal collectivization does advance by giant steps. It is nourished by what the average person is fed day and night by the communications media which the civilizational process has developed, and from which there is little escape. We have pointed out how the universalization of information affects political systems and processes; it must affect equally strongly the lives, emotions, and attitudes of people in a general way. By and large, we hear and see the same things and are exposed to the same version of things and events. Thus we find ourselves in a prefabricated world—and it is a world which reflects the uniformities of the age of modernity more than anything else. American youngsters abroad, asked for some American folksongs (on the pattern of the French "Allouette" or "Frère Jacques") have been known to respond with tunes from television commercials; this was all there was in their collective minds.

We observe the same phenomena in other fields. In regard to language we have the spread of pidgin-English all over the world. And the growth of "organizational language," not only by bureaucrats but in everyday usage (everything and everybody being "effectuated," "processed," etc.) points in the same direction. It is, as one German observer has called it, the uniform, drab, colorless, mechanized "language of an administered world." [6] In it, man as an individual person vanishes.[7]

It is perhaps the most significant and, from one point of

6. "Sprache der verwalteten Welt."
7. Yet pseudo romanticism often still transports him into an environment largely lost. One is reminded of the similar fate of chickens, once a few in a yard, now thousands enjoying "togetherness" in the modern "chicken factories." To this the following item (from Noel Perrin, "Department of Amplification," *New Yorker*, 6 July 1963) refers: "I also find the Wooden Bucket Principle operating in the books we have begun to buy for my daughter, who is now two. Some of these are books written and published in the United States in the last four or five years—animal ABC's, I-Can-Do-This-Or-That books, and so forth. Supposedly they are both about and for contemporary American children. Yet I was reading from one just tonight that shows a little girl saying, 'Pick. Pick. Pick. I'm a little chick.' Behind her are five chicks, about a dozen hens, and two roosters, all wandering freely about in front of a quite charming henhouse, picking for corn. Real American chickens, of course, do no such thing. They neither wander nor pick. Instead, they spend their time, in lots of ten thousand or a hundred thousand, locked in battery houses, never walking an inch. The cages are too small. I think their feed has aureomycin in it."

view, the most frightening element in this situation that, among the different groups in the modernized countries, it seems to affect youth above all; theirs is the most "rationalized," utilitarian, unideological, practical "get on" and "no nonsense" behavior pattern of all. But there are also signs of revolt.

Man should be the measure. He should live neither in isolation nor in an organized fake "togetherness," but in touch with nature, culture, people. To enable him so to live, he must experience the "great reversal."

2. THE GREAT REVERSAL

Its Meaning

To talk of "reversal" in the face of a process as powerful and relentless as the technological-civilizational process seems almost ludicrous, a futile bemoaning of something which cannot be helped or even should be welcomed. Is there any profit in asking whether there isn't a future different from what the sweep of the civilizational process foreshadows? Is not trying to stem this tide as illusory, indeed, as "reactionary" an enterprise as advocating the return to the Middle Ages, or to the "golden age"? Is not the author's attitude vis-à-vis the trend in any event nothing but a rehash of a by now a hundred years old "culture criticism" with which disgruntled intellectuals, thinkers out of tune with their time such as Tocqueville, Burckhardt, Nietzsche, and their lesser followers, saluted the rise of democracy and the concomitant "leveling," the advent of industrialism, the machine age, in short, "modernity"?

In the face of the civilizational process one can distinguish three major types of reaction. There is, first, the one already mentioned: the ultracritical, pessimistic, "reactionary," all-out rejection of the process in all its implications, social, political, cultural. The second type, its opposite, is a conformist "progressivism" which sees only desirable and beneficial results in modernization and expects even more of the same in the future. A third kind of attitude does not agree—or agrees only in part—with the first two. It does not reject, indeed welcomes, many of the economic, social, and political implications of the process, while opposing most of the cultural, spiritual, attitudinal ones. It does so out of a concern for the attainment and/or preservation of what is truly human in man, and may therefore be referred to as "humanistic."

To any student of the history of ideas the reactionary character of the ideology of "culture criticism" is clear. Tocqueville, great realistic observer of facts and trends, reluctantly admitted the irreversibility of the trend leading from aristocracy to egalitarian democracy; but it is obvious that he regretted its inevitability and preferred the values and institutions of a libertarian aristocracy. Jacob Burckhardt was an equally forceful and similarly resigned "liberal of the old school" (*Altliberaler*), as much opposed to political egalitarianism as he was to cultural leveling. Nietzsche's hostility toward the "nihilism" of the "last man" comprised, most radically, any and all egalitarianism and humanitarianism, which he condemned as the "herd morality" of the masses. His "tables of a new law" for the strong few with their "will to power" in practice, although much against the great individualist's anarchistic inclinations, caused many of those influenced by his culture critique to glorify ultranationalism, state-perpetrated violence, in short, twentieth-century fascism. The Adamses in America (both Henry and Brooks), equally powerful adversaries of democratic leveling, and Spengler in Germany, all regretted the decline of the "old" Western civilization and its values and foresaw, if ever so resignedly, the rise of the technological civilization and the "Caesars" of the dying age.

Inherent in all this is genuine reactionism, the yearning for going back to the "good old times" (which are seen, respectively, as the times prior to 1789, or 1848, or 1914, or now possibly 1939), with their "organic" forms of life, their preindividualistic societies, their human relationships built on status differentiation and "estate," their diversity not only of cultural patterns but also of economic, social, and political status, that is, inequality of rights and conditions. Sometimes this reactionism includes an advocacy of actually going back behind the developments of technology and industry, of driving out the competition of the factory-made cotton by continuing to hand-weave the cloth.

But we are not, and cannot be, *Maschinenstürmer*. We cannot—even if we want to—go back behind what technology has wrought in the fields of social and political relations. Are we, then, compelled to line up with the civilizational conformists? Progressives, indeed, sometimes share with the reactionaries a belief in the "fatalistic inevitability" of developments. Although evaluating them differently, they consider it useless to oppose any part of them. To them it is as if powers of a "demonic" character stand behind such tremendous trends and determine future developments.[8] Here, exactly, lies the fallacy of either attitude. As long as we consider "trends," "developments," "processes" as superhuman forces or powers, we shall be their slaves. But after all, unless one engages in mysticism or some kind of irrationalistic metaphysics, one must recognize that they are products of man, and dependent on man's attitudes, valuations, will, and action. And so we do find some who, in the face of an apparently overwhelming trend, have had the courage to call it mortal and to direct our attention to its man-made nature. We find them among culture critics and even among scientists and technologists.[9] Thus, one prominent scientist has called it "childish" to believe that "that which is feasible technically must therefore be done." A mature attitude "considers technical tools means to an end," so that man remains "master of technique." [10]

8. Georges Bernanos, in *La Liberté pour quoi faire?* (Paris, 1953), has ridiculed this fatalism: "Supposez que demain les radiations émises sur tous les points du globe par les usines de désintégration modifient assez profondement leur équilibre vital et les sécrétions de leurs glandes pour en faire des monstres, ils se résigneront à naître bossus, tordus, ou couverts d'un poil épais comme les cochons de Bikini, en se disant une fois de plus qu' on ne s' oppose pas au progres" (p. 103).

9. See, among the former, Lewis Mumford (in *The New Yorker*, 7 December 1963): "Most of our compatriotes are under the impression that the forces that are ruining their cities and harrying their lives are even more difficult to resist than the decrees of Providence. But there is nothing automatic about these forces; as was true of the seemingly mechanical chess player who once awed all challengers at the old Eden Musée, on Twenty-third Street, there is a man inside the works!"

10. Carl Friedrich von Weizsäcker, address of 13 October 1963 (text in *Frankfurter Allgemeine Zeitung*, 14 October 1963).

Conservative Liberalism

Our attitude, in regard to a possible "reversal," will therefore be this: we propose to be both "positive" and "negative" about the "process." Positive in regard to the material advance which science and technology have rendered possible for the masses of the people of the entire world; positive also in regard to the social and political implications of this advance, i.e., the possibility of and the actual trend toward equality among human beings. Negative, on the other hand, in regard to the phenomena in the cultural-spiritual and general-attitudinal sphere which have been commented upon in the preceding chapter. Previously, we commented upon the fact that the egalitarian sweep of the last couple of centuries has been entirely in line with modernity; it has also been in line with age-old ethical ideals opposed to domination and exploitation. Inasmuch as the process of civilization brings about equality of human beings in material opportunity, social status, and dignity, a humanistic attitude can only welcome it and seek to promote it. I have previously called an approach that, within the bounds of the feasible, seeks to establish as much chance as is possible for the free personal development of all humans equally a "realist liberalism." [11] Taking now into consideration the concomitant opposition to the cultural and general "antiperson" implications of the civilizational process, we may well call our overall philosophy "conservative liberalism." This may sound paradoxical to those attuned to the traditional political meaning of the two terms. But the term "conservative" is used here in the literal sense of being intent on "conserving," or "preserving," that which is valuable in our cultural heritage and our spiritual tradition, that without which the specifically human element of humans, that which distinguishes them from the depersonalized, uniform man of the machine age, cannot prevail. To be sure, the conservative liberal will always confront the danger of being in the "wrong company" of those self-styled conservatives who exploit opposition to certain cultural trends in order to promote reaction-

11. See *Political Realism and Political Idealism* (Chicago, 1951), pp. 129 ff.

ism in the "material" sphere (economics, politics, race relations, etc.). Hence the discomfort of a good many liberals when they have to take a stand in questions such as "progressive education." That education, as we have seen, is in danger of neglecting the true values of learning, thought, cultural tradition. Reactionary attacks upon it often try to replace it by an old-fashioned authoritarian system or by one where higher education would be restored to the few, an elite of social or plutocratic prerogative. There is no reason why conservative liberals should keep such company merely because their attack is coupled with opposition to what conservative liberals themselves oppose, cultural neglect or neglect of the modes of true learning.

Conservative liberalism is humanistic in a dual fashion: In its concern for the elementary physical survival and well-being of all humans; but also in its equally urgent concern for the survival and development of those traits and values which, in the course of his age-long travel from animal to his present status, have rendered man a "person," and his environment—social, cultural, and natural—particularly adapted to this status. In either aspect it is in conformity with that attitude of "universalism" for which I have previously pleaded [12] as a new approach to the common tasks of mankind facing the danger of nuclear annihilation. These tasks comprise not only policies concerning arms regulation, international organization for peace, etc., but also those intimately connected with the accelerating civilizational process, e.g., demographic problems, problems of the conservation of the world's resources, the salvation of at least some remnants of man's natural habitat on this globe, and so forth.[13] Universalism thus turns out to be the application of humanistic "conservative liberalism" to the area of international relations. Here, the new attitude implies subordination of the traditional preoccupation with one's "national interest" to a supranational concern with the common interests of the human race. The dilemma, of course, is acute whenever a crisis situation places the present,

12. See *International Politics in the Atomic Age* (New York, 1959).
13. Sir Robert Watson-Watt has put it neatly when he said: "Not only must we remember that the proper study of mankind is man; the converse is also manifestly true" (*New York Times*, 20 June 1964).

nation-state, unit of international affairs before the alternative of "surrender" or "fight," exactly as an individual, attacked by a hostile person, has to choose between nonviolence and use of force in self-defense. But exactly as organized society is supposed to forestall this extreme situation among its individual members, it must be the supreme task of international society to prevent the ultimate "confrontation" and to search for a solution of issues in which the various national interests are resolved in the common interest. The new required type of "universalist" man is the one who, in the face of international and domestic pressures, manages to rise *au dessus de la mêlée*, put himself into the shoes of others, including opponents, and this way is able to distinguish special pleading from universal concern.

We have seen before that the young tend to be depoliticized under the influence of the technological process and the formation of affluent societies. If we are to have a "reversal," where, so we must ask, is youth to find new ideals if these are not to be the outmoded ideals of the past, such as nationalism and others? How vital it is to find approaches and values that go beyond the mere animal sphere of good or better living in the material sense is seen from the more or less irrational channels into which "anomie" leads the young of the modernized countries with increasing frequency ("beatnik"-ism, hooliganism, senseless vandalism, drug addiction, delinquency, and so forth). Those values and ideals, we believe, can and must be found in the objectives of universalism and of the overall "reversal." How is this reversal to come about? What is the new type of values it has to take into consideration? What, in particular, can and must be done in specific fields, such as that of demography?

The reversal has not necessarily to be a universal "conversion." If we had to wait for that, it might never come about. In principle it is possible as long as there are people who are aware of the problem and are endowed with a feeling for its urgency. All would be lost only in the extreme event that the civilizational process had managed to achieve such a degree of conformism that the last remnants of resistance had disappeared. This is a state of affairs which at this point still seems remote. As the civilizational process grew over the past fifty years or so it also called forth more or less forceful, although generally insufficient, efforts toward "conservation." Today, intermittent but occasionally quite powerful revolt against conformity testifies to the latent strength of resistant forces.[14] Another encouraging factor lies in the relatively "rational" nature of the required attitudes and approaches. Frequently, one merely needs to point out the unreasonableness of certain effects of the civilizational process[15] to show that rational and elementary ethical considerations demand a change in the form of stoppage, return, or reversal of process. Often, also, there is a good deal of planning involved here, and this may likewise elicit the favorable reaction of a generation used to the beneficial effects of planned progress in science, technology, and elsewhere. The main trouble is that the progress is so general, fast, broad, and multifaceted that it appears to many as overwhelming, "natural" in *all* its aspects, and therefore hopeless to resist. Yet resistance, to be successful, must come soon and fast. Each day of delay may render the job more difficult. This is apparent in areas such as the population explosion, where policies of birth control and family planning encounter growing difficulties the longer they are delayed. The same applies to coping with depletion of resources and to many other fields, especially since the civilizational process with its technological progress frequently endangers not only cultural values but the material environment necessary for physical human survival, as witness the increasing threats to human life and health through pollution of air, water, soil, and similar phenomena caused by unchecked industrialization. Mankind confronts the danger of literally suffocating in its own wastes. Therefore, what is needed most is a constant reminder, creating a constant, nagging kind of concern urging

14. A rash of recent publications in the United States (such as Rachel Carson's *Silent Spring*, Stewart Udall's *The Quiet Crisis*, or Harry Caudill's *Night Comes to the Cumberland*), all centering around the problems of natural and human resources and their salvation or conservation, may be indicative of this; or they may prove to be just another instance of the sudden rise and equally sudden decline of public interest in certain problem areas.

15. In this study we have from time to time come across examples, e.g., in regard to unlimited extension of speed in transportation (supersonic planes, etc.), unnecessary and, in its effects, cruel extension of life (e.g., of persons incurably ill), and so forth. Space flight, except for scientific purposes, may well turn out to be another example.

men to act before it is too late; in other words, a realization that, the more tardily a problem is attacked, the more difficult its solution, and the more radical and painful the measures which have to be taken.

Substantive and Instrumental Values

Thus the reversal can be brought about by a simple—and yet so difficult—change in the attitudinal climate, that is, through a turning away by more and more people from the assumptions and patterns of life of the civilizational process. They will seek to preserve and even promote this process whenever it brings advantages to the material aspects of human life. They will oppose to it new objectives whenever it is found to run counter to what the new attitude considers essentially human. No longer will that which is scientifically and technically possible be done for this reason alone. It must show its credentials in terms of its effect upon truly human life and the humane living-together of human beings. Aggrandizement, acceleration or expansion per se no longer will be considered as beneficial or an "advance" in the human sense. This goes for the number of people on earth, production of goods or development of resources, length of the lifespan, speeds, and so forth. All are quantitative values, to be measured against something beyond technology and quantity.

For purposes of the "reversal" the distinction between instrumental and substantive values is basic. Instrumental values are those which enable men to live, survive, live well in a material sense—they refer to the material goods, resources, commodities, services which people need, including the economic, social, political, legal systems, institutions, and arrangements created and organized for this purpose. Substantive values, on the other hand, are concerned, not with mere physical life and survival, but with people's survival as those peculiar ("human") beings with needs beyond these: spiritual, cultural, aesthetic, being in touch with "unprocessed" nature, uncrowded contact with fellow humans, leisure to think and feel—in short, a life and a world à la mesure d'homme. Only if and when this distinction becomes "operative" will the reversal be successful. Against its chances of success stands that "law of civilizational conformity" which enjoins us to go along with the process wherever it leads. If we manage to set up against this injunction an attitude of "civilizational disobedience" which would subordinate the instrumental to the substantive values whenever they clash, we shall have reversed a trend which is inimical to and threatens to overwhelm the other great processes, and in particular the process of culture.

What would the reversal imply in regard to one particular value, namely, the preservation of our heritage of premodern culture and unprocessed nature? Reversal here would entail the relatively simple job of preserving unspoiled landscape as "wilderness area" or "natural park," for instance; or of laying out highway systems or airports or planning new dwelling areas or entire new cities so as to fit them into the existing landscape; or of taking the measures necessary to preserve the relics of ancient places (e.g., by redirecting traffic around a city)—all this provided population pressure is relieved, which otherwise would make most of this impossible.

But it is easy to realize that even such a task belongs in a much larger context. There is an intimate connection between reversal programs of this type and the great overall problems of rigidity and acceleration in the economic, social, and foreign-political affairs of nations. Thus, any reversal-type urban or rural planning becomes inevitably enmeshed with problems and programs of urban or rural redevelopment for social purposes, such as abolishing slums and the poverty, disease, criminality, lack of educational opportunity they create. These, in turn, are related to more general policy problems; in the United States, for instance, to that of the relation between the public sector of the economy and the private. We have seen that one of the major destabilizing factors in the West is large-scale poverty perpetuated in the midst of growing prosperity; that a separate society of the poor exists side by side with the "normal," major, developing one. Reversal policies here must join policies of a realist liberalism that call a halt to pseudo-liberal laissez-faire, stop production for production's sake (where cars, for instance, are produced in ever accelerated fashion regardless of whether people need them, or streets and highways can accommodate them), and channel productive efforts into what should come first: the basic needs in housing, education, etc., of the larger masses of the people, including the impoverished. But all this would require a major policy change: breaking the rule of the corporations and their component parts (the manufacturers, the dealers, the advertisers, and also the connected trade unions) and performing these tasks through local and regional legislation (such as zonal laws, traffic regulations, housing rules) and, above all, through that most potent type of social regulation: tax and budget legislation. In regard to urban and landscape conservation, for instance, the reversal would have to aim at replacing transportation by means of the individual passenger car, which strangles and destroys cities (and also, by piling one new highway system on the other, the land in between), by mass transportation. Khrushchev, visiting the United States, was right in his remarks about the waste implicit in hundreds of thousands of Americans traveling daily to and from work in cars—one solitary person each (sour though the grapes may have been when he made the remark).

But the East, in regard to substantive values, has its own set of problems. There it is not free enterprise running wild but the problem of a technocratic bureaucracy that, armed with a doctrine, has been filling the cities with dead-as-the-dodo-style buildings or has been responsible for art and literature with papier-mâché heroes expressive of "social realism." Thus, where in the West the cultural reversal must imply planning what has remained unreflectingly spontaneous, in the East it means unplanning the wrongly planned or coerced in favor of releasing personal initiative. The reversal task here merges with that of political and general liberalization.

In the world's South, finally, there are perhaps the greatest problems but also the greatest hopes. We do not have to repeat here what was said before about the tremendous forces of acceleration which push the underdeveloped into the one broad stream of modernization; or point out again the destabilizing elements inherent in an often chaotic situation of political or economic nonviability, cultural-spiritual breakup of traditional systems, influx of alien ideologies, and so forth; or dwell once more on the tasks awaiting a rational aid and development policy with meaningful priorities. What interests us here is the question whether, within the (necessary) process of the modernization of the emergent nations and people, remnants of what they emerge from, that is, of the premodern mode of life, of their varied and different cultures and values, cannot and should not be preserved. How can something of the nontechnicalized man and his attitudes, institutions, and creations be salvaged in a more and more technicalized environment?

There is an encouraging paradox in the rise of many of the new countries: while one believes almost religiously in Westernization and modernization, there frequently is also a strong and fervent reversal to one's own precolonial culture and tradition. It appears, for instance, in the search for *négritude* in parts of Africa, and in many related ways. The answer to the question of whether this trend can become the basis for the preservation (or restoration) of ancient culture must at this point remain open. Much will depend on the attitudes of the generation which will follow upon that of the strongly Westernized present leaders. If it should prove possible to carry indigenous values over into the machine world, it would benefit the "advanced" world, too, which would be confronted with a living example of something successfully refusing to yield to the technological process in its cultural implications.

This antiprocess trend might be strengthened in other ways also. It is not necessary, for instance, that modern ways of production be introduced *everywhere*. Consider the realm of agriculture. It *is* necessary to modernize old-fashioned systems of agricultural production where primitive agricultural techniques fail to yield enough for present or increasing populations. But where they do yield enough, and the people are not yet imbued with the acquisitive spirit of producing for sale (i.e., profit), only the spirit of the machine world would consider leaving them alone, that is, failure to "push" them toward a money economy where they can exchange surplus products for manufactured goods, as something unnatural and perverse. To the people of Burma, for instance, it still seems "natural" to work only for immediate needs, then to "loaf." This "loafing" is the foundation of their traditional culture and way of life. As in many other rice-producing countries, their fertile lands produce enough for what their people consider a decent standard of living. Why should they adopt, let alone be compelled to adopt, the Western "work ethics"? And here again, a premodern attitude might well instigate a new attitude in advanced societies. Impressed by the durable, solid, and aesthetically satisfying products that such cultures still fashion (household goods, tools, furniture, etc.), the machine-world people may yet come to demand such things for themselves. Once a new attitude of this sort (which should not be confused with a mere interest in the exotic or outlandish) spreads, they will soon be surrounded by solid and beautiful objects; handicraft people and artisans will enjoy a new lease on life; education will find new and oftentimes more meaningful objectives; in short, the "old world" may yet teach the new. All this, however, presupposes one thing, namely, that population pressure does not compel the new nations to engage in the deadly race between resources and people where even mechanization of agriculture and industrialization may fail to provide additional billions of humans with the necessities of life.

Impact of the Demographic Factor

Thus we are thrown back to the population problem. We encountered it at the beginning of this analysis, when the population explosion of our times furnished us with one of the most conspicuous illustrations of the "Adams curve"-type of acceleration; we met it again when discussing its destabilizing impact on world affairs, and in particular on the condition of the underdeveloped world and its relations with the advanced nations; when discussing the problem of foreign aid; and so forth. Indeed, this *ceterum censeo* may appear as an author's *idée fixe* which places entirely too strong an emphasis on one particular factor. I do not believe that it is an idiosyncrasy, however. It is in the center of the complexity of things.

It can be easily seen why this is so. Exactly as the population explosion constitutes the prototype of the acceleration process, the problems it raises, if left unsolved, would render the entire process of civilization with all its technological and other achievements and advances of doubtful effectiveness because there would be an accelerating race between the pressure of the billions (or tens of billions), on the one hand, and an ever so far-reaching control of the environment, on the other. We have seen this not only in relation to food and other necessities but regarding natural resources in general as well as the air we breathe, the purity of water, and so on. Next to the self-extinction of the race through nuclear war, there is the nightmare of humanity suffocating under the weight of its numbers on the planet.

Population *planning,* on the other hand, is squarely in the middle between the civilizational process and the reversal. Qua planning, it is part and parcel of the general process of controlling "nature," of manipulating the environment.[16] Qua stabilizer, on the other hand, it constitutes a bridge from an unchecked process to the "humane" approach to things, because only through stabilizing the population can there be a return to diversity, development of the individual personality, quality production, and the like. Viewed in this light, population control is not only a problem of quantities. We would still view it under standards of the civilizational process should we consider merely how many people on earth or in a given area or nation can be kept alive. For we can hardly separate from this aspect "decency" of life, the "good life." How many, so we must ask, can be given their equal share in cultural and spiritual development, through individualized education and recreation? For how many can satisfying, substantial, beautiful goods be produced? Without paying attention to this dimension of the problem, concern with "development of personality" might remain mere talk.

Thus the quantitative and the qualitative, the problems of

16. As for the means of birth control and other ways of population planning, many are in the area of domestic and foreign policies. In the advanced countries, it would not only be a matter of providing advice on family planning and birth control as a free social service (and, in addition, of abolition of laws that would hamper such service by prohibiting sale of contraceptives or voluntary sterilization), but also of tax and similar measures based on the realization that, in contrast to most previous periods of history, children (from the fourth or so per family on) now constitute burdens on society. As for the underdeveloped, in addition to whatever they can do with their own resources, much will depend on whether foreign aid programs will finally come to grips with the problem and make population planning a major condition of aid.

material advance and those of humane living, here join hands. We have only to imagine that, by some miracle, the obverse of the population explosion should take place, a population "implosion," so to speak, that is, a recession in figures that would suddenly lift the pressure from our policy makers and planners, from overcrowded schools and overcrowded slums, the labor market, the hospitals. What a splendid vision of infinite opportunities for decent life and human values! Visualizing this kind of utopia can show us into what a corner we have been driven by the opposite development. Were the achievements of the technological process available to a manageable number of people, many a vision of the utopians might for the first time come true.

As it is, of course, the momentum carries on, and things must inevitably get worse before they can get better. Thus the aim must be to stabilize populations at some minimally high figure sometime in the future. Is this, in turn, a utopia? Can there be such a reversal?

Against a rational approach we have here the array of the same forces that are lined up against "universalism." Seemingly, the security dilemma of powers and power groups which makes them hesitate to subordinate national interests to universal concerns, because they cannot be sure that "the others" will do the same, also drives them into competition over numbers. Will not your own cutting down on population increase put you into an unfavorable position vis-à-vis those who do not so limit their numbers? Why, for instance, should the colored races of the world be prevented from further increasing at this point? Why should the white people be given an "advantage" exactly at a time when the nonwhite populations of the world emerge from age-old backwardness and servitude? Why should Protestants prevent Catholics, with their generally higher birthrate, from gaining greater proportional strength within a given population of mixed religious denomination? These are a few examples from "nonpolitical" groups. The argument, seemingly, is even more potent in the case of nations as power units. Thus de Gaulle, in his New Year address of 1964, gleefully forecast that French babies born that year will see "a France with hundred million inhabitants."

Actually, national competition for demographic greatness makes even less sense than that of social, racial, or religious groups within nations that have differential rates of increase. Even in terms of power and similar "national interest," is Japan worse off for stabilizing its population at the 100 million mark? Will India be, supposing it succeeds in its present efforts at population planning? Or France, if it should lag in this respect behind Italy or some other neighbor? We have seen before that the process of civilization renders mere numbers of people secondary to their quality, especially in scientific and technological training. Would it not, therefore, be more realistic for de Gaulle to provide a France now struggling with overcrowded schools and universities with new schools instead of gloating over France's "great demographic upsurge"? Is it not more useful for nations—even under viewpoints of their own national interests—to base their policies on the existence of a limited, calculable, healthy, and highly trained population rather than on growing multitudes condemned to live and die in slums? There is only one approach which might find political advantage in an opposite policy: that which banks on the growing despair of rapidly increasing "poor" nations in order to fan the flames of their antiimperialist resentment. Should Maoist Communism (which for China itself now seems to have come to realize the necessity of population planning) engage in such policies, it should not be beyond the resources of the Western world to convince the victims of this approach that they constitute mere pawns in a power struggle. True, such teaching would be even more convincing if the teachers themselves would live up to the lesson and, finally, turn to planning in an area which, alone among the important fields of human concern, so far has been left to nature's unregulated hazards and whims.

Enough about population control. To check unlimited acceleration here constitutes a first requirement of humanist reversal policy. Once this has been achieved, most of the other reversal concerns in the field of material conservation and environmental preservation (purity of the air, water, other resources, remnants of unspoiled nature, etc.) would be greatly alleviated.

The only area in which reversing the acceleration process

is equally urgent is that of the arms race. Will science and technology, now used by and put into the service of the unplanned and unchecked civilizational process, provide a counter-system of universal security, a system through which the greatest destabilizing factor of the present, the threat of nuclear annihilation, would be eliminated? As in the case of population control, reversal here finds itself at the side of scientific and technical planning for a livable world. It does so not only in the interest of physical survival but also because it is necessary to establish an environment safe from those "survival fears" and "jitters" that now beset mankind and endanger the mental health and stability required for all higher cultural effort. Man can live the "good life" only in mental sanity. It may well be that this type of reversal will occur less through spectacular changes of international systems and policies than through the spread of an attitude pattern which, encouraged by a prolonged period of nonuse, will simply refuse to consider the use of the available machinery of destruction as a practical possibility. Agreement on still necessary procedures to prevent accidental use, use by miscalculation, and so forth, in that event would become not only easier but secondary in urgency. Even the problem of whether weapons should be left in the hands of individual powers, whether they should all be eliminated, or whether a central world agency should be given an armaments monopoly could then be approached with less passion and greater likelihood of success.

The "Good Life"

For a long time the ideal of the "good life" has been couched in the terminology of "rights." Guarantees to individuals of time to enjoy life outside work, of educational and similar opportunities to develop their personalities, of an equal chance to participate in the cultural activities and the spiritual life of mankind—these, like the traditional demands for political rights and civil liberties, have more and more come to be embodied in catalogs of "natural" or "human" rights, whether in constitutions of individual countries or in the United

Nations' Universal Declaration of Human Rights, with its specifically listed rights to rest and leisure, to education, and so forth. Recently a political philosopher has asserted that they may all be considered aspects of one overarching and most fundamental right, the right to "self-realization" as *the* "most comprehensive right." [17]

This "right," qua ideal, clearly corresponds to the basic reversal ideal propounded here. We may well doubt, however, the same author's assertion—in which he agrees with age-old "natural law" theory—to the effect that the claimed right constitutes a fundamental right "flowing existentially from the recognized nature of man." [18] Man's "nature" exists only in historical evolution. The process of civilization may well be—and seems to be well on the way of—changing this "nature" so profoundly that talking about a "recognized nature of man" becomes doubtful. A process that tends to cut man from his traditional ties to "humaneness" may ultimately deprive him of the historically established "self" that strives toward "self-realization," leaving him a completely altered "machine man" without meaningful relation to the mentioned types of "rights."

In the face of what threatens now, we cannot share the optimism of the natural-rights school of thought. What has evolved may perish or wane, be it ever so precious. But ours is at the same time a more activist approach. It is up to man to save what is in peril. And this requires not only the high spirit of idealism but equally as much the cunning of realism. Especially when confronting the large-scale mass organizations set up under the process, the trends adverse to human self-realization must be fought by counter-means of organization and in a similarly systematic and "sophisticated" fashion. This is exactly what distinguishes the fight in an age of accelerated process from reform movements and fights for "rights" in, e.g., the eighteenth or nineteenth centuries. So powerful have been the inroads of the civilizational process that, although people usually now have "merely" to assert rights that already exist, their "depolitization," their satisfac-

17. Carl J. Friedrich, "Rights, Liberties, Freedoms: A Reappraisal," *American Political Science Review* 57, no. 4 (December 1963): 841 ff., 844.
18. Ibid.

tion with the relative state of affluence brought about by the process, and other factors have rendered many ignorant of what they are being deprived of, or indifferent toward the value of the threatened loss. Thus they must be prodded into taking up the struggle, whether it be the enforcement of basic material opportunity and fundamental civil and political rights—as in the case of the black man in America—[19] or whether it be the struggle for the salvation of individuality, personality, privacy, and diversity from the inroads of the machine and the spirit of the machine. Yet in the face of all the difficulties there remains a confidence deep within one's "self" that something can be preserved of the quality of feeling and emotion, of capacity to sense joy and sorrow, yes even conflict and tragedy, of ability to be proud, jubilant, or desperate. The struggle to retain something of this nature and thus to maintain one's self will decide the fate of man as man.

We may conclude our study with words drawn from a matter-of-fact, down-to-earth English thinker, who, over one hundred years ago, wrote with astounding perspicacity on the impact of the civilizational process and the values threatened by its acceleration:

> Toward what ultimate point is society tending by its industrial progress? When the progress ceases, in what condition are we to expect that it will leave mankind?
>
> I confess I am not charmed with the ideal of life held out by those who think that the normal state of human beings is that of struggling to get on; that the trampling, crushing, elbowing, and treading on each other's heels, which form the existing type of social life, are the most desirable lot of human kind. . . .
>
> Those who do not accept the present very early stage

19. The cause of American blacks—the one great current issue of this type in the advanced part of the world—can be considered the model of all similar endeavor, since it deals with the entire range of the values that are at stake today: elimination of poverty and deprivation in the most elementary sense; recognition of equality of opportunity of all human beings regardless of racial or similar distinctions; maintenance and development of personality through participation in all that which renders such development possible; and preservation of that diversity, those peculiar traits, which in the instance of the musical and emotional talents of blacks has always added something specially ingratiating to the "American character."

of human improvement as its ultimate type, may be excused for being comparatively indifferent to the kind of economical progress that excites the congratulations of ordinary politicians: the mere increase of production and accumulation. . . . It is only in the backward countries of the world that increased production is still an important object: in those most advanced, what is economically needed is a better distribution, of which one indispensible means is a stricter restraint of population. . . .

There is room in the world, no doubt, and even in old countries, for a great increase of population. . . . But even if innocuous, I confess I see very little reason for desiring it. . . . A population may be too crowded, though all be amply supplied with food and raiment. It is not good for man to be kept perforce at all times in the presence of his species. A world from which solitude is extirpated, is a very poor ideal. Solitude, in the sense of being often alone, is essential to any depth of meditation or of character; and solitude in the presence of natural beauty and grandeur, is the cradle of thoughts and aspirations which are not only good for the individual, but which society could ill do without. Nor is there much satisfaction in contemplating the world with nothing left to the spontaneous activity of nature; with every road of land brought into cultivation, which is capable of growing food for human beings; every flowery waste or natural pasture ploughed up, all quadrupeds or birds which are not domesticated for man's use exterminated as his rivals for food, every hedgerow or superfluous tree rooted out, and scarcely a place left where a wild shrub or flower could grow without being eradicated as a weed in the name of improved agriculture. If the earth must lose that great portion of its pleasantness which it owed to things that the unlimited increase of wealth and population would extirpate from it, for the mere purpose of enabling it to support a larger but not a better or happier population, I sincerely hope, for the sake of posterity, that they will be content to be stationary, long before necessity compels them to do it. . . .

It is scarcely necessary to remark that a stationary condition of capital and population implies no stationary state of human improvement. There would be as much scope as ever for all kinds of mental culture, and moral and social progress; as much room for improving the Art of Living; and much more likelihood of its being improved, when minds ceased to be engrossed with the art of getting on. . . . Hitherto it is questionable if all the mechanical inventions yet made have lightened the day's toil of any human being . . . they have not yet begun to affect those great changes in human destiny which it is in their nature and in their futurity to accomplish. Only when, in addition to just institutions, the increase of mankind shall be under the deliberate guidance of judicious foresight, can the conquests made from the powers of nature by the intellect and energy of scientific discoverers, become the common property of the species, and the means of improving and elevating the human lot.[20]

20. John Stuart Mill, *Principles of Political Economy*, bk. 4, chap. 6 (New York, 1870), 2:334–40.

THE TERRITORIAL STATE REVISITED—REFLECTIONS ON THE FUTURE OF THE NATION-STATE

First published in *Polity* 1, no. 1 (Fall 1968): 11–34, this article tried to correct the wrong impression created in some readers of "Rise and Demise of the Territorial State" (see chapter 3) that I had anticipated the disappearance of the nation-state. Far from this, the state had persevered into the 1960s and, in some respects, even increased in strength and functions. Why and how is discussed in this essay, as detailed further on pages 17–19 of the *Introduction*. I have since changed some ideas contained in this essay, especially those on "legitimacy," and the reader finds some results of this re-revisitation in the concluding parts of the *Introduction*.

Reprinted by permission of *Polity*, The Journal of the Northeastern Political Science Association.

Despite the conspicuous rise of international organization and supranational agencies in the postwar world and despite the continuing impact on international affairs of subnational agents such as business organizations (in the West) and "international" parties (in the East), the states remain the primary actors in international relations. Indeed, as the rush into "independent" statehood shows, being a sovereign nation seems to be the chief international status symbol as well as to furnish the actual entrance ticket into world society.

In 1957 I published an article entitled—perhaps rashly— "Rise and Demise of the Territorial State."[1] Its chief thesis was to the effect that for centuries the characteristics of the

1. See chapter 3 in this volume.

basic political unit, the nation-state, had been its "territoriality," that is, its being identified with an area which, surrounded by a "wall of defensibility," was relatively impermeable to outside penetration and thus capable of satisfying one fundamental urge of humans—protection. However, so my argument proceeded, territoriality was bound to vanish, chiefly under the impact of developments in the means of destruction which render defense nugatory by making even the most powerful "permeable." What was going to take the place of the now obsolete nation-state? I said that, rationally speaking, only global "universalism," affording protection to a mankind conceiving of itself as one unit, was the solution.

This thesis was subsequently referred to by many who seemed to agree with its main thrust—that of the demise of the nation-state. The nuclear age seemed to presage the end of territoriality and of the unit whose security had been based upon it.[2] Naturally there was less agreement concerning what (if anything) would take its place. "Futurology" (to use the term—now accepted into the language of social science in Europe—coined by Ossip K. Flechtheim for a science or art of prognostic) provides uncertain standards of predicting developments. But it is clear that, at least in a negative way, the "demise" thesis seemed to preclude a revival of something close to the traditional political unit. Rather, it seemed to anticipate trends toward international interdependence, if not global integration.

Developments have rendered me doubtful of the correctness of my previous anticipations. The theory of "classical" territoriality and of the factors threatening its survival stands. But I am no longer sure that something very different is about to take its place. There are indicators pointing in another direction: not to "universalism" but to retrenchment; not to interdependence but to a new self-sufficiency; toward area not losing its impact but regaining it; in short, trends toward a

2. See, for instance, the similar conclusion reached by Klaus Knorr in *On the Uses of Military Power in the Nuclear Age* (Princeton, 1966), p. 174. See also Raymond Aron, *Peace and War: A Theory of International Relations* (New York, 1966), pp. 395–96, and even Hans J. Morgenthau in, for example, "The Four Paradoxes of Nuclear Strategy," *American Political Science Review* 58 (1964): 23 ff.

"new territoriality." The following constitutes an attempt to analyze the trends that point in the direction of a possible territorial world of the future and to present something like a model of such a world with the aid of hypotheses, which, on the basis of demonstrable facts, do not seem entirely implausible. There will be a variety of hypotheses, each probably open to some doubt, but the sum-total seems at least minimally plausible.

I. CONSIDERATIONS

Consider the following: (a) In the spring of 1967 there was on the shore of the eastern Mediterranean a unit that appeared under any customary standard unviable. Endowed with an "impossible" strategic configuration it faced encircling units not merely hostile but solemnly sworn to destroy the "alien" unit in their midst at first opportunity. The opportunity seemed to have come when two obstacles suddenly vanished that so far had enabled Israel to live: the protective force of UNEF and the proverbial disunity of the Arabs. The world anticipated the second stage of Hitler's "final solution" of the "Jewish question." What happened? Determined to face death and extinction, a population deeply attached to its "homeland" not only resisted but beat all comers. The latter, *not* faced with the choice of victory or national extinction, fled.

(b) There was, in 1967, one of the poorest countries extant, chiefly agrarian, little developed, long under colonial rule, never, in modern times, politically organized as an independent unit. Split in half, it was also split in its approach to the problem of its unification and independence. Then the most powerful nation on earth undertook to impose one solution upon the Vietnamese. Whereupon one half, so far only half-heartedly resigned to Communist rule, became united as one in resistance to the "aggressor" (even to the point of permitting the controlling group to risk arming the people), while in the other half guerrilla war and the "fish-in-water" situation frustrated the "invader's" efforts to such an extent that even the marshaling of overwhelming force failed to enable him to achieve his goal of subjection.

What are we to conclude from the above? That in an age of nationalism nations are invincible? That the nuclear arsenal is "unavailable" as an effective means of forcing decisions? That a new type of warfare restores the protective function to entities that, at least in the eyes of large portions of the people, legitimately represent the nation, or to the group that strives for national autonomy? Before trying to establish hypotheses, let us look further into the two situations used as examples. In neither case has nuclear power been used. But the other type of weapon and warfare which causes the decline of classical territoriality by enabling belligerents to circumvent the "hard shell" of defense and to destroy the enemy "vertically"—airpower—has been clearly in evidence. What has been its effect? In the case of Israel control of the air, established at the very beginning of hostilities, was decisive in her victory. What did it achieve? Survival of one national unit, certainly. But also defeat of the enemy in the traditional sense of compelling him to abide by the will of the victor? The present plight of Israel, not knowing what to do with its "victory" in the face of apparent Arab determination not to negotiate a settlement, is significant. In an age of nationalism and guerrilla war one seems to be able to counter aggression but not to subdue. Supposing Israel had occupied Cairo and Damascus, might she have forced her enemies' hands? For example, by establishing, in the classical fashion, compliant regimes with which to negotiate? In all likelihood, little would have been gained. In such cases, the "Algerian" type of situation is liable to ensue, with the victor facing the "territorial" urge of a nationalistic population, its readiness to bear any hardship rather than submit.

The same applies to Vietnam. There, too, the Algerian analogy is correct, and not the far-fetched one of Hitlerian expansionism and a possible Munich. Nuclear power so far has proved "unavailable" because it would be "overproductive." While United States control of the air has been the primary cause of its and its client's forces not being defeated on the ground, it has proved incapable of defeating the enemy. The resulting stalemate, in the long run, is likely to be more frustrating to the side that fights away from home halfway around the globe for a cause that, at best, is confused in its mind, than for those who are convinced that they fight for their homes, ground, country, nation.

Israel, the Arabs, Algeria, Vietnam—we may add, from recent years, Poland, Hungary, Rumania, China, France, Panama, Cuba: nation-state and nationalism, territorial urge and the urge to maintain (or establish, or regain) one's "sovereignty" and "independence"—all of these do not seem to have diminished in importance in these decades of the nuclear age. Let us try to develop some hypotheses concerning their role in the future.

II. THE END OF EMPIRE

By "empire" we mean control of areas and populations outside those one considers as constituting one's own nation; the term also indicates the (nonnational or multinational) entities thus formed. It is our first hypothesis that remnants of empire, where it still survives, are bound to disappear, in this way rendering the entire surface of the globe (inasmuch as it is under governmental control of specific, separate political units) a mosaic of nation-states. (On the problem of their identity, coherence, and legitimacy see below.)

Let us distinguish empires of the old style from those formed under the impact of nuclear and bipolar factors. The old empires were chiefly founded by and based upon territorial conquest and domination. They were successful because of the then prevailing strategic-technological and/or cultural-civilizational superiorities of the expansionist countries and the simultaneous absence of nationalism in the modern sense from the areas into which the imperial countries expanded (with tribalism in Africa, for instance, or feudal systems with weak national coherence in India). At a certain stage of industrial and capitalistic development there were strong economic motivations for such expansion and control. The importance of foreign resources and manpower, and of capital export and investment, to technologically and industrially developing nations led theorists of "imperialism" such as Lenin and other Marxists, but also non-Marxist ones, to believe that imperialist expansion and colonial control were features innate in and congruous with the advance of industrial systems. We know now that this conjunction was characteristic of only one phase in this development, a phase which under new technological developments (such as substitution of synthetic for natural raw materials) is drawing to a close.[3]

Thus, beginning with a pre-Western empire, the Ottoman, and then extending to the great "classical" empires of the British, French, Dutch, etc., the process of liquidation has been going on relentlessly, spurred by the triumphant march of nationalism over the globe. Indeed, so little "interest" remains in the imperial stance that nowadays we sometimes find the imperial country in the somewhat absurd situation of trying hard to "get out of there," and as soon as possible, but having a difficult time doing so without leaving behind chaos or strife (for example, Britain and its few remaining possessions "East of Suez"). And even the conclusion of arrangements on retention of bases which may be more vital to the defense and/or the economy of the newly independent unit than to its former ruler, often proves difficult because of the extreme nationalism found in the area. Such areas thus tend to become useless to the former owner, untenable, or both. (On their role in regard to "new-style" empires see below.)

We may thus anticipate the extension of this trend to still existing areas of old-style empire, such as that of the Portuguese in Africa. Only where original empire led to white settlement on a large scale which subsequently developed its

3. See, for example, Knorr, *Military Power*, pp. 21 ff. In Knorr's convincing presentation this is only one of several factors making for the diminished value of territorial expansion. Others are: the decline of offensive foreign-political goals, with welfare societies, no longer led by military elites, turning to domestic affairs; the growth of an antiwar spirit, due to the more direct impact on people at large of the costs and suffering of war; restraints through world opinion; and decreased submissiveness of ruled populations (pp. 29 ff., 57 ff.). I shall deal with some of these factors, in particular the last one (which, of course, is closely related to the rise and spread of nationalism), below. A similar line of argument is to be found in E. O. Czempiel, *Das amerikanische Sicherheitssystem 1945–1949* (Berlin, 1966), for example, on p. 12: "In its initial phase capitalism depended on raw materials, so that there was temptation to compel their possessors to exploit them. . . . In the era of mass consumption raw material production as well as capital exports recede in importance behind promotion of sales. For the sale of private cars, that symbol of mass society, territorial expansion is not necessary . . ." (translation mine).

own separate territoriality will there be serious problems concerning the liquidation of these settlers' control over (numerically minority or majority) indigenous populations (as in South Africa). There it is, however, no longer a problem of imperialism or colonialism but rather one of racial adjustment and ethnic integration in a territorial unit.

The demise of old-style empire is now largely achieved, and few doubt the completion of the process in the future. But many will say that this has not meant the disappearance of empire as such; that it merely indicates a change in appearance and aspects. Territorial conquest and expansion may no longer be the fashion of the day. But has not indirect penetration, with indirect controls, taken their place when totalitarian regimes try to conquer the world through propaganda and subversion and when the nuclear superpowers extend the "hard shell of defensibility" from the traditional territorial unit, the nation-state, to blocs that, under bipolarity, tend to comprise halves of the globe? One effect of this "new-style" imperialism was that, within each of the two blocs that gave the postwar international system its bipolar character, the relation between a leading power and nations that formerly would have been allies on an equal plane became one of dominating unit to client, or satellite unit. I have previously tried to trace the novel features of intrabloc relationships which prevail under bipolar and nuclear conditions (for example, the novel features of NATO, as compared with alliances of the old style[4]), while the "imperialistic," expansionist tendencies of world-revolutionary systems have been vividly described by authors such as Hans J. Morgenthau.[5]

I still believe that my description of postwar bipolarity and its effects was correct in reference to a situation in which two,

4. *International Politics in the Atomic Age*, pp. 112–43.
5. These authors use the somewhat misleading term "nationalist universalism"; see, for example, *Politics Among Nations* (4th ed.; New York, 1967), pp. 323 ff. World-revolutionary expansionism does constitute a new type of expansionist nationalism, but the term "universalism" might better be reserved to an antinationalist or nonnationalist, *internationalist* attitude. The ensuing confusion can be seen in a book like J. W. Burton's *International Relations: A General Theory* (Cambridge, Mass., 1965), where Morgenthau and I are referred to throughout as joint advocates of "nationalist universalism" in a sense in which neither of us has used the term; see, for example, pp. 110, 132, 149.

and only two, powers held a nuclear monopoly, and the development of weapons and delivery systems required the establishment of empires complete with forward areas of troops stationed at or near their rim and bases lining their frontiers. Even at that time, however, there were forces at work that counteracted the empire-consolidating factors. They have since turned out to be extremely important. One category is primarily military-strategic. With the development of intercontinental ballistic missiles and the corresponding delivery systems the importance of missile bases outside the territory of the superpowers themselves has diminished. With the emergence of second-strike capacity on both sides and the ensuing stabilization of mutual deterrence, the usefulness of nuclear weapons as umbrellas protecting areas outside the superpowers has become doubtful. I shall have more to say about the impact of such "unavailability of force" on nation-states and the nation-state system. Suffice it here to draw attention to the ensuing lesser importance of allies (or clients) and their inclusion in organized blocs or defense systems, and to the equally diminishing value of bases on foreign soil and of integrated forces. Even where the latter are still strategically meaningful, their maintenance becomes more difficult under the impact of the second type of factors: the resurgence of nationalism within the blocs. Resistance of nations to being reduced to client or satellite status by now has meant their emergence from such a status to genuine autonomy (especially in the East) or to the traditional nationalism and the national independence of prenuclear times (as in the West). To this must be added the trend toward nuclear multipolarity through nuclear proliferation—a joint effect of the spread of technological know-how and of nationalism. What this presages will be discussed in more detail below. What had to be pointed out here is the trend away from the coherence and consolidation of the new-style empires that had been founded on nuclear monopolies or nuclear superiorities, toward the assertion, or reassertion, of nationhood and independence.

III. THE UNAVAILABILITY OF FORCE

"The dangerousness of war has reduced the danger of war." [6] The overkill machinery of nuclear armament, with all its potential pervasiveness in regard to the territory and boundaries of traditional international units, has had the unexpected, paradoxical, and encouraging effect of stabilizing a world most had believed destabilized in the extreme through the advent of the new weapon. At the dawn of the atomic age, when the new machinery for destruction had first become available to powers utterly at odds in regard to ways of life, types of regimes, and objectives of foreign policy, there had been general expectation that the holocaust was inevitable unless the enormity of the threat would make the superpowers agree on radical measures of disarmament and control. They did not, and, yet, in twenty years of nuclear confrontation, the world has escaped nuclear war and even conventional war among major nations.

Chief cause of this development, of course, has been nuclear stalemate through nuclear deterrence. The boundaries of the blocs turned out to be the limits of spheres of tacitly agreed upon nonintervention. The United States and the Soviet Union emerged as the two great "conservatives," both intent on consolidating the status quo as it had been established after World War II, including its often abstruse and seemingly unmanageable arrangements, settlements, and boundaries (for example, the two Germanies, Berlin, and access routes to West Berlin; or the 38th parallel in Korea). A nuclear war, or any war that might escalate into one, was not to be risked over issues located in the sphere conceded to the other side (such as the crises concerning Hungary, Berlin, or Cuba). In this way, at least in intention, the bloc frontiers have taken the place of the "trip-wire" lines of protection which national boundaries used to constitute in the age of territorial impermeability.

But this also meant protection of the respective actors and regimes and, by way of indirection, of the units controlled by these regimes. If Castro is protected in Cuba, or Chiang on Taiwan, or Ulbricht in East Germany, or whoever is in power

6. Inis L. Claude, *The Changing United Nations* (New York, 1967), p. 9.

at Seoul, this entails also the preservation of Cuba, the Republic of China, the German Democratic Republic, and the Republic of Korea *qua* territorial units. Force in the relationship between the United States and the Soviet Union, or their respective blocs, has been "unavailable" in the sense that the effects of nuclear action are considered unacceptable to either side. Although the weapon must remain available as a retaliatory threat, one not merely hopes that it will never be used but is more or less agreed that it will not function—except as retaliation—in one's policy calculations.

One can go a step further. Realization that any kind of hostilities involving the major powers or their bloc affiliates can easily get out of control and escalate into nuclear war has made them discount, to some extent, the use even of conventional force. . . . We can further observe that even outside the blocs (or whatever remains of them) the use of force has declined in the relations between the big and the small. There certainly has been growing hesitation to resort to it. . . . Compared with prenuclear imperialistic practices, the forbearance of the United States toward Panama or that of the Soviets toward Albania or Rumania has been quite astonishing. Some of the reasons are nuclear, to be sure. Less forbearance might lead to nuclear "confrontation" or worse things. But there are additional reasons. Thus, in former times the powerful could afford to disregard hostile reaction on the part of what is loosely referred to as "world opinion." They can no longer discount it today exactly because, with force less available, they must look for substitute means of safeguarding interests and conducting policy. These may be found in areas such as "parliamentary diplomacy," where—as in the debates and votes of the United Nations—the goodwill of the small may turn out to be important. In this way, a hostile reaction to warlike policies of the mighty can be brought to bear on the international plane. . . .

But the effect of the "unavailability of force" on the territorial stability of countries is not exclusively positive. It is somewhat ambiguous. For instance, we can see that, by way of curious reaction, force unavailable to the large may encourage the small to defy them and use force with impunity. What hampers the powerful—anxiety concerning nuclear confrontations, anticolonialist opinion, etc.—favors the small. They leave the nuclear worrying to the nuclear powers and bank on being backed up by world opinion and the world organization. To this may be added a frequent lack of responsibility or the parochialism of new nations and their leaders, who may be tempted to pursue grievances to the point of violence in disregard of the dangers this involves for world peace. They may even set out to create threats to the peace so as to draw attention to their particular problems.

Another ambiguity lies in the combined effect of nuclear "unavailability" and second-strike capacity. The latter protects the superpowers but seems to deprive the others, in and outside the blocs, of reliance on nuclear protection. This has been one of the reasons for the assertion of independence of bloc members and, in some instances, for the development of their own nuclear forces. While this has added strength to them qua nation-states, it also endangers them vis-à-vis the other superpower. Their getting out from under the wings of the protecting power leaves them out in the cold, more independent but also more endangered.

What about nuclear proliferation as such, and its effect on the nation-state system? Undoubtedly, acquisition of a nuclear arsenal adds to the relative strength of the acquiring nation, in particular in its relation to the remaining nonnuclear ones. Even countries like France, which, because of lack of sufficient economic base or for similar reasons, are destined to remain inferior to the nuclear superpowers, gain in status and thus, to some extent, in freedom of foreign-political action. And those which, like China, are on the way to "superpowerdom" comparable to that of the United States and the Soviets, may perceive an opportunity to try out the path of "new-style empire." This, in turn, threatens others, such as India, and thus reinforces the tendency toward proliferation.

Even should a nonproliferation treaty come about, its effect on the stability of the present international system must be doubted. If France and China cannot be brought under the agreement, it is hard to see what protection can be effectively given to countries like India, which would assume a status of permanent nuclear inferiority. If the nuclear umbrella furnished their own allies by the United States and the Soviet

Union has become dubious, can there be one for nonaligned countries? Verbal assurances of this sort tend to become "incredible," and even though they may be given in good faith, a counterpower not believing in them may be lured into risking confrontations that may end in nuclear war. In this way, far from creating protection and stability, a system of such guarantees may actually increase the danger of war. More likely than not, and whether there are nonproliferation agreements or not, if a nuclear power threatens a nonnuclear one, the latter will quickly be transformed into a nuclear power by a nuclear "friend" (who, in a case like that of the United States and West Germany, has merely to make bombs or missiles in the area accessible to the nonnuclear power already in possession of delivery systems and trained personnel); in such an event, a treaty is unlikely to make much difference.[7]

Thus we are warranted in anticipating a world of nuclear proliferation, with increasing numbers of both greater and lesser nuclear powers. This will certainly involve great instability and growing risks of actual nuclear war.[8] On the other hand, it is at least imaginable that what happened in the postwar decades may repeat itself; that is, that at least for a period of time, *systems* of mutual deterrence may stabilize the situation. There may be regional systems, with regional nuclear balances, there may be agreed upon and inspected denuclearized areas, and so forth. Details depend on factors that are difficult to predict, such as the identity and distribution of the nuclear powers, the stage and level of their nuclear equipment, and the internal cohesion of the units in question. In any event, we may, by way of hypothesis, assume the

7. See also L. Beaton, "Nuclear Fuel for All," *Foreign Affairs* 45 (1967): 4, 662 ff.; Beaton points out that even a legal commitment to nonproduction of nuclear weapons will mean little, especially after some lapse of time and possible change of the commitment-making regime, if the country can use plutonium derived from nuclear power stations in its territory. The only safe guarantee against proliferation would be nuclear disarmament of the "haves," but this is not in the cards.

8. Among the most dangerous risks a multiplication of variables under nuclear proliferation would bring about are those of a personal nature (insanity or incapacity or emotional overreaction of leaders, unintentional or unauthorized action of subordinates, etc.). For a summing up of these factors see Jerome D. Frank, *Sanity and Survival: Psychological Aspects of War and Peace* (New York, 1967).

emergence of a multipolar world of nuclear proliferation in which the territorial nature of the component units is preserved and is not entirely in jeopardy. The global victory of the nationalism of the self-determining and self-limiting variety (in contrast to expansionist nationalism), in addition, would clearly circumscribe the units and thus provide this world with the underpinning of enhanced stability of the constituent entities. This presupposes uncontested boundaries and the settlement of outstanding territorial issues. International organization and international law might here come to the rescue. But the emergence of a world of nationally defined and delimited units requires a number of additional hypotheses.

IV. LEGITIMACY OF NATIONS

So far we have dealt with trends and phenomena that provide the exterior environment in which a new territoriality may arise. Decline of empires, reduction in the role of penetrating force—developments such as these create preconditions for continuation of a national role as a basic constituent of international relations. They are necessary but not sufficient factors. In a positive way, nations, in order to be effective actors in international relations, must prove to be "legitimate" units, that is, entities which, generically and individually, can be and are being considered as basic and "natural" for the fulfillment of essential purposes, such as the protection and welfare of people. We must, therefore, search for factors that enable them to play this role, and also deal with the obstacles they encounter.

Why do we speak of "*new* territoriality"? If territory and statehood are to continue or resume their accustomed role, in what respect are they new? I suggest the term because now they will exist in an environment of nuclear penetrability, and they will have to assert themselves in an environment of vastly and rapidly increasing technological, economic, and general interrelationships of a shrinking world.

To one watching the seemingly unending appearance of (by now over 130) "nation-states" upon the international scene—a veritable population explosion of nations—raising doubts about the ongoing power of the nation-state idea may sound strange. But all of us are aware of the turmoil and travail, the difficulties and doubts that accompany the process. Can one put into one and the same category Gambia and France, Barbados and China, the Congo and Argentina? It is a commonplace to point out the synthetic nature of units formed on the accidental basis of boundaries drawn at the European conference table in the age of colonialism; the artificiality of "nations" built on the tearing apart or throwing together of several coherent entities, such as tribes; the doubtful identity of nations themselves proclaiming to be parts of an overarching nation (such as Arab states in relation to an overall "Arab nation"); the linguistic and similar centrifugal forces that threaten even apparently solid nations such as India; the nonviability of tiny or excessively weak nations, devoid of sufficient population and/or resources; the lack of territorial integration of widely separate island groups.

But these problems do not appear entirely insoluble. There is the problem of the "microstates" (especially those still unborn, in the Pacific and elsewhere). There is a parallel here to the mini-units that emerged as "sovereign" entities in the area of the Holy Roman Empire after the Peace of Westphalia; most of these were eventually consolidated or absorbed. It should not prove beyond human (even political) ingenuity to find solutions here through federation, semiautonomy under other units, etc. More complex seem the problems of larger and yet highly synthetic units, many of them in Africa. We shall discuss some of the more basic questions relating to their nationhood below. It is sufficient to point here to the analogous condition of at first equally synthetic units in another continent, South (and Central) America; they originated in similarly artificial colonial districts, an origin which did not prevent their exhibiting, in due course, the sentiments and characteristics of nationhood. They might have grown into one or two overall "nations" on the pattern of the North American colonies (which originally had, perhaps, even more distinctive characteristics of their own than those in Latin America); instead they grew into the genuinely distinct nations most of them constitute today.[9] Raymond Aron is probably right in

9. It is true, however, that in those Latin American countries where

pointing out that some of the smaller among the new African states are more viable than they would have been had they been established as bigger and therefore (economically, etc.) seemingly more viable entities. In this way it is easier for them to overcome tribalism. The contrast between the relative success of, let us say, Ghana, on the one hand, and Nigeria or the Congo, on the other hand, illustrates what he means.

What, then, renders a nation-state legitimate? Legitimacy originates from the feelings and attitudes of the people within as well as neighbors and others abroad in regard to the unit, its identity and coherence, its political and general "way of life." Where there is positive valuation, that is, an impression or even a conviction that the unit in question "should be" the one on the basis of which a particular group organizes its separate and distinct existence as a "nation," there is legitimacy. The legitimacy of the territorial state that emerged from the Middle Ages in Europe was chiefly founded on defensibility against foreign attack (its protective function) and on the two successive principles of "legitimate" dynastic rule and, later, common nationality. One might distinguish between the legitimacy of the unit as such and that of its internal system (regime, sociopolitical structure). In regard to the former, in an age of nationalism units may range all the way from illegitimacy to complete legitimacy. Mere possession of the outward paraphernalia of statehood (independent government in de facto control of an area) does not suffice. For instance, with the growth of national unification movements in the areas later constituting the German Empire and the Italian Kingdom, existing sovereign states in these areas became increasingly illegitimate. Today, the partition of Germany leaves the legitimacy of both German units in doubt.[10] Independence movements rendered empires increasingly illegitimate as indigenous nationalism rose against colonialism. But in many of the new states that emerged from decolonization, absence of minimally strong feelings of identity and solidity still prevents their being

Indians—not yet mobilized politically and otherwise—constitute a high proportion of the population we have the problem of nationhood still to be established out of ethnically diverse constituent groups.

10. Even more spurious, of course, would be West Berlin as an independent "third German state" (a suggestion of the Soviets and their friends).

considered as fully legitimate. There is, of course, a good deal of variation. Where, as in Algeria, or now in Vietnam, a population previously little integrated even in its own image has to fight long and doggedly for independence, it is likely to emerge more strongly consolidated as a national entity than where a "nation," carved out with accidental boundary lines, had independence thrown upon it without much popular exertion. Being compelled to fight for or defend one's territory generates true nationhood.

Internal legitimacy (without which the legitimacy of the unit as such can provide little real solidity) in our day is closely related to democracy in the broad sense of people having the conviction that they control their destinies and that government operates for their welfare. Old-fashioned autocracy, once legitimate in the eyes of the people in many parts of the world, today hardly survives anywhere as legitimate. Even Ethiopia, Saudi Arabia, and Iran have to "modernize" themselves in this respect. And modern dictatorship, as appears clearly from trends and developments everywhere and in respect of the most diverse types of that form of government (from Spain through Eastern Europe to the Soviet Union), feels compelled to shed its more authoritarian and totalitarian traits in order to establish a popular image of legitimate rule. In the democracies themselves, legitimacy is the stronger the older and more safely rooted democratic habits and processes actually are. In many new countries legitimacy is in doubt not only because of the problematic nature of the unit but also because of the nature of the regime, which may be oppressive (military control as the only way to keep the unit together) and/or unrepresentative (in the sense of rule by one among several ethnic groups). Thus one can arrange the countries of the world along a continuum ranging all the way from externally and internally stable and legitimate to "soft," "spongy" units and regimes.[11] Only as the latter ones "harden," that is, with the spread of national self-determination and democracy, will

11. Referring to the domino theory of aggression in Southeast Asia, Kenneth Waltz remarks: "States in the area of the fighting lack the solidity, shape, and cohesion that the image suggests. Externally ill-defined, internally fragile and chaotic, they more appropriately call to mind sponges. . . ." "The Politics of Peace," *International Studies Quarterly* 11, no. 3 (1967): 205.

the "new territoriality" arise in regard to them. For, as Rupert Emerson has put it, "the nation has in fact become the body that legitimizes the state." [12]

But these developments are not autonomous or self-contained. The outside world can, and does, influence them, for instance, through the extension or denial of "recognition" or through the grant of membership in international agencies, particularly the United Nations.[13] There is reason for the German Democratic Republic to try so desperately to gain recognition (and therewith the status of a legitimate international unit) from other than Communist countries, and, by the same token, for the Federal Republic to try to prevent this and thus remain the only German unit recognized by the majority of nations. The older nations of the world, in this way, have a chance, through policies of recognition and acceptance to membership based upon whether or not the applicants are viable as nationally coherent entities, to promote the emergence of some legitimate units and hamper that of others. The UN, in particular, might devise objective admission standards for such purposes. But such policies can also be used for the power-political objectives of particular nations, as is shown by the history of United States "recognition policies." The same applies to policies of foreign aid. Such help would seem to lend itself to stabilizing and thus legitimatizing new and/or under-developed countries. But aid *policy* can be used also to make these units "penetrable" through the creation of economic, technological, or military dependencies. Thus the future of the legitimacy of nations is intimately tied to problems of intervention and indirect penetration.

V. INTERVENTION AND NONALIGNMENT

At this juncture, foreign intervention, especially by "indirect penetration," [14] constitutes, perhaps, the most serious

12. Rupert Emerson, *From Empire to Nation* (Boston, 1960), p. 96.
13. On the effect of what he calls "collective legitimization" through acceptance into the UN, see Inis Claude, *Changing UN*, pp. 83 ff.
14. In his truly penetrating and enlightening study, *The Revolution in Statecraft* (New York, 1965), Andrew M. Scott calls this phenomenon "informal access" or "informal penetration."

threat to the future of nations and their "new territoriality."

In addition to nuclear permeability, certain new technological penetrabilities (for example, through observation and collection of information from space satellites and through telephotography) and the manifold opportunities created through economic, technical, and military assistance, indirect penetration adds the power-political opportunities that emerge from an "international civil war" situation among competing systems and ideologies. This quasi-war situation renders possible political-military penetration of a country through promoting or lending assistance to indigenous insurrectionist forces, an assistance which, in turn, may range from diplomatic aid (for example, recognition) rendered to a rebel regime to making portions ("volunteer" or otherwise) of one's own armed forces available. It may further mean penetration of the top level of a country's regime through bribery or similar "purchase" of top personnel, or the doctrinal penetration of such levels on the part of revolutionary regimes. In the pursuance of such policies one may exploit all the weaknesses and dissensions which exist in the penetrated unit, whether they originate in ethnic, religious, or other groups discriminated against, in depressed socioeconomic classes, or among ideologically opposed or alienated groups or individuals. As Scott puts it, "in a period of increasing informal access, a situation sometimes develops in which the critical boundary may not be the geographic one but one defined by the circumstances of the market, the location of the adherents of an opposing ideology, the location of a given racial or religious group, or the zone of effectiveness of counter-penetration efforts. . . . In an era of informal penetration, the attack on the legitimacy of the government in the target country frequently denies the very principle of legitimacy on which that government is based." [15]

Such penetration assisting the "revolutionary" side, or its threat, may in turn provoke similar penetration by powers interested in shoring up the existing unit and its regime. Defense agreements, military aid, training of troops, establishment of bases, economic-financial ties through investments,

15. Ibid., pp. 168–69.

aid, exclusive or predominant trade relations, currency arrangements, all of these are common means to establish or maintain influence which, especially in the case of newly independent, small, and weak units, frequently amounts to dependency coming close to what the "revolutionary" side (although engaging in similar policies in regard to "its" clients) denounces as "neocolonialism." Not only American penetration of countries allegedly or actually threatened with "subversion," but also continued French influence in formerly French African units are cases in point. On the "Eastern" side, in addition to (and even in competition with) Soviet (and their clients') efforts, Chinese and Castroite forces may be at work.

Civil war assisted from abroad in this way may result in the dissolution of statehood (through secession) or of the prevailing regimes (through revolution). Could there be a more glaring example of the "demise" of the territorial state?

While not playing down the importance of these phenomena, one can point out countertendencies and advance the hypothesis that they may prevail in the long run.

One of these is the lessening of revolutionary penetration and interference that has resulted from the "deradicalization" of Communist regimes. Of late, there has been much discussion of a worldwide trend toward "deideologization," the "end" or, at least, the "erosion" or "decline" of ideologies and of the corresponding movements, whether leftist or rightist, West or East. There is little doubt of the presence of this phenomenon as far as the once world-revolutionary doctrines and policies of the core-Communist power are concerned.[16] It has been apparent not only in doctrines of peaceful coexistence, peaceful liberation from colonialism, and peaceful transi-

16. As Robert C. Tucker has pointed out, the process should be referred to as "deradicalization" rather than "deideologization," because less radicalism in action may be accompanied by doctrinal emphasis on symbols of "nonchange." "Intensified *verbal* allegiance to ultimate ideological goals belongs to the pattern of deradicalization." "The Deradicalization of Marxist Movements," *American Political Science Review* 61, no. 2 (1967): 343 ff., 358. But even in this connection there is a decreasing line in regard to amount of and emphasis on doctrine running from Stalin through Khrushchev to the present Soviet rulers, and a corresponding decrease in expected reference and obeisance to ideology on the part of writers and scholars. Cf. Jean-Yves Calvez, "La place de l'idéologie," *Revue française de science politique* 17 (1967): 1050 ff.

tion from capitalism to socialism but, more importantly, in Soviet moderation of her actual attitudes in the face of tempting situations abroad, most strikingly, perhaps, in Vietnam. Inasmuch as there has been aid to revolutionary forces, this has been due chiefly to the Chinese factor, the felt necessity not to lose face in the eyes of leftist movements and parties throughout the world. Even with the Chinese themselves, for whom Soviet deradicalization has been a golden opportunity to claim world-revolutionary leadership, action has not matched proclamation. In a situation as close as the Vietnamese, assistance has consisted mainly of verbal advice rather than more forceful and substantial intervention. Only when danger struck really close to home, as in Korea after the UN forces crossed the 38th parallel, did they intervene more massively.

There seems to be growing realization among *all* Communist regimes that interference is promising only where conditions in the respective country or area are "ripe" for a revolution (or "war of liberation"), and that ripeness presupposes the readiness and ability of the indigenous forces to carry the brunt of the struggle. This has been stated repeatedly by both Soviet and Chinese spokesmen,[17] and it does not seem to be mere subterfuge. A long history of disappointment with Moscow-initiated and foreign-guided coups, uprisings, and riots from the Twenties (Hungary, Bavaria, Hamburg, China) to more recent times seems to have taught the Communist regimes a lesson. The situation that promises success cannot be created artificially; it must be based upon the "territorial imperative" motivating an indigenous population together with its leadership's revolutionary objectives.

But where indigenous forces are primarily responsible for a revolutionary victory, they are not likely to accept control or influence on the part of an assisting power—*vide* Yugoslavia and China herself. This, in turn, may lessen the temptation to intervene. And, by the same token, lessening of Communist

17. Interestingly, Trotsky, than whom no one was more "world-revolutionary," had declared in the 1920s that "only that revolution is viable which wins out of its own strength." Quoted in Ossip K. Flechtheim, *Bolschewismus 1917–1967: Von der Weltrevolution zum Sowjetimperium* (Vienna, 1967), p. 47.

interventionism may in due course diminish the West's concern with "world Communism" and its alleged "conspiracy" to control the world, and thus affect its policies of counter-interventionism. For twenty years there has not been a single Communist attempt to revolutionize a developed nation or society, or a corresponding attempt on the part of the West to "liberate" a Communist unit. Even in regard to the Third World there seems to be a decrease in such ventures. The United States has not seriously tried to "regain" a Communized country as close as Cuba. Much, however, in respect to the underdeveloped, overpopulated "South" of the world depends on its chances of development and modernization. On this vital problem see below.

We seem to be in a stage of transition from doctrinal-political splits, confrontations, and interventions toward a world of lessened antagonisms. In such a world, nation-states would be left in peace to develop their own systems and remain neutral themselves in regard to the great powers. Nonalignment is in line with nationalism as a legitimizing force; it also lessens the concern of the big that, by leaving small states alone, they might simply hand the opponent a chance to extend his influence. Under bipolar conditions, nonalignment could appear risky to the small because of absence of protection and guarantees. But even then alignment was not without dangers of its own—of becoming, for example, a target for the other side because of bases on one's soil. With the disintegration of the blocs noninvolvement will appear preferable to more and more of the weaker states. . . . Alignment, in such a case, cannot help but create concern in one superpower about the other's aggressive intentions, and may this way lead to "preventive" intervention; nonalignment reassures.[18] If this tendency should spread, increased stability of nations and of the nation-state system would ensue.

18. Burton, *International Relations*, has developed a theory according to which the international system of the future will be distinguished by a lessening of alliances and the substitution for "power politics" of nonalignment based chiefly on nationalism.

VI. OUTLOOK AND CONCLUSIONS

A good deal of attention has recently been paid to discoveries in the relatively young science of animal behavior (ethology); they relate to the so-called territorial nature of certain animal species. Biologists such as Konrad Lorenz and, following their lead, popularizers such as Robert Ardrey, have given us vivid descriptions of how animals in every major category (fish, birds, mammals) stake out an area as "their own," fix boundaries, defend their territory (singly, with a mate, or in small groups) against intruders, are motivated by their "territorial instinct" more powerfully when close to the center of their territory than when at a distance from it, and so forth. To perceive analogies to these striking phenomena in human affairs, and particularly in relations of nations to each other, is tempting, and the authors mentioned have not hesitated to jump to such conclusions. "The territorial nature of man is genetic and ineradicable." [19] The "territorial imperative" not only motivates individuals, such as peasants threatened with collectivization of their holdings, but accounts for the behavior patterns of nations and other human collectivities. For those of us in the social sciences who have previously emphasized the role of "territoriality," especially in international relations, it is tempting to find in these phenomena a biological and thus vastly more fundamental confirmation of their theories. If the "territorial imperative" that motivates the basic units of international relations is rooted in the nature of humans as animal species we do not have to worry about the future of the nation-state. Contrariwise, approaches that look forward to eventual replacement of territorial units with something nonterritorial, such as world government, would truly be proved utopian.

I suggest that we suspend judgment, however—at least for the time being. It seems that the ethological findings themselves are contested exactly in the area of our ancestors, or closest relatives, the primates.[20] And an unwarranted jumping

19. Robert Ardrey, *The Territorial Imperative: A Personal Inquiry into the Animal Origins of Property and Nations* (New York, 1966), p. 116.

20. See, for example, S. Carrighar, "War Is Not in Our Genes," *New York Times Magazine*, 10 September 1967.

to conclusions becomes patent when no evidence is offered that a genetically inherited instinct prevails in humans as it does in certain, but *only* certain animal species, or that what motivates individual animals (or possibly humans) or very small groups (like families or clans) the same way, that is, instinctively, motivates large societies, such as nations. Ardrey, for instance, is inconsistent when he claims that the territorial imperative that motivated Russian peasants tenaciously clinging to their plot of land was destroyed by collectivization (thus "proving" the eternal, because instinct-based, nature of private property) while at the same time asserting that the much larger collectivity, the nation, as such reacts instinctively to intrusion on "its" territory. Why, then, do not *kholchozes* develop their territorial instinct? True, in cases of threats to their very existence (such as we have discussed in connection with Israel, Algeria, etc.) nations' defensive behavior seems to be motivated by very elementary and powerful "imperatives." But even here there is no proof of *instinctive* behavior. And outside such marginal and truly "existential" situations the analogy is even less convincing. The more "normal" condition of nations competing for power (including territory) and thus getting involved in expansionism, armament races, and wars seems to go back rather to what I have called the "security dilemma," that is, the fear that competing units may deprive them of their land, resources, independence, and political existence. Animals do not "know"—as does man—that conspecific groups may become competitors for "hunting grounds" or other means of living; they do not "realize" that, if "their" territory proves insufficient to support a given number of them, they can solve this problem by invading others' territory, or, by the same token, that conspecific groups may attack them for these purposes.

It is thus a realization specific and unique to man that explains (in part, at least) competition for territory and scarce resources and accounts for intergroup conflicts, territorial defense and aggrandizement, and so forth. The social constellation deriving from this realization is different from one that would derive from genetically inherent instincts. For, if it is conscious competition for scarce resources rather than a territorial and/or aggressive instinct[21] that in the past has been the prime motive of humans and human societies, the outlook for the future of international relations must differ vastly from one based on the assumption of biological drives. Under the latter, territorial units must forever go on fighting for land and resources. But the security dilemma can at least be attenuated through scientific-technological progress that "modernizes" mankind and thus frees it from scarcity. Modernization thus raises the hope that nationhood could become stabilized, not on the basis of a territorial instinct, but on that of providing plenty for those it comprises. Our final hypothesis, therefore, refers to the modernization of the premodern world.

As we have pointed out before, industrial technology renders modernized nations ever more independent from natural resources outside their boundaries; they need no longer expand and conquer. For the presently underdeveloped nation modernization means liberation from economic dependencies (such as those of the present one-crop and one-resource countries). Modernization and economic development would also serve to confer on many units that legitimacy which, as pointed out before, they lack because of the absence or weakness of a "national" elite that would integrate them, despite ethnic and similar disparities, into a modern nation. Once national self-determination and national integration has been achieved all over the globe, expansionist nationalism will be discredited and, if practiced, will encounter the overriding strength of the other, defensive, nationalism. The latter is likely to remain the effective ideology of an age of technological modernity in which the hold of other traditional ideologies, creeds, and value systems tends to vanish.

But whether such consolidation of the nation-state and corresponding stability of the state system will be attained depends on whether at least a large proportion of the underdeveloped will be able to modernize themselves. Modernized countries have proved relatively stable; also, generally, they do not desire territory from others: not the Soviet Union from the

21. Aggressiveness is likewise claimed by Lorenz and others to be a genetically inherited human instinct; in this article, which deals primarily with territoriality, I cannot deal with this theory in detail.

United States, or vice versa, nor even, by now, Germany from France. But the underdeveloped are beset by every type of turmoil, radicalism, and foreign interventionism. It is therefore a problem of development and development policies; a question of whether the affluent nations will be able and willing to make the sacrifices that are required of them even though they themselves have their own problems of development and equity; above all, it is the problem of preventing overpopulation. The rapidly growing pressure of population outrunning resources not only prevents the underdeveloped from modernizing but may actually lead to conditions deteriorating so badly that territory may assume overwhelming importance again. Unless there is rapid and drastic population planning, excess populations will press against boundaries separating them from—for the most part equally overpopulated—neighbors, and wars may ensue with the violence of the primitive, elementary struggle for "hunting grounds" and "water holes," only now on a global plane. Territory would become an object of expansionism and conquest again, and nationalism assume, or reassume, the nature of antagonism and despair. The big and wealthy would withdraw into their poverty-surrounded nuclear fortresses, or else engage in renewed "international civil war." For the time being, so it appears, it is not internationalism, "universalism," or any other supranational model that constitutes the alternative to the territorial, or nation-state, system, but genuine, raw chaos.

Such chaos would lead to a system or, rather, a nonsystem of international relations in which the terms territoriality and statehood would hold scant meaning. If we consider how little has been done in these decisive decades to forestall such a development—hardly anything, for instance, in the vital areas of population control and of the widening gap between the underdeveloped and the affluent nations—the pessimistic conclusion that it is almost too late for the development of a system of "new territoriality" seems, realistically, to impose itself. Assuming, however, that the "almost" still leaves room for more hopeful potentialities, let us recall the hypotheses made above by summing up the most basic requirements for a development under which the new-old nation-state, the polity of the last decades of this century, might emerge.

First among these, I would list the spread of political, economic, and attitudinal modernity to the areas where legitimate nation-states have still to be established through such processes of modernization. What this presupposes demographically, technologically, economically has already been mentioned.

Second, to make sure that new states, as well as some of the old, do not fall prey to continual quarrels over territorial issues, such issues among them must be settled in such a way that boundaries encompass populations which consider themselves and are recognized by others as nationally satisfied and self-sufficient entities. This is a large order, and all devices of diplomacy, all procedures of international organization, all rules of law and institutions of adjudication must be utilized, developed, and possibly improved for their solution.

Third, we must count upon the continuing deradicalization of systems originally based on world-revolutionary doctrines, and a corresponding inclination of the other states to leave the choice of internal structure to the respective nations without trying to influence, interfere, or control. Among other things, this would imply that programs of foreign assistance be separated from political policies and/or transferred increasingly to international agencies, and that even in case of civil war outside powers abstain from assisting either side, including the one they consider the "legitimate government" of the unit in question; new international law might be developed to spell out the corresponding legal rules and commitments.

Last, but not least, under such hypotheses recourse to international violence would be reduced to two major categories: action in self-defense when, and only when, one's own territory is directly attacked or invaded; in the event the invader succeeds in occupying the area, continued resistance of its population through a combination of guerrilla warfare and nonviolent resistance to render the aggressor the "fly on the flypaper." The unavailability of the "big" instrumentalities of international violence—in the sense of our discussion above—might induce their possessors to forego intervention in such situations, just as they might forego intervening in civil wars according to our third hypothesis. If genuine, legitimate nations in this way become units of their own protection, urged on by a "territorial imperative" of the pattern set by countries like Switzerland and Israel, they may have a better chance to survive as independent states than under the system of alliances and similar pacts, in which "collective self-defense" all too often serves as a subterfuge for big-power intervention.

The function, then, of the future polity would still or again be that of providing group identity, protection, and welfare; in short, the legitimate function of the nation. And this neo-territorial world of nations, in addition, might salvage one feature of humanity which seems ever more threatened by the ongoing rush of mankind into the technological conformity of a synthetic planetary environment: diversity of life and culture, of traditions and civilizations. If the nation can preserve these values, it would at long last have emerged as that which the philosophers of early nationalism had expected it to be: the custodian of cultural diversity among groups mutually granting each other their peculiar worth. In the past that other, opposite type of nationalism, the exclusivist, xenophobic, expansionist, oppressive one, has rendered their expectation nugatory, causing instability and infinite suffering of nations and people. This small world of ours can no longer live with it. Chaotic instability is too high a price to pay for its fleeting triumphs in an inflammable world. Neo-territoriality will function only if and when the danger of nuclear destruction and the interdependence of humans and their societies on the globe will have made nations and their leaders aware that the destiny awaiting us is now common to all.

RELEVANCIES AND IRRELEVANCIES IN THE STUDY OF INTERNATIONAL RELATIONS

This chapter first appeared in *Polity* 4, no. 1 (Fall 1971): 25–47. Chiefly concerned with method, it is critical not so much of the "scientific method" as such as of its frequently trivial and irrelevant results. In a situation where the very survival of mankind is threatened not only by the nuclear weapon but by overpopulation, environmental deterioration, and other perils, political science—and international politics in particular—must become relevant. Relevant is that which is concerned with survival problems. The "great reversal" in attitudes and approaches called for in chapter 7 must also apply to the study of international relations. See further comments in the *Introduction*, pages 26–27.

Reprinted by permission of *Polity*, The Journal of the Northeastern Political Science Association.

I

In the never-ending parade of Great Debates which shake up, rend, and otherwise enliven the profession of political science, give flavor to its somewhat staid meetings, and occasionally embitter the collegial relations of its members, we have arrived at what one of the leaders of the second-but-last upheaval refers to as "post-behavioral revolution." [1] The "behavioralist revolution," in turn, had shaken what now is commonly called the classical or traditionalist school, whose adherents never ceased bemoaning that which characterizes or at least goes hand in hand with behavioralism: quantification and "hyper-factualism," on the one hand, and over-conceptualization and

---

1. David Easton, "The New Revolution in Political Science," *American Political Science Review* 63, no. 4 (1969): 1051 ff.

"hyperabstraction," on the other. If the leaders of the revolution of the 1950s[2] now mend their ways and admit to some of their sins, why another indictment?

What follows is not intended to knock down a straw man of extreme "scientist" (whether behavioralist, conceptualist, or quantitative), but rather to deal with a danger common to all approaches, that of irrelevance, or triviality. If, for the most part, behavioralists are singled out for criticism, this may be due to the fact that "scientific" methods apparently entail more of a risk of getting entangled with trivia (while the opposite danger of traditionalism is getting involved in "metaphysical" vaporousness, but that is another story). Also, I want, more specifically, to deal with the problem as it presents itself in an area not so frequently singled out for criticism, international relations.

International Relations, of course, is an eclectic field, but even if one deals with it under viewpoints of political science (that is, as international *politics,* disregarding international economics and so forth)—as I shall do in this essay—I submit that it partakes of the nature of applied rather than "basic" or "pure" science. One might compare it with medical science, pathology for instance, which on the basis of findings of pure sciences like biology, serves a practical objective: health, physical or mental, or (in the case of political science) societal or international; in other words, in this sense a policy science.

A science such as international politics is problem-oriented; it deals with the ills (present or anticipated) of its area (in this instance, the world); it may proceed from there to general "laws," or systems analysis, or model building, but the starting point and the emphasis is on the concrete and the practical. Does this imply despising "basic research"? First of all, it does not imply that international relations study should continue the tradition of the "Great Issues" debates of yore, with their overgeneralizations, simplifications, and fuzziness. On the contrary, to serve its objectives it must be founded on the most meticulous research into the details of its field; like

2. Besides Easton see also the articles by other initiators of behavioralism, such as Joseph LaPalombara and Roy Macridis in the issue devoted to the "comparative method" of *Comparative Politics* 1 (October 1968).

medicine, it must be aware of and familiar with the findings of the sciences on which it builds, whether demography or international finance, mathematical statistics or social psychology. Second, reduction of "theory" to a lower place may be warranted because of one special characteristic of what is now called "theory" or "science" in the social sciences:[3] in contrast to the immense practical impact natural science has through applied science and technology, it has so far had little impact on practice. Therefore, perhaps not as much is lost if "basic science" is relegated as Easton seems to fear when he says: "The failure to continue to add to our capital accumulation of basic social knowledge will see us tragically unprepared for even greater crises in the more distant future." [4] What, in basic knowledge so far accumulated, has prepared us for coping with the present crisis?

The problem is how to define "relevance" and distinguish it from the trivial. Does not every age, civilization, class, country, nay, individual look at the world in different ways and under different value standards? Is not what appears important to one irrelevant to others? Must not this rule out a problem-oriented approach that claims to be able to single out the important issues and the relevant problems? This is a particularly bothersome problem for one who, standing for relevance, yet is a "value relativist" who believes that, in principle, no "ought to" can be derived from an "is." But cannot perhaps a "should" be derived from a "will otherwise be" in the extreme case where "otherwise" denotes physical extinction of the entire human race? I submit that, when certain values become so overwhelmingly important that their nonrecognition (although in theory not disprovable) appears absurd not only to a "compact majority" but to practically everybody engaging in human discourse, they can be posited as certain, or undeniable. Such a value is survival, not in the

3. The revolution of the 1950s has brought about a significant shift in the use of the term "theory" as monopolized by the new "scientists." It used to denote what Frank M. Russell dealt with in his "Theories of International Relations" (1936), but in 1968 I could get a survey of this subject matter into the *International Encyclopedia of the Social Sciences* only by disguising it as "International Relations: Ideological Aspects"!

4. "New Revolution," p. 1055.

sense of individual survival or even that of particular groups but of the human race, plus that of the total environment in which mankind can live.

This is the extreme condition in which, for the first time in its history, mankind finds itself today. The combined effects of the population-resources-environment-nuclear arms crises have created a situation of such urgency that general agreement on relevance should now be possible. When a serious natural scientist can make the statement "I suppose we have between 35 and 100 years before the end of life on earth," [5] it illuminates a threat of extinction and, with it, an emergency situation which, as such, defines what is relevant now. In contrast to what classical phenomenology (Edmund Husserl) called "Lebenswelt" (the experienced world we used to live in, which did not yield uncontested standards for ultimate relevance), our present "Ueberlebenswelt" (survival world) does yield them in the form of survival values. Albert Schweitzer's dictum "what supports life is good" applies now to the continuance of human life on earth.

If the problems of the present are so overwhelming, it is all the more important that we grasp clearly the significant characteristics of the age. They can, I believe, be summed up under the heading of the "acceleration process": decisive developments of our world can be cast in the form of a curve (usually an "exponential" one) which illustrates almost everything that counts in today's affairs, whether it concerns trends in world population or energy consumption, exhaustion of resources, urbanization or rate of pollution, scientific findings or technical innovation, speeds of transportation or communication. It is a curve that starts moving upward gradually, hardly noticeable over earlier periods but at some point turning upward ever more steeply until it becomes almost vertical. It is this onrush of events, the increase in the *rate* of speeds or other transformations, which puts its imprint on present-day life, within and among nations; and which may involve our rush into oblivion. Nothing, even in areas and regions not yet affected by the scientific-technological process,

5. See Anthony Lewis' column, "Not with a Bang but a Gasp" in *New York Times*, 15 December 1969.

seems to escape it. It constitutes the most basic structural phenomenon of our world, and we had better recognize it as such if we want to cope with the trends and try to solve the problems it creates. Almost stark in its simplicity, the acceleration process may yet escape sufficient attention in some areas. To be sure, certain phenomena, such as the increase in arms production and ensuing armament races among nuclear powers, are eminently noticeable, but others, such as the population increase, are characterized by what has been called "the paradox of aggregation," that is, that acceleration there moves in small, almost imperceptible steps and for this reason fails to worry us; or it permits us to postpone doing something about it to a never-reached mañana.

What I have said does not imply demeaning method and study of detail in favor of grandiose suggestions for overall planning. Great problems are usually easy to discern, but the details are infinitely complex, and in dealing with them all modern method has its place. The devil, as the Germans say, is in the detail. Analysis of overall systems without intimate knowledge of the concrete remains vague. But exclusive devotion to detail is liable to miss the relevant and yield trivialities. Researchers, then, may get lost in the woods, counting the twigs and the branches of the trees while no longer aware that they started out to engage in forestry. We can no longer afford a *l'art pour l'art* type of assembling facts and analyzing data for their own sake, because time is running out. Moreover, such an approach is liable to divert attention (and funds, and energy) away from the relevant issues and thus have a politically conservative, quietistic effect. What we need is discussion of great issues on the basis of precise method and exact analysis.

Lastly, the speed with which we are swept toward situations that put mankind's existence in jeopardy must render international relations research future-oriented. Only that which has a potential bearing on the future can be considered as relevant. We must explore what future, or which alternative futures, are possible on the basis of present conditions and trends. Objective inquiry remains the basis from which to start. But empirical research remains meaningful only if we relate it to problems standing in urgent need of solution, such as birth control and environment planning; arms control and development aid; area control from outer space to the ocean floor; and, for students of international politics in particular, the effects of all the accelerating world trends upon the structure of, and the relations among, nation-states. Only that which has relevance for this kind of substantive problem can be called relevant to the study of international relations. Perhaps more than in any other field of scholarship and research, those engaged in international affairs must substitute for the ideal of the uncommitted, ivory-tower researcher that of *homme engagé*, if not *homme révolté*.

What has been said will, perhaps, gain in clarity by some criticism of the more recent research and method, some remarks concerning methods and subject matter that appear particularly promising and some of which have been neglected, and a few words on the "futurological" orientation upon which relevant research must model itself.

II

About twenty-five years ago a well-known political scientist said that political science is not a science because it has not developed a language of its own, unintelligible to the laity. Under this definition we are now scientists. As an editor of a political science journal I am condemned to read in the manuscripts submitted to us things like this—and I select at random:

> This dichotomy of open- and closed-mindedness may be thought of as a discrete classification of Latent Attitude Structure (LSA) reflecting the basic personality structure. These two poles represent ideal types. From one pole to the other, the concept of open-closed forms a continuous variable.

All this amounted to—and the author was honest enough to say so in the subsequent sentence—was, "In other words, individuals are more or less tolerant or dogmatic." But to invent "LSA" surely was more scientific, or at least sounded so. So does "interest aggregation" and "interest articulation" instead of the traditional terms for the activities of political parties and interest groups, "integrated role networks" for institutions, "authoritative allocation of values" for decision-making by holders of authority, and so *ad infinitum* and *ad nauseam*.

One need not object to new terminology as long as the user knows what he is talking about and makes it clear to the reader. Every science needs a vocabulary of basic concepts, and the question boils down to whether traditional or common language terms best fit the purpose. But one cannot avoid the impression that much of what has been invented (or taken over from an equally guilty sociology or psychology) has been introduced in order to "become unintelligible to the laity" rather than to specify or clarify. And much of the "sin" is due to the tendencies toward unnecessary abstraction, quantification, mathematization, etc., on which something will be said now and to which this language criticism was only meant to be the introduction.

One chief danger of quantification lies in something which can almost be called a law of scientism, to wit: what *can* be counted *will* be counted. I have chosen at random some pieces from a well-known reader in international politics,[6] whose editor has assembled what is done at the "frontiers of knowledge." One researcher has studied the "interaction behavior" of delegates to international conferences,[7] that is, he observed and counted who, during a number of sessions of a UN committee, got up and talked privately with whom else. It's a lengthy study, complete with tables, diagrams, figures. But since the subject matter of these "interactions" remained unknown, nothing more could be observed than that certain delegates were more frequented than others; the mystery of

6. James N. Rosenau, ed., *International Politics and Foreign Policy, A Reader in Research and Theory* (rev. ed.; New York, 1969). I would like to emphasize that what follows entails no criticism of the reader as such. On the contrary; it's a splendid selection (and besides, I have an article in it myself!).

7. "Interaction and Negotiation in a Committee of the United Nations General Assembly," in ibid., pp. 483–97. The study has been called "in many respects a model of careful behavioral research." Robert E. Riggs and others, "Behavioralism in the Study of the United Nations," *World Politics* 22 (January 1970): 197 ff. May be, but what for?

the "smoke-filled room" type of negotiation was not lifted.
When observing animal behavior, this kind of approach makes
sense, *faute de mieux;* but here, humans were reduced to
animals. In another study one counted "visits between heads
of state and other high-level government officials" over a
period of time, as reported in the *New York Times.*[8] This was to
throw light on "influence relationships among nations" (who
has to go to see whom), but there was the same abstraction
from the contents and the meaning of the visits, and the results
added little to the impression a conscientious reader of the
Times or any other regular follower of world news would get
anyway.

Content analysis also counts; this, indeed, is its very
essence. In our reader there is an item content-analyzing
statements by John Foster Dulles on Soviets and Communism,
revealing his well-known prejudices.[9] While it is important to
study perception, prejudices, belief-systems, images of opponents, and so forth (on this problem of "blinkers" of policy-
makers see below), it remains doubtful whether content
analysis can add much that non-numerical research fails to
show. And what it shows must be carefully evaluated. What,
for instance, might a similar study reveal about whether Stalin,
in his public statements, was influenced by doctrine or merely
mouthed it? My first encounter with a content-analyzer was
when I worked in one of the war agencies during World War II
and a young and eager student fresh from Harold Lasswell's
seminar suggested searching utterances by Hitler and assorted
other Nazi leaders for their strategic intentions; a comprehensive effort yielded nothing that anybody familiar with Nazi
doctrine and policy did not know, and I doubt whether it
helped curtail the war by one hour. Although content analysis
has become a bit more sophisticated by now, weighing in
addition to counting, one may still wonder how many man-
hours are used for similar nonpurposes in government agencies at this very moment.

Among other quantifying studies I mention the celebrated

8. Rosenau, "The Structure of Influence Relationships in the International System," pp. 583–99.
9. Rosenau, "The Belief-System and National Images, A Case Study," pp.
543–50.

study by Singer and Small on alliance commitment and war involvement covering the period from 1818 to 1945.[10] With its vast array of tables and correlations it resulted in a finding—and even this was hedged around with some qualifications—that "alliance commitment predicts to war involvement"; that is, alliances are generally meaningful, and corresponding commitments are usually observed. It seems to me that a much simpler way of finding out what happened to alliance commitments would have been to take each war and ask: was there a preexisting alliance? and was it observed? More relevant, in my view, would be to find out which ally backed up which country in which war and why; and still more relevant, perhaps, to single out the cases in which alliance commitments were *not* kept and analyze these "in depth." For that, it is true, a study of specific cases would be necessary, but it would in all likelihood be more revealing than a "data making" which treats some hundred alliances as equal particles in statistical fashion.

Much of this kind of study in international conflict and violence is dubious because it must treat each conflict (with the exception of a few quantifiable factors, such as number of casualties) alike, regardless of the period, the environment, or the civilization in which it occurs.[11] And little by way of conclusion can be drawn when basic underlying concepts, such as victory, defeat, aggression, even initiation of war, are left undefined. I remember hearing Karl Deutsch report to the APSA convention of 1969 findings according to which in the nineteenth century three-fifths of all wars were won by their

10. Rosenau, "National Alliance Commitment and War Involvement, 1818–1945," pp. 513–42. An elaborate study by the same authors (J. David Singer and Melvin Small, "The Composition and Status Ordering of the International System, 1815–1940," *World Politics* 18 [1956/66]: 236ff.) counted the number of diplomatic missions sent and received by governments over more than a century. In its results it is even more disappointing than the alliance study. The rank order of nations it "reveals" has been known anyway to any knowledgeable student of diplomatic history (to the extent that ranking can be quantified at all).

11. It all started with Quincy Wright. I remember him presenting what subsequently went into *A Study of War* in a seminar at the Geneva *Institut Universitaire de Hautes Etudes Internationales* in the 1930s, where his chiefly European students, although greatly impressed by the wealth of his data, were flabbergasted by the unsophisticated use of the historical and cultural variables.

initiators, while after 1911 three-fifths were lost. The obvious conclusion would be that starting a war "paid" in the 19th century but no longer does so in ours. But what *does* it prove? In my opinion little, if only because all depends on what meaning is given to terms like "initiating," "loss," or "victory": who initiated the (1967) June War? who, indeed, World War I? who won the Korean war?

Gaming and internation simulation are examples, not so much of quantification techniques as of a laboratory (and that means, apparently, ultrascientific) approach to the study of international behavior. In our reader we have, first of all, the by now famous, or notorious, simulation of the outbreak of World War I (That is, the crisis days preceding the outbreak).[12] I have no doubt that simulation can serve as tool for educational purposes. Students can learn from it. So can teachers, and maybe even practitioners of international politics. But in regard to the question of what theoretical insights it provides into the process of policy- and decision-making during international crises, doubts are in order. Meaningful results would seem to depend on whether and to what extent a "fit" can be established between the real and the simulated events and whether the players can be matched with the historical figures. In the example under discussion, "the CPI (California Psychological Inventory) profile of each prospective participant was compared with that of each historical figure" (*Quaere:* when and where did the emperors, chancellors, and prime ministers have their "profiles" taken?) Even so, when American high school kids in the 1960s are selected to play the roles of Nicholas, Tsar of all the Russians, and William II, Emperor of the Teutons, a high degree of insensitivity to the cultural-historical dimensions of the case is revealed. It so happened that in one "run" of this simulation the kids were apparently inclined to settle the issue peacefully through conference and thus avoid war. Perhaps this shows that, not Plato's philosopher-kings but high school kids should rule, having more sense than the usual run of "statesmen." Maybe so, but the simulators, in their report, do not arrive at this or any other

12. Rosenau, "An Attempt to Simulate the Outbreak of World War I," pp. 622–39.

conclusion. Generalizations such as "communications be-tween opposing blocs will be less than among alliance part-ners" are perhaps interesting, but didn't we know this before? Was it worth the "input" in terms of time, funds, and efforts?

Computer simulation hardly yielded more. The case I refer to likewise concerned the World War I crisis, processing communication flows between the Tsar and the Kaiser.[13] Obviously, there comes out what you put in and since, in this case, the computer was fed hypotheses such as "people pay more attention to news that deals with them" and "less to facts that contradict their previous views," the results were predict-able. It would seem more important to test the hypotheses themselves and, if they are found correct, ask what to do about the respective behavior-patterns of policy-makers.

In another case of using allegedly new approaches to the study of international relations the author claimed that "devel-opments in theory building in international relations . . . seem to have neglected international organization."[14] He thereupon proceeded to apply to problems of international organization Almond's structural functionalism, using his concepts of so-cialization and recruitment, interest articulation and aggrega-tion, rule-making and rule-application: "the whole works." The "output" of all this "input" was minimal. It amounted to applying new terminology to known and much worked-over phenomena, such as: who emerges as leader and influences others in an international system or, which governmental and nongovernmental pressures play on international organiza-tions?

What is most striking in all of these examples is the poverty of relevant findings despite the frequent refinement of method. This shortcoming has been noted by many. According to one critic, it is due to the "compulsion to theorize" which animates "law-makers, model-builders, and paradigm-mold-ers."[15] Anther critic indicts "an escape to abstraction to avoid

13. Rosenau, "The Kaiser, the Tsar, and the Computer: Information Processing in a Crisis," pp. 664–78.

14. Rosenau, "A Functional Approach to International Organization," pp. 131–41.

15. Albert O. Hirschman, "The Search for Paradigms as a Hindrance to Understanding," World Politics 22 (April 1970): 329ff.

the consequences of close contact with the realities of politics." [16] And even a supporter of the "new science," summing up a survey of behavioralist studies of the United Nations, had to conclude: "Yet, the literature, with the exception of the voting studies, is largely noncumulative." [17] This is it: in contrast to the integration and the progress of the natural sciences, each effort here stands by itself, without leading to more general insight and conclusion.

If in the last mentioned critique voting studies are exempted, this points up a more general phenomenon, namely, that quantification lends itself best to situations involving large numbers of actors; survey research of populations, of course, has proved the most conspicuous and (provided the samples are representative and the questions relevant) most successful technique to date. In international relations, this would mean studies of attitude patterns of people within nations concerning foreign policy problems. Studies of action- and behavior patterns of smaller groups, such as legislatures domestically and General Assembly types of international bodies, in contrast, are hampered by the fact that changes in the policies of a few members may affect the conclusions drawn from studies like those on UN bloc voting. The danger is that one projects into the future what one has found in the past. As in the case of the now so fashionable research into judicial behavior (where the unforeseen shift to "conservatism" of one Supreme Court judge out-dated volumes of analyses), voting patterns in international bodies are liable to change in ways difficult to predict. This is not to imply that prediction based on past performance is impossible. It is not, provided one keeps in mind that consistency in behavior depends on identity of the actor, which, in international affairs, is often interrupted through change of system, revolution, merger, etc.

The failure of many adopting the new methods to predict correctly must constitute a most conspicuous failure of political science in the eyes of a public that considers political scientists experts on politics; it may come to consider pure waste the vast expenditure of time, effort, and resources which

16. Henry L. Bretton, "Political Science Field Research in Africa," *Comparative Politics* 2 (April 1970): 437.
17. Riggs, "Behavioralism in UN," p. 231.

goes into scholarly research, especially when it uses such an impressive apparatus of scientific-looking method. Who among us, studying, for instance, "political socialization," predicted the sudden and radical break in the attitudes of the young? There we were, right in the midst of them, but, busy with trivia, we failed to see what was going on.

Let me refer to only one case illustrating "predictive" failure. In its December issue of 1968 the APSR published an article entitled "Measuring Social and Political Requirements for System Stability in Latin America." [18] Its authors, after meticulous search for an analysis of large numbers of indicators of stability and instability, made certain predictions. The following is from a letter I sent to the editor of the Review (and which remained unpublished):

> To the Editor of APSR:
> In Ernest A. Duff's and John McCamant's article "Measuring Social and Political Requirements for System Stability in Latin America" the following "Predictions" are found under the heading of "System Stability Profiles": Panama: "Continued democratic stability with minor difficulties . . ."; Brazil: "A semi-democratic system should be able to survive minor manifestations of discontent . . ."; Peru: "Continued democratic government with a strong probability of lessening military interference. . . ." By the time the issue in which the article is published was out, "democratic stability" in Panama had given way to assumption of power by military junta; whatever "semi-democracy" there had been in Brazil had been replaced by dictatorial rule; and the "democratic government" in Peru, with its "probability of lessening military interference," had yielded to control by the military.[19]

18. *APSR* 62 (December 1968): 1125–43.
19. "Stability" and "instability" studies, especially when dealing with developing nations, usually disregard one major variable, namely, foreign influence; that is, the fact that many of these units are "penetrated systems," whose development, modernization, etc., is influenced by foreign capital investment and what it is used for, by foreign aid policies, by actual or threatened intervention on the part of economically interested or even controlling powers, or (as in the case of some African states) these powers' readiness to fly in paratroopers whenever a regime they favor is tottering. How does all of this affect structural stability or change? In the usual

It is perhaps presumptuous to claim more for traditionalists, but some of them have been able to predict outcomes on the basis of common sense analysis for which no gaming or computer-feeding was necessary. Hans Morgenthau's prediction that nothing will come of the Paris peace negotiations as long as we permit the present South Vietnamese government to be a copartner because no government will negotiate its own demise is a simple conclusion for which no ever-so-sophisticated analysis of the decision-making process, of alliances, of coalitions, or of conflict resolution is required. Perhaps political "science" shares with meteorology the problem that, frequently, there are just too many variables even for computerizing; one or a few minor ones may throw developments into one or the opposite direction. Hence the importance of being familiar with the cultural-historical dimensions of the situation and area in question, and the importance of "informed guesses," hunches, intuition (which, of course, must be based on all available data).

Some of my scientific colleagues have tried to explain a yield they admit is small in terms of relevance by referring to the novelty of the method. All considered, they say, it is only fifteen to twenty years old. But if one takes into consideration the size of the output, the number of persons and institutions engaged in it, the support it has found through organizations like the SSRC, etc., this research must by now surpass the sum total of traditionalist research since the latter started some forty or fifty years ago. After all, we have the same "acceleration curve" at work in the area of scholarly output as everywhere else.

III

All great political theory (or political philosophy) in the past started from concrete situations and relevant problems: Plato's from those of a degenerating Athenian democracy;

comparative politics studies the data on calorie intake, literacy percentages, and the like, which they use, remain generally uncorrelated to this very relevant international relations-type of factors.

Hobbes' from civil war and the threat of anarchy; Rousseau's from what seemed to him a degeneration of European civilization and a decay of civic spirit; Marx's from exploitation of industrial workers through class rule and ensuing human alienation; and so forth. But it is difficult to perceive a connection between what today is called "theory" and the great problems of the age.

It would be presumptuous on my part to tell my confreres how to deal with great problems in such a way that new Platos and Rousseaus may emerge. All I intend is to indicate a few areas where research seems particularly necessary because of past neglect, and to mention ways which may facilitate meaningful research.

I begin with the latter: we might, perhaps, try out selecting, as topics, the immediately "salient" and concrete (that which our better journalists uncover as life and death problems of a country, or society, or region) and then work our way back to whatever more general conclusions and more abstract findings become possible. This would be in the place of assembling vast numbers of quantitative data from handbooks of political and social indicators or dimensionality of nations compilations, and juggling them around until they yield some usually bland and irrelevant results.[20] In other words, let us begin with the pathology of politics. Violence (domestic and international) has been covered quite fully (although as mentioned, often in overly quantifying fashion), but what about that which follows upon, or provokes, international violence: police (or military) repression? What about a comparative study of police methods (including surveillance, investigation, torture), from Moscow over Athens and Madrid to Rio and Chicago? In this way, perhaps we could learn something about variants of the repressive features of different types of political systems (instead of measuring them by some "unpolitical" factors), which, in turn, might enable us to define or refine general concepts (for example, of democracy, totalitarianism, etc.). How about studying the phenomenon of corruption, the vari-

20. I do not mean to belittle the importance of having these data. Assembling them constitutes respectable quantitative effort but it forms merely the basis for more relevant research.

ous forms in which it appears at different spots in the political system and its impact on the functions and the functioning of the system? [21] Starting from there, we might conceivably arrive at some "systems analysis" type of conclusions. What about studying the intelligence agencies of different powers (turning ourselves into a kind of counterintelligence) and their role in other countries? If enterprising newspapermen can dig up the facts, why can't students of politics and international relations? Coming closer to "survival" problems, one might engage in a comparative study of pollution controls (including the objections, resistances, evasive tactics on the part of government agencies and private interests which they tend to provoke). There probably exist, within the respective disciplines, comparative studies of welfare systems, of poverty, etc., but we, as political scientists, have long neglected the politics involved.[22] In all these instances (and the above, of course, is meant as mere random exemplification, with some more particularly "international" examples to follow below), theoretically meaningful results are likely to ensue.

It is true that data in areas such as police systems, or systems of repression in military or other dictatorships, may not so easily be come by as are those available in official government statistics, and the respective research may involve personal risk. But the yields will be more rewarding. Dimensionality data are, per se, one-dimensional, and research based exclusively on them is liable to set up one-dimensional men and one-dimensional nations. We then study and analyze election figures regardless of whether the elections were phony, or engage in studies on the "incidence" of violence without considering situations where open violence was prevented because of the overwhelmingly repressive nature of a system (which we then, in the absence of open violence, tend to consider as "stable").[23]

21. Some relevant material has been collected by Arnold Heidenheimer in a useful volume, *Political Corruption, Readings in Comparative Analysis* (New York, 1970).

22. Easton, "New Revolution," p. 1057, has figures on the small number of articles in *APSR* which over a decade dealt with poverty (one!), race relations, etc.

23. See, for example, conclusions drawn in an otherwise interesting and informative article on "Patterns of Political Violence in Comparative Historical Perspective," *Comparative Politics* (October 1970): 1 ff.

Turning now to international politics proper, analyses of international systems in the nuclear age (such as Morton Kaplan's variations on the theme of types of systems, or Kenneth Waltz's and others' debate on bipolarity and multipolarity) are familiar, but there is little about how the possession or nonpossession of nuclear weapons affects national leaders and publics, policies and decision-making processes. Intuitive observations, such as one by Charles Yost, who remarked, apropos Czechoslovakia in 1968, that "the only country a big power can still attack with impunity is one of its allies," illuminates entire landscapes in the field of power and bloc relations; but they must be underpinned, or qualified, by more detailed study. In the following I would like to outline a few areas in which such study seems particularly necessary.

One we still know too little about is that of the "determinants" of foreign policy and foreign policy-making. Thus an article by Graham T. Allison, wherein the Cuban missile crisis serves as a starting point for model-building in the field of strategic and foreign policy decision-making,[24] is full of interesting observations and suggestions, especially on how a leader's role and position in the complex of the foreign policy elite of a country determines or influences decisions, but it raises more questions than it answers. The author quotes Robert Kennedy as having said that, if any of six advisors to the president had been president, the world might have been blown up. But, on the other hand, he quotes somebody who said, "Where you stand depends on where you sit"; that is, had one of the chiefs-of-staff, for instance, sat in the president's chair, he would have acted as JFK did. What *is* the impact of role and position? Furthermore, the author contrasts what he calls the "rational policy model" (that centers around the "national interest," etc.) with two other models according to which foreign policy is the outcome of preexisting organizational factors and/or the competition, deals, and compromises among governmental bureaucracies. That the impact of "national interest" perceptions has been emphasized at the neglect of other factors certainly is a valid argument. But we

24. "Conceptual Models and the Cuban Missile Crisis," *APSR* 63 (September 1969): 689 ff.

need to know more about the other influences; for instance, about *how* the military influences foreign policy-making in all sorts of countries and systems. The need to know is most urgent in relation to foreign policy decision-making in imperial states like the United States, in view of the growing number of domestic participants and the complexity of their relationships. If only to counter Marxian or similar reductionism, we need to know more on the impact of the profit motive and of general "bourgeois" ideology of the type of "what is good for General Motors is good for the country." Generalities on the role of a military-industrial complex or of investment interests are not very helpful as long as they remain vague and general or, where dealing with specific instances, fail to tie them up with the decision-making process.

From the study of problems like these we can move toward studying the impact of perception, role, and psychology generally. As for "perception," its role in foreign policy-making can hardly be exaggerated, and study of its impact has hardly begun. Even the "national interest," to the extent that it does influence policy making, does so only in the shape it is perceived by the decision-maker; it is not something that presents itself "objectively" to the actor (as even the otherwise so perceptive Hans Morgenthau seems to assume). There is here a gamut of factors that determine how it is perceived in the specific instance, ranging all the way from ideology and doctrine over class and similar background and interest to personal background and personality structure of the perceiver. Thus, specific group or "caste" prejudices may mold foreign-policy elites; one might investigate the impact of "cold war" prejudices on entrants into such an elite: in the case of the United States, even the (by background) "liberal" newcomers to the foreign service soon seem to acquire the "hard-nosed" so-called realism of the older administrators (consider also the now typical conception of oneself as "manager": "security manager," "crisis manager").

Connected with this, and with the acceleration phenomenon, there is the problem of how to absorb a rapidly increasing flow of information. What is heard, and what gets lost in the "noise"? Perception, basis of action, in turn is based on incoming information. Karl Deutsch has built an entire theory upon the cybernetic function of communication flows among actors.[25] How and by whom is that flow controlled on its way to the decision-maker? Perception also determines how actors conceive of their country's role in world affairs: whether they visualize it as big, medium, or small power, or as non-aligned or "naturally" belonging to one or another group or bloc; they may have differing images of the international system as such, which may appear to them as one of balance or imbalance (perhaps to be rebalanced), of bi- or multipolarity, or even as no "system" at all, that is, as a chaotic play of forces in a world where the actor has to make the best of it for his unit.

From images and perceptions we are inevitably led to problems of role playing and psychology. We have remarked upon the role of "role" in connection with the article by Allison. There is a rather long but still incomplete effort to elucidate this cluster of problems. Already prior to Parsons and his school, students of international affairs such as Georges Scelle had discovered the importance of what Scelle called *dédoublement fonctionnel,* the overlapping role functions of foreign policy-makers *qua* domestic agents *and* agents of international society (for example, in treaty and agreement making; that is, in international legislation). In a more complex form such a *dédoublement* appears in Reinhold Niebuhr's theory of "moral man and immoral society," of individuals acting "for," that is, in the name of, a group for which they feel responsible but which also may absolve them of individual moral or psychological constraints (the family father doing "for" his family what he would not do by and for himself, the business chief acting "immorally" or even illegally "for the good of the firm," the statesman "for the good of his country"; a classical definition of a diplomat was to the effect that he is "an honest man sent abroad to lie for the best of his country"). Wanted: a joint political-sociological-psychological study of the impact of foreign policy roles upon the attitudes and action-patterns of foreign policy elites.

The trouble with applying psychology to political science

25. Something which can be overdone unless, as William Fox has observed with fine irony, "the bits of metal exchanged through the air by modern states in wartime are also treated as messages." William T. R. Fox, *The American Study of Internation Relations* (1968), p. 104.

or international relations is that the psychologists, psychiatrists, and psychoanalysts themselves are so frequently in disagreement about basic problems and findings of their discipline(s). But if, as students of international relations, as I have pointed out in the beginning, we must rely on basic sciences, we cannot avoid delving into what a science such as psychology can offer. If we have to deal with political consequences of urbanization, we cannot afford to neglect what psychologists have found out about the psychological effects of crowding or noise. We must do our best to single out what has been found and is no longer a matter of controversy. Above all, we must avoid loose talk, ours and that of the psychologists. The latter, all too often, jump to conclusions in fields not their own. Konrad Lorenz and his disciples, then, apply the concept of innate human aggressiveness (itself contested by other ethologists and psychologists) to the realm of social groupings, such as nations. But "aggression" and "aggressivity" may have a quite different, nonpsychological connotation in, for example, international relations. Let me refer to a recent publication by a German psychologist, which may illustrate what we can learn and what we must reject.[26] Its author, Arno Plack, shows that much in the social and political life of people and nations, especially in the area of crime, violence, etc., can be explained by sexual repression and the corresponding taboos, norms, laws, threats of punishment, and so forth. He then tries to show that absence of such repression in the family and sex structures of certain tribes (with polygamy or sexual permissiveness systems) accounts for the peaceful nature of domestic as well as intertribal relationships that anthropologists like Malinowsky and Ruth Benedict have observed among the Trobrianders and some Eskimo tribes. From there, however, he jumps to modern societies and modern nations and to the conclusion that not only crimes committed in modern war (war crimes) or the "legalized crime" of killing or wounding "lawful combatants" in war are explained by the system of sexual repression and frustration prevalent in modern society but the outbreak, that

26. Arno Plack, *Die Gesellschaft und das Boese, Eine Kritik der herrschenden Moral* (Munich, 1968). The book deserves to be made available in translation.

is, the occurrence of war itself. The confusion, typical of other psychologists or anthropologists, arises because one overlooks the fact that psychological factors may be necessary but not sufficient conditions. Frustration (caused by repression, sexual or other) may account for brutalization and may in part explain what happens in war but not (or not sufficiently) war's occurrence. Plack, for example, mixes up the elites responsible for the outbreak of a war and the soldiers fighting it; and he tends to overlook the other motives (ranging all the way from economic ones to the "security dilemma" of nations) that may have caused a specific war. It is indeed vital for the student of war and peace to know more about the psychological factors that play on leaders and masses; both psychoanalytical findings (applying to individuals in modern societies) and the findings of anthropologists (applying to members of so-called "primitive" civilizations) must be taken into consideration. But we must be wary of the generalizations many psychologists are prone to, the pan-sexualism of the Freudians as well as others.[27] We also should not overlook some simpler findings of classical psychologists who, without benefit of the more refined psychoanalytical theories, occasionally expressed verities relevant for political scientists (and others); for example, the one—already known to early American "realists" like Hamilton—which teaches that beneficial action, rather than engendering gratitude, is liable to cause resentment on the part of the beneficiary against the benefactor. *Vide* de Gaulle and the Anglo Saxons.[28]

IV

If we want our efforts to be relevant we must, as I have said in the beginning, deal with the "survival" problems of our

27. There is now a theory abroad which, in contrast to Freud's oedipal-patricidal instinct, claims an instinct of "filicide" as underlying war and related phenomena; evidence such as the widespread incidence of cruelty to children notwithstanding, one might ask whether, in war, parents want their own children, rather than those of the enemy, killed. *"Allons enfants de la patrie,"* also referred to as evidence, says *"allons,"* not *"allez"*!

28. In Israel I heard a story about an Arab farmer on the Left Bank who had benefited from Israeli aid in making his farm more productive. He admitted this but said: "And I hate you all the more for it."

time and world. This calls for three things: that our research be future-oriented; that we approach problems from a global viewpoint, realizing that the world is now one and the threats to survival global; and that, as scholars, we try to become influential with those who, over the coming decades, can still be expected to make the vital decisions—the leaders of nations. I will conclude with a few remarks upon each of these requirements.

"Futurology" (or "futuristic"), the science, or art, of prognostic, is still suspect to some as a kind of social-science astrology, but if it ever went through that stage, it has developed by now into a respectable type of scholarly approach to the fields in which it is applied. In Europe, in particular, scholars such as political scientists, "peace researchers," and others, have joined in efforts to establish scholarly standards and methods.[29] Futurology has become less concerned with forecasting what *will* happen than with elaborating what *may* happen, what we can prepare for, what can be planned. Futurological research, of course, must be preeminently careful to start from most meticulous consideration of factors present and past so as to derive from them what is feasible. It also must avoid being overly impressed with the most spectacular of the trends, the accelerating scientific technological progress, and thus land in a science fiction type of prognosis that overlooks or plays down the nontechnological areas and trends. In respect to technology, what counts is the channelling, limitation, control of a runaway technology which must become a "technology with a human face."

With the crisis problems in which the world is entangled, relevant futurological research in the social sciences turns out to be either peace research or environment research. As a fundamental standard, or norm, for such research one can perhaps define a value-maximizing, committed futurological approach as one which analyzes choices among possible

29. There is by now a whole literature on these matters, there are institutes and periodical publications. Status and development of futurology, the theoretical problems it encounters, its methods, its relation to planning, etc., have been summarized in a comprehensive volume by the inventor of the term "futurology" and its indefatigable promoter, Ossip K. Flechtheim (see his *Futurologie, der Kampf um die Zukunft* [Cologne, 1970]).

futures on the basis of policy preferences under which mankind can live. That is, future-oriented international relations research must establish models for a world in which mankind can survive. Thus, in thinking about alternate futures, researchers must distinguish what is inevitable (for example, choosing an example from demography, continued global increase in population at least for a period of time), what is feasible (for example, a choice between noninterference and interference with population growth), and what is desirable under value-maximizing standards. And then they must study means and policies to attain the objective: for example, in regard to the population explosion, how can one influence the birthrate in developing countries? Should foreign aid be made conditional upon adoption and implementation of practicable family control programs by aid-receiving countries? [30]

It is here that study of international law and international organization becomes relevant. They constitute the natural vantage point from which to view matters globally and to approach problems from an internationalist or (as I once called it) "universalist" viewpoint; that is, one which considers the interests of mankind as overriding those of any of its political or other subunits. I think it can be demonstrated that, in the long run, national and subnational interests are *not* inconsistent with the universal interest in survival, security, and development; there is a long-range common interest in arms control, control of populations and resources, peaceful settlement of territorial issues, and so forth. With this in mind, one

30. Although somebody has suggested that the United States "celebrate 1976 as a year of reproductive pause to come as close as possible to a zero birthrate" (*New York Times*, 22 September 1969), I doubt whether even the pill could make such counsel of despair practicable; but a policy of taxing families for children beyond, say, three because they become now burdens upon the shrinking resources of the world (of which the United States consumes most), might prove feasible and, sooner or later, inevitable unless there is more voluntary restraint. A measure of this kind, to be sure, would be a bitter contraceptive pill to swallow for past—and even present—indifference. Yankee ingenuity may hit on more palatable devices, such as Kenneth Boulding's "green stamp plan" for population control, "whereby every person receives . . . a license to have the socially desirable average number of children. Then a market is established in these licenses or fractions thereof, so that the philoprogenitive can buy them from those who do not wish to have children." Kenneth E. Boulding, in *A Great Society?* ed. Bertram M. Gross (New York, 1968), p. 224.

might approach the study of international law in a future-oriented, functional, untraditional way (nobody wants the "legalistic-institutionalist" approach back!) by investigating (perhaps even using quantitative methods) where and why it has failed in the past, researching nations' and regimes' incidence of law observance under different circumstances, and engaging in case studies of systems behavior when faced with questions of whether to live up to rules or not. What impact does law have on foreign policy decision-makers, what is the role of their legal advisors? Or, for more immediately practical purposes: why not—perhaps under United Nation auspices—research and list, under viewpoints of international law, all presently existing territorial conflict areas among nations, since conflicts over territory, boundaries, etc., so often give rise to tensions, crises, and wars? A comparative study of war crimes, unfortunately, can now also be put on the agenda of relevant international law research.

True, the study of international law and organization has fallen somewhat into disrepute, and there is a lot of cynical "realism" abroad in respect to "starry-eyed idealists." But there is perhaps no more realistic approach than one which looks for new international institutions and machinery (or asks how existing ones can be used) for devising international rules for such things as oil pollution (for example, establishing maximum sizes for tankers, obligations to pay, perhaps into an international fund, damages caused by oil leaks, and so forth), or for similar situations where the former distinction between domestic and international spheres no longer applies (comprising by now the entire ecological field, since environmental damages, such as air or water pollution, even though occurring deep inside some nation of continental dimensions, eventually affect the atmosphere or oceans of the world). We have seen, in the case of the quick agreement on a treaty on highjacking of planes, that international actors can act speedily when a problem becomes "burning." What they must be made to realize is that all problems of this nature are "burning" ones.

This leads to the question of how to bring to bear on national actors the urgency of viewing survival problems as supernational, universal ones. We have referred to the "duplication of functions" national policy-makers have, in our day, as policy-makers for their units *and* participants in the processes of international action. But most of them, in particular those of the two great imperial powers, continue viewing international affairs as primarily a zero-sum game. And with these attitudes they influence research, including the potentialities of future research. In practice they control all (as in the Soviet Union) or a large portion (as in the United States) of what is going on in this respect. They determine and set priorities for projects. Research goes primarily into areas in which the respective establishments are interested and is diverted from that which may turn out to be embarrassing. There is a great imbalance here that must be rectified. Here lies the importance of independent academic research, but to what extent are we still independent, and can we hope to match the efforts subsidized by government agencies and special interests? Establishment-free research has a difficult time where the great advantage in organization, funds, and manpower lies with the vast governmental setup which engages in it or farms it out, often attracting the best academically trained talent (there is a "brain drain" in this respect, too).[31] It is all the more important to keep at least a minimal area of *academe* free from the influence or control of agencies (including even the foundations) and reserve to it a minimum of untied funds (it is all the more important, too, that this minimum be not tied up with irrelevancies). We must not forget that futures, too, can be preempted: he who does the studying of futures, or controls it, may determine which future will be planned and, therewith, the outcome or, at least, the direction. More relevant than many a project would be a study of who convinces whom of what in the world's key spots of policy planning.[32] In a world of

31. Cf., in this country, the Pentagon and its research institutes (such as RAND, the Institute for Defense Analysis, etc.), the research setups in CIA, NSA, USIS, and so on. One of the best summaries of the United States research establishment and its consequences is found in a foreign study. See Ekkehart Krippendorff, *Die amerikanische Strategie* (Frankfurt, 1970).

32. How vital the problem of what information and counsel reaches the power holder and of who controls access to him may be even in an "open society" became frighteningly clear when the narrow access to the president that a few hawks on Vietnam like Rusk and Rostow controlled from 1964 to March 1968 was revealed. See the disclosure of the story by an insider: Townsend Hoopes, *The Limits of Intervention* (New York, 1969), esp. pp. 16 ff., 59 ff., 93 ff.

so many competing voices it may not be enough to write books or articles. Considering the acceleration of events and the little time left, we may have to become propagandists of a cause and even turn activist. But here this article-writing prosecutor rests.

Secretary-General U Thant has recently said that the people of the world "have perhaps ten years left in which to subordinate their ancient quarrels and launch a global partnership to curb the arms race, improve the human environment, defuse the population explosion, and supply the required momentum to world development efforts." While perhaps a bit hyperbolic, this statement realistically sums up the four areas decisive for human survival.

One might object that science, as I advocate it, likewise constitutes exhortation on the basis of more or less correct assumptions; and that "futurology" is an uncertain trumpet. Agreed. But if science implies certainty, so does death. And our efforts, I prefer to believe, should be for life and the living.

10

DÉTENTE AND APPEASEMENT FROM A POLITICAL SCIENTIST'S VANTAGE POINT

This chapter constitutes the abridged version of a paper read at a symposium on "Detente in Historical Perspective" held at the Graduate Center of the City University of New York in October 1974. Papers and discussions were subsequently published under the editorship of George Schwab and Henry Friedlander, *Detente in Historical Perspective* (New York, 1975). The excerpts here reprinted bring the discussion of the appeasement-détente problem of chapter 5 up to date, with special emphasis on *Ostpolitik* as well as American policies toward the Soviet Union in Europe.

Reprinted by permission of Cyrco Press, Inc., New York.

I

United States policy toward the Soviet Union is "one-sided appeasement," "phony détente." Thus spake George Meany, one of our foremost self-appointed experts on foreign affairs.[1] But the criticism is neither limited to him nor is it recent. Over the last couple of years the general trend among experts in international politics has been going in the same direction, and some statesmen as well as scholars drew the Munich parallel as early as the end of World War II. Thus Truman, in his memoirs, tells us how the appeasement of the 1930s was present in his mind at the outbreak of the Korean war. . . . Winston Churchill told us in *his* memoirs: "If we add the United States to Britain and France; if we change the name of

1. *New York Times*, 2 October 1974.

the potential aggressor; if we substitute the United Nations for the League of Nations, the Atlantic Ocean for the English Channel, and the world for Europe, the argument is not necessarily without its application today." [2]

Still, history knows wrong parallels. As a political scientist I want to go a bit into definitions and concepts, trying to apply them to longer periods of time. We political scientists are perhaps overly inclined to make theories and develop models for what to the historian is a unique flux of events, but our analogy problem seems to point up the need to clarify our thinking by putting into the general context of international relations such concepts as détente and appeasement. Otherwise they remain mere fighting terms that reflect conflicting attitudes and are used in the service of clashing movements and ideologies.

The political science approach tries to generalize and distinguish types of policies and attitudes that might apply to entire historical periods and whole systems of international relations. Détente and appeasement seem to me to denote behavior patterns of international actors that can be used in what has been called "conflict theory." There they can be placed into a continuum of conflict attitudes ranging all the way from aggressivity over intransigence or "stand-pattism" to readiness for conciliation and compromise, that is, détente, moving from there to appeasement in the sense of making unilateral concessions, hence to joining the stronger side in a conflict in hopes to share in the spoils, finally to unconditional surrender. It seems to me that, within this spectrum of behavior-patterns, three are of particular interest: First, "stand-pattism" in the sense of irreconcilability, unwillingness to change a status even to the slightest degree, defense of one's claimed rights to the utmost; second, détente readiness, that is trying to arrive at rapprochement through mutual understanding and reciprocity in concessions; third, appeasement, not in its original meaning of détente readiness but in that of a readiness—perhaps in order to arrive at genuine détente—to make unilateral concessions to one who cannot be appeased; one here tries to satisfy, or satiate, an insatiable actor. . . .

2. Winston Churchill, *The Second World War* (Boston: Houghton Mifflin, 1948), vol. 1, *The Gathering Storm*, p. 211.

II

. . .

The role of appeasement and nonappeasement emerges most prominently in the modern state system with its balance-of-power policies. This system, for centuries, was one of balances neglected, defended, destroyed, restored. It was characterized time and again by the emergence of a power that would try to overthrow the balance and establish its hegemony over all of Europe, whether it was Spain, or, later, France (twice, under Louis XIV and Napoleon), or still later, possibly also twice, Germany. In such instances, whenever it was too late to frustrate the would-be hegemonic power through other means, a war of the "Grand Coalition," under British (and, since World War I, United States) leadership was required to restore the balance. Appeasement, then as in the 1930s, constituted a "wrong" policy under viewpoints of the interests of the nonhegemonic powers. Thus, appeasement may be defined as a policy ignoring (or being ignorant of) what balance policy requires. . . . Often it was appeasement policy that made the subsequent war of the Grand Coalition inevitable, as in the 1930s, when, I believe, one could have had it cheaper if one had acted forcefully against Mussolini in 1935.

Is there, then, no alternative except appeasement and intransigence, no role of détente and genuine rapprochement? It depends on the international situation of a given period. Vienna, after Napoleon's attempt to establish French hegemony in Europe, had restored a balance that, despite tensions, local wars, and hostile alliances, functioned for almost one hundred years. In 1919 one had tried to replace an unorganized balance system by institutionalizing the balance through collective security under the League of Nations, an effort that failed. Yet there was in the 1920s a policy that succeeded for a while in establishing a balance in Western Europe, specifically between France and Germany. . . . Locarno had been arrived at through Briand's and Stresemann's policies and mutual understanding and lasted for a number of years, based as it was on mutual concessions (with Germany recognizing the West-European status created at Versailles—in particular the loss of Alsace-Lorraine, and the French making concessions in regard to reparations). Admittedly, it was a shaky détente, because of the irreconcilables on both sides, such as the Poincarés and the *Deutschnationale*, who, having prevented détente prior to Locarno, put an end to it when depression set in and nationalism rose on both sides. Yet one cannot place into the same flux of development the period before and after 1933. With Hitler's rise to power, there entered an entirely new element: striving for hegemony. Even the German nationalists' and militarists' aims were limited as compared with Hitler's. Thus, whatever, under a détente policy, the Western powers might have granted a still mildly revisionist Germany ("mild" as compared with Nazi objectives), they instead, foolishly, set out to grant an unappeasable regime. Austen Chamberlain's efforts were for genuine détente, while those of Neville Chamberlain amounted to appeasement.

III

Let us now turn to our analogy problem and ask: What has been the role of détente, stand-pattism, and appeasement in the postwar period? It is my thesis that the present is *not* comparable to the 1930s. Again, our assessment is predicated upon the general international system. That emerging from World War II turned out to be a bipolar system where two superpowers, organized in power blocs, have opposed each other but so far have been deterred from risking all-out war by the mutually suicidal nature of the nuclear weapon. Being antagonists in most everything—in doctrine, way of life, internal system—the Soviets and the Western bloc, leaders as well as publics, were inclined to view the respective adversary as bent on world hegemony, the West suspecting a Communist "world conspiracy" to destroy the "free world," the East convinced that "capitalist imperialism" was out to wipe out "socialism." Under such symmetrically opposed views (one the mirror-image of the other) any concession, any ever-so-moderate effort to lessen tension, would be considered appeasement; only stand-pattism, not yielding an inch, seemed to protect one's security. Thus, at the time of the Cuban missile crisis, both Kennedy and Khrushchev were accused by their respective intransigents of having given in to the opponent. (The Chinese even used the term Munich, and it is likely that Khrushchev's subsequent fall from power was due to the intransigent element in the Politburo.)

Such mutual, mirror-image types of recrimination must make one pause and ask whether the truth is not in the middle. Both images may well be wrong. That is, instead of both sides, or at least one of them, being expansionist and ultimately bent on world domination, in reality, with their rational insight into the irrationality of the use of all-out force in the nuclear age, both sides are defensive-minded, i.e., interested primarily in the maintenance and defense of the status quo that had resulted from the war.

It is not my intention here to warm up the controversy about the origins of the cold war into which those mutual suspicions led the two power blocs. In my opinion they were neither in Soviet expansionism or Communist world conspiracy nor in U.S. imperialism but, rather, in what I call the "security dilemma" of nations, that is, their mutual fears and suspicions that the other side might turn aggressive. The Soviets' moving into what Hitler had presented Stalin on a silver platter through invasion and subsequent defeat, namely, control of Eastern Europe, looked like unappeasable expansionism to some in the West, but might it not, from the Soviet viewpoint, be considered as building a defensive belt around a much invaded country, particularly when the Americans engaged in what looked to them as encirclement, through troops stationed all along the Iron Curtain and bases scattered across the globe from Thule to Okinawa; by building blocs and alliances and, above all, rearming the former chief enemy, the Germans? In a situation of "security dilemma," whatever is done for precaution and defense by one side, is liable to be interpreted as offensive by the other.

However this may have been, it is clear even from what happened during the cold war that both sides had come to recognize the lines of deepest military penetration of their forces at the end of the war by and large as the lines demarcating their respective power spheres, and that these might be crossed only at the risk of a war nobody wanted. Bipolarity thus meant stalemate, a balance of sorts, and consequently, a mutual, if tacit agreement not to interfere in the sphere of the other. Even at the height of the cold war, this policy of restraint could be observed at the time of the East German uprising, the Hungarian revolution, the invasion of Czechoslovakia, and on the Soviet side whenever, during one of the perennial crises over Berlin, a Stalin or Khrushchev refrained from trying to take over a city that, geographically, was located deep within their sphere.

In such a situation, must we have stand-pattism with all its risks of crisis and confrontation, its nonrecognition policies . . . its arms races and competition for influence in ever so remote areas? Or are there chances for rapprochement and genuine détente? Stand-pattism, as we have seen, is the correct policy in the face of an adversary's hegemonial and expansionist policies, whereas détente is possible—and does *not* involve appeasement—when both sides are basically status quo-minded.

One could not "do business" with Hitler by trying to establish lines of demarcation or spheres of influence. One can, with proper precautions, I believe, do business of this sort with Soviet leaders. I am aware that to recognize this possibility goes against the grain of those who still believe in the unalterable final goal of Communism to conquer the world, and this belief, ironically, is bolstered by the fact that Communist leaders, in order to maintain their ideological credibility, are inclined to emphasize those goals (Khrushchev's "We will bury you," etc.), although such objectives belong to the category of ultimate but presently unrealizable ideals, while a Hitler, dissembling his real objectives, could deceive the world for years with his famous "peace speeches." But if one wants to see the difference between genuine world-revolutionary involvement and one-single-nation policy one should compare what Lenin and other early Bolsheviks were expecting and aiming at with what Stalin and his successors actually were striving for. . . . When the formers' attempt to spread the world revolution had failed, Stalin drew the only realistic conclusion: to build socialism in one country and subordinate everything else, including the fate of foreign revolutions and the function of foreign Communist parties, to the survival of the Soviet Union. After Stalin's victory over Hitler the new, and favorable, status quo[3] was the one hence to be defended and protected, and in view of the new threat to Soviet security perceived, rightly or wrongly, at her Eastern flank, Stalin's successors, by and large, have maintained this nonrevisionist, defensive policy toward the West. Thus both sides, at least for the time being, had accepted the postwar distribution and balance of power.

IV

There was, however, one flaw in this situation. While, basically, the new status quo in Europe was recognized by East and West, there was the exception of the German question. West Germany, backed by her allies, refused to give up her claim to "reunification in freedom" (that is, inclusion of East Germany in the Western sphere) and to recognize the new boundary with Poland (that is, give up claims to the Eastern territories), which meant nonrecognition of the GDR, of the Oder-Neisse line, etc. But a balance is never stable when a major actor is wedded to revising it, and thus general détente was still hamstrung by intransigence and confrontation.

But stalemate, even though acknowledged by both sides, must not necessarily be perpetuated. If both sides are determined to seek accommodation, stalemate may be used as a starting point for loosening up a situation. When, in the late 1960s, Bonn became ready to recognize the postwar European status, and Moscow was ready to accept a strong and rearmed Western-aligned Federal Republic, the major obstacles in the way of détente were removed, and what is now known as *Ostpolitik* could be inaugurated. . . .

Those who were "present at the creation" of the Federal Republic and the cold war, the Achesons, the former U.S. High Commissioners in West Germany, together with the West German opposition (and, I am sure, in accordance with

3. Comparable, perhaps, to the one achieved by Bismarck after his victory over the French, which rendered German foreign policy for about twenty years one of nonrevisionist status quo policy.

mirror-image reservations within the Politburo) have called that policy "surrender." The fact that, once more, "Munich"-type charges originated from extremists on both sides must make us pause. *Ostpolitik*, in my judgment, merely meant the formal recognition of a de facto status created right after, and as a consequence of, World War II. The West accepted nothing that had not, in fact, existed for a quarter of a century. "Nothing is given up," said Willy Brandt at the signing of the Moscow Treaty, "that was not gambled away long ago." No territory changed hands, nor were there changes in political alignments; the overall strategic or political balance was not affected. But—if I may quote from another article of mine—"if West Germany now, through *Ostpolitik*, signalized that she was ready finally to make peace with the East on the basis of defeat in World War II, realizing that Germans had to pay for the excesses committed by a criminal regime, it did mean creating a new basis for peace and stability in Europe." [4] And even if one considers the legitimization of the GDR and its regime and of Eastern boundaries as a Western concession, it was not a unilateral one. There was reciprocity in the Soviet guarantee of the status of West Berlin as a Western unit, of free access to it, of improved personal contacts between East and West in regard to travel, visiting, etc. That there was mutuality of concessions, a genuine give and take, can be seen from the great reluctance of the East German government to accede to the agreements (Ulbricht had to go); it is still the one that places the greatest obstacles in the path of détente.[5]

Three place names which have become symbols for policies in the interwar period may serve to clarify: Munich, Rapallo, Locarno. That *Ostpolitik* did not involve a Munich (in the sense of a unilateral giveaway) I hope to have shown. What about Rapallo? Rapallo, the place where, in 1922, Germans and Soviets agreed to establish diplomatic relations, has ever since

4. John H. Herz, section on *Germany* in Gregory Henderson, Richard Ned Lebow, and John G. Stoessinger, eds., *Divided Nations in a Divided World* (New York: McKay, 1974), p. 17. See this section also for an overall discussion and analysis of *Ostpolitik*.

5. As for mutuality of concessions, there is a story of Soviet negotiator Abrassimov having remarked, after signing the Quadripartite Agreement on Berlin: "Now they will liquidate me."

been used as shorthand for German-Russian rapprochement, if not German "betrayal of the West." [6] Hans Morgenthau perceives such a risk in Soviet détente efforts now.[7] I cannot agree. There is nobody in any responsible position in West Germany today who would be seducible this way and advocate giving up Western ties for an Eastern orientation. Short of a rise to power of a neo-Nazi group or else the Communist party, something rather inconceivable now, this is simply not in the cards. As for the Soviets, they must, after all, have learned something from the failure of the Stalin-Hitler Pact. I doubt whether they would welcome as an ally even a Communized Germany, a unit that would duplicate China at their Western flank (not to speak of the fact that such a German reorientation could only be had in return for reunification, and how would that affect the other bloc members?). Therefore I would rather draw the parallel of Locarno. Locarno, as we have seen, meant German recognition of the post-World War I status in Western Europe and thus initiated Franco-German détente. *Ostpolitik* involves an "Eastern Locarno," that Eastern Locarno the German intransigents had refused in the 1920s when they dreamed of chopping up or gobbling up Poland. Now the frontier with Poland has been recognized. The way is thus open to closer personal, economic, and cultural relations with the nations of the East, which, so it seems to me, have a better chance of internal liberalization this way than through a continuation of a Western policy of ostracism.

But the latter tendency, the emotionalism of intransigence and hostility, is never far below the surface of détente . . . and a spirit of constant suspicion—to be distinguished from wholesome caution and watchfulness—may become self-fulfilling prophecy. Euphoria, on the other hand, is no great help either. What is needed in creating and maintaining an atmosphere of

6. The original Rapallo agreement, of course, did not imply this. It provided for the establishment of diplomatic relations between Germany and the Soviet Union, implying a certain assertion of independence on Germany's part but no realignment. In this respect, rather than comparing it with what happened in 1970, it might be compared with the establishment of Bonn-Moscow relations by Adenauer in 1955.

7. See, e.g., his "The United States and Europe in a Decade of Detente," in *The United States and Western Europe*, ed. Wolfram F. Hanrieder (Cambridge, Mass.: Winthrop, 1974), p. 7.

détente is calm, down-to-earth assessment of the given situation and its opportunities, if any.

The greatest threat to détente I perceive today lies with the military and its supporters on both sides. Détente policy has been attacked for alleged neglect of so-called defense and security interests. I would criticize SALT negotiations and related policies rather for having achieved almost nothing and, by not calling a halt to the insane arms race with its piling one new weapons system upon the other, for increasing not only the danger of the ultimate blowup of the world but also the more imminent one of bankrupting the industrialized countries—apparently first the Western ones. It would be truly absurd if, without having had a conscious policy of the sort, the Soviets (and/or the Chinese) would this way inherit the Western world. As long as second-strike and overkill capacities are maintained, even radical reduction of armaments would not imply appeasement or surrender; on the contrary, it constitutes, in my opinion, the only way to genuine détente among the superpowers. I am critical of Mr. Kissinger's efforts not because of his détente policies toward Moscow and Peking or his efforts to arrive at Near Eastern détente through establishing some sort of peace, or at least mutual toleration, between Israel and the Arabs, but because of insufficient efforts in the area of weapons control, as well as continued nondétente policies in Southeast Asia and even open intervention in countries like Chile.

In this utterly inflammable world of ours, all of us, whether West or East, North or South, are bound to go down or survive together. Trying to reduce tension so as to be able jointly to meet the really great global challenges—the food and resources crisis, the energy crisis, the threatening destruction of the biosphere—is, I submit, the only path to survival.[8]

8. I would also like to refer the reader to Senator Walter F. Mondale's article "Beyond Detente: Toward International Economic Security," *Foreign Affairs* 53, no. 1 (October 1974), where he says:

> Certainly detente is important. The gains in East-West relations must be consolidated on a realistic basis; negotiations on strategic arms, the European Security Conference and the questions of force levels in Europe must be pursued. . . . But international economic policy is now

our top external challenge. . . . We must seize the opportunities presented by detente . . . to deal effectively with our economic problems, or the progress we have made toward a more secure world may be undone. In the 1920's there was also a version of detente, symbolized by the Treaty of Locarno, and at the same time an emerging depression. When the nations of the world failed to cooperate to deal with the depression, its consequences rapidly unraveled the elements of that detente, and in the end economic collapse contributed mightily both to the emergence of grave threats from Germany and Japan and to the paralysis of other nations, including the United States, in the face of those threats (pp. 1 f., 6).

My only reservation concerns the use of the term "economic," which is actually meant to comprise all the great global questions, from population explosion and its effects to the threat of environmental destruction.

11
TECHNOLOGY, ETHICS, AND INTERNATIONAL RELATIONS

Originally a paper read at the "International Symposium on Ethics in an Age of Pervasive Technology" held at the Technion, Haifa (Israel) in December 1974, the essay has been published in *Social Research* 43, no. 1 (Spring 1976): 98–113; also, in German translation, in *Frankfurter Hefte*, Frankfurt, Germany, August 1975. The essay, here printed in abridged form, traces the development of ideas on statehood, security dilemma, etc., up to present views on the world emergency. A "minimum ethic of survival" is suggested as normative foundation for policies giving the universal interest in survival priority over standards of group ethics and group (national, etc.) interests. See further comments in the *Introduction*, pages 27–29.

Reprinted by permission of the New School for Social Research, New York.

I

Marx theorized that what happens in politics, as elsewhere, constitutes the superstructure over the modes and means of economic *production.* Though wary of determinism, I propose the thesis that much of what happens in politics, and in particular in the relations of nation-states, can be interpreted as superstructure over the development of the means of *destruction;* that is, the development of military technology.

Mankind, throughout its history, has been organized in units whose chief purpose it was to provide security and protection, in the physical and economic sense, to those living within them. For their protection from outside aggression or interference, therefore, these units had to provide themselves with means of defense. The very nature of the prevailing unit thus depended on military technology. The latter would determine whether these units were large-scale or small, decentralized or tightly organized, etc. Thus we find tribes or clans as "highest" units of international relations at certain points of development, city-states, large-area territorial states, or even empires, at others. In Europe, with the "gunpowder revolution," it became possible for rulers, with the aid of artillery and standing armies, to control larger territories and to subdue the medieval "feudal" powers found within such territories. Thus we have the rise of the "modern" territorial or nation-state, a unit that afforded protection and security to its inhabitants by surrounding itself with a "hard shell" of fortifications and thus became "impermeable" or "impenetrable." Of course, there still were bigger and smaller, more or less powerful units, and the latter could be penetrated by the former. However, this now required a major effort, and we are thus justified in claiming that "sovereignty" and "independence," those hallmarks of the modern state, were based on two major factors: its own indigenous strength and power, that is, the stage and development of military technology; and, second, its international "connections," such as alliances. Thus, the very nature of the chief actors on the international scene was based upon the "territoriality" of the acting units, their defensibility, their (relative) impenetrability. On this depended the specific nature of international politics from the Westphalian Peace to the end of the nineteenth century. It was an era of limited wars (limited at least as compared with the "total" wars of our century), of power balancing power, of the expansion of European "Powers" into the less "developed" world (where, again, the less developed stage of military technology accounted for the easy conquest and subjugation of huge areas and empires, such as the Asian or Western Hemisphere "Indias," by militarily superior Western armies and navies). When non-Western units such as Japan or, more recently, China, learned the ways of Western science, technology, and organization, they too became Western-style modern sovereign and independent nation-states. On the basis of a geographically pervasive technology the entire world, including what we now refer to as the Third World, could become one world of nation-states.

II

But history, and with it technology, marched on. If the gunpowder revolution, toward the end of the Middle Ages, accounted for much of the international system that prevailed in succeeding centuries, a double weapons' revolution in our century accounts for a radical change in the character of political units and, consequently, in their international relationships. It has been a revolution that affects the underlying character of the territorial state, its impenetrability, in such a way that it has turned into its opposite, radical permeability. I refer, of course, to the invention of the airplane and the nuclear bomb, to air war and nuclear war. With these inventions, the roof, so to speak, was off the traditional units of protection. In the place of the necessity frontally to attack if one wanted to win, it now became possible to penetrate the enemy "vertically" and, at least in the case of nuclear war, to destroy him completely. Not even the strongest territorial unit seemed safe from such penetration, and if there were two, or more, possessing these means of utter annihilation, war now would mean, not power measuring power, not victory or defeat, that is, a certain rationality in pursuing war and war aims, but mutual, irrational suicide. . . .

III

When I first wrote about these matters, I drew what seemed to me the logical conclusion from this state of affairs. Nuclear penetrability had rendered the traditional nation-state obsolete because it could no longer fulfill its primary function of protection. Even entire power blocs, new-style alliance systems such as NATO or the Warsaw Pact alliance—which in essence meant pushing the protective wall formerly surrounding individual states around entire blocs of states, each controlled by one "superpower"—had become penetrable with the unlimited range of the weapons available to the superpowers. The world had become too small for more than one of them; therefore, ultimately there would have to emerge either world hegemony of one power, or a world government to

which *all* states would cede the power to control the world and
ensure protection from nuclear destruction; this would entail
yielding control over the "ultimate" weapon to a world
authority, that is, on the part of so-far sovereign and independent nations, giving up their traditional sovereignty.

However, the first of these alternatives, global hegemony
of one power, seemed unrealizable since, even if there were
only two superpowers vying for this role, neither could be
expected to yield to the other without fighting it out, i.e.,
without a nuclear war which, in all likelihood, would destroy
both. The other alternative would be practicable only if and
when there would occur a radical transformation of attitudes
and their leaders toward the problem of organizing a livable
world, an attitude I called "universalist." Universalism would
substitute for the traditional, so-called national interests the
overriding interest of all in survival; survival in a world that
had become mortally vulnerable for even the mightiest. In
former times, substituting the ideals of universal peace for
pursuing national interests had been considered "utopian,"
and rightly so, because national interests were still tied up with
nations as effective units of security and protection. . . . But
now the dichotomy of "national self-interest" and "internationalist (or universalist) ideals" no longer seems to fit a
situation where ever so vast a power cannot protect nations
and their inhabitants from annihilation. The former ideal has
become a compelling interest. While the pre-nuclear stage of
technological development had meant the rise of the territorial
state, the present one would lead to its demise. Otherwise,
utter chaos would replace a world of at least minimal rationality. While I was skeptical in regard to whether mankind would
be rational enough to realize in time that universalist order had
to replace the old system, I was still optimistic enough to
consider it possible, provided there was a period of what I
called a "holding operation" during which the superpowers
would engage in stopgap measures such as an amount of arms
control that at least would stop further "overkill" armament,
mutual agreement on spheres of influence and drawing of lines
of demarcation, nonproliferation of nuclear weapons to the
nonnuclears, etc., policies that would substitute at least minimal "peaceful coexistence" for the then existing cold war and

thus, gradually, prepare the way for bolder universalist approaches. But, in view of developments since, I had to qualify my thesis of the impending "demise" of the nation-state.

IV

I now perceive international politics as an area of fundamental contradiction. On the one hand, arms technology has advanced in almost unimaginable ways, the arms race has continued unabated, nuclear arms have spread, and states, big and small, seem more beholden to the idea and the practices of sovereign independence than ever; indeed, the last vestiges of old-fashioned colonial empire have given way to a world fully organized in such state-units, by now numbering about 150. On the other hand, mutual deterrence, a system under which "second-strike capacity" renders starting nuclear war too risky for even the strongest of the nuclears, has accounted for the surprising fact that no nuclear weapon has been used after the initial bombs dropped on Japan. Nuclear war has become less likely, and even conventional war, because of the ever-present danger of its "escalating" into nuclear war, has not occurred between the nuclear powers and has even become less likely elsewhere because of possible involvement of nuclears interested in the nonuse of the weapon. Underneath the wings of this shaky "nuclear peace," countries other than the two superpowers, whether allies, clients, or nonaligned, have had a chance to reassert their independence. The basic contradiction thus lies in this: On the one hand, availability of nuclear arms and possibility of nuclear war call out for "universalism" or, at least, for policies tending in that direction: disarmament, détente, strengthening the authority and the role of international organization, etc. On the other hand, lack of any appreciable power of such organizations and the very accumulation of power in the individual state-units requires, for each of them, "preparedness" in the sense of at least a minimum of defense-readiness and corresponding armament. What I once called the "security dilemma" of nations—the age-old situation where units that are under no higher authority have to rely on their own power for defense even though their potential opponents are as defensive-minded and as little aggressive as they themselves may be (because you cannot read the opponent's mind and thus must be prepared for "the worst")—besets nations today as much as ever before. . . .

Vietnam as well as Israel have provided examples of the force and viability of nationalism if used for defense and its obsolescence for purposes of conquest. Must we thus admit the continued validity of the "national interest" and the policies based on it, and the illusory nature of anything going beyond it in the direction of internationalist ideals (or interests) and global controls? And this way admit the irreconcilability of above-group, "universalist" ethical principle with the "real world"?

V

I do not believe that we have to make such an admission. But before discussing this question, I would like to refer, if ever so briefly, to the nonwar and nonsecurity areas of international relations, where we observe the same dialectical conflict between one-world trends and trends and policies based on the national-interest viewpoint. Again, it is the scientific-technological process that accounts for global trends. Indeed, hardly anything is more striking in its effects on the modern world as the not only pervasive but acceleratingly rapid development which has created our machine world and everything that flows from it. The famous exponential curve of acceleration—a curve that rises first slowly and then ever more rapidly and steeply—characterizes almost everything in today's world—whether it be the rapid accumulation of scientific-technological knowledge ("information explosion") or whether it concerns demographic trends ("population explosion"), whether trends in the use of material resources such as energy, or trends in the ways such use affects the environment (explosive increase of pollution, for instance). These trends are obviously related to technology: the population explosion, e.g., with new inventions and techniques in health and hygiene and its results of cutting down infant mortality, increasing average life expectancy, etc. What are their impacts on international relations?

First, they have created a global environment that now constitutes one universe: one universe of information and communication where whatever happens anywhere on earth can be known almost instantly everywhere else; where speed of transportation can get people (e.g., political leaders) together in no time; where more and more "ordinary" people get to know other people and countries; where the world becomes more and more alike as a synthetic habitat man builds in the place of his former "natural" environment. This involves universal concern with what happens anywhere; e.g., catastrophies like crop failures and ensuing famine can no longer, as in colonial times, be disregarded because they happen in some part of somebody else's "empire." Crises are speeded up because "instant diplomacy" speeds up action and reaction. The conduct of foreign affairs becomes ever more hectic, with statesmen constantly on the go, meeting their colleagues for frantic consultation or debate but also enabling them to solve problems; technology enables them, specifically, to meet in international conferences whose growing number and increasingly comprehensive agendas deal with matters of vital importance to the world. More generally, technology has been responsible for a tremendous increase in industrial production, ever higher yields of mechanized agriculture, and ensuing higher living standards in at least parts of the world; but it has also become responsible for the problems thus created, such as the aforementioned population explosion which, in turn, has led to the threat of exhaustion of vital resources; or overurbanization in deteriorating, crowded metropolitan areas; of environmental destruction due to unregulated, "wild" economic growth. In other words, the very problem of physical survival has become universalized. What affects one or a few (e.g., oil infestation of some high-seas area with its effects on the living resources of some part of the ocean, or failure of a grain or rice harvest in one country or area) is liable to affect all, and thus it seems that only global approaches are meaningful in the attempt to solve vital problems facing mankind in an interdependent world.

But, again, "group" considerations and group interests intervene and frequently conflict with and hamper the global approach. We could observe this in drastic fashion during the many international conferences called to deal with the global problems of population (Bucharest), of environmental deterioration (Stockholm), of food supply (Rome), of the law of the sea (Caracas). Third World countries, although burdened more than others with demographic pressures, opposed proposals to set global standards for birth control; developing countries with rich but so far not fully exploited resources, such as Brazil or Iran, insisted on their "right to contribute their share of pollution"; coastal countries claim ever larger portions of the ocean for exclusive exploitation. The same spirit of group competition causes racial, ethnic, or religious groups to oppose population control in fears of being outcompeted by competitors (e.g., blacks and other "nonwhites" in the United States, Catholics, or Jews where they live in non-Jewish environments). Struggle among ethnic groups and resort to violence among members of such groups is on the increase. This kind of group competition (basically, of course, grounded in the "security dilemma") has been the hallmark of political events in the past. The question is: can we, that is, mankind considered as one global community, still afford it?

VI

It is my thesis that in today's world in which the ancient Darwinian dilemma still sets group against group but where, for the first time, the survival of all is in jeopardy, even those who (like myself) are value-relativists (i.e., believe that, in principle, no "ought to" can be derived from an "is"), can agree that, when certain values become so overwhelmingly important that their nonrecognition appears "absurd" to practically everybody, they can be considered as "certain." Where the alternative to the "ought to" denotes physical extinction of the entire human race, survival, not of individuals or specific groups but of mankind as such becomes an absolute value. Edmund Husserl's *Lebenswelt*, with its group and national interests, its security dilemmas, etc., has now become a stark and simple *Überlebenswelt* where man must realize that his affairs, and especially world affairs, are no longer a zero-sum game (one wins, the other loses) but one where the loss or gain of one in the long run means the loss or gain of all.

I said "in the long run," and this leads us back to the dialectic contradiction in the situation. The traditional ethical dichotomies (or aporias) of "realism vs. idealism," "egoism vs. altruism," or, in the area of international politics, of "nationalism vs. internationalism," "bellicism vs. pacifism," and so forth, were insoluble when advocacy of martial virtues, e.g., was in principle as theoretically "valid" as that of their opposites. Today they may make sense to some "in the short run" but are destructive of global survival in the long run. Former "mere" idealism, as I have indicated above, turns into the realism of the interest in the survival of all. Albert Schweitzer's simple *dictum* (by some ridiculed as simplistic) that *Leben erhalten und fördern ist gut* ("morally good is that which maintains and promotes life") is valid in the sense of its application to the collective life of mankind.

Such a "minimum ethic of survival" becomes comprehensive in two ways—latitudinally or geographically, so to speak, because it turns global, and longitudinally, in its time dimension, in that it turns futuristic, taking into account the future of mankind, the generations that, so we may still hope, will come after us. As for the first, spatial, dimension, I agree with the formulation of one of my colleagues, to wit, that

> the most basic division in the world today is not between communists and non-communists, between blacks and whites, between rich and poor or even between young and old. It is between those who see only the interests of a limited group and those who are capable of seeing the interests of the broader community of mankind as a whole.[1]

As for the second, or temporal, dimension, it means that, for the first time, we are compelled to take the futuristic view if we want to make sure that there will be "future generations" at

1. Richard Gardner, "Can the United Nations Be Revived?", *Foreign Affairs*, July 1970, p. 676.

all. Acceleration of developments in the decisive areas (demographic, ecological, strategic) has become so strong that even the egotism of "après nous le déluge" might not work because the *déluge* may well overtake ourselves, the living.

But if, in principle, the principles of a universalist ethics can be shown to be the only valid ones, what are the chances of their prevalence in practice? The difficulties seem enormous, and I must in all honesty admit to considerable pessimism. For, there must, in the first place, be realization of what is required, and, second, worldwide readiness to act, and act quickly. But who can even comprehend, in one overall worldview, the necessities and priorities, who can develop one overall plan, or even mere guidelines, to put them into practice? At the time I wrote about universalism replacing the obsolete state I looked hopefully toward those whose job it is to take the universal view, such as the chiefs and the staffs of international organizations. But even there the voices of responsible actors sound more and more desperate. Former UN Secretary U Thant said—and this was in 1969—that the people of the world

> have perhaps ten years left in which to subordinate their ancient quarrels and launch a global partnership to curb the arms race, improve the human environment, defuse the population explosion, and supply the required momentum to world development efforts.

If you add to this the food and resources (in particular, energy) problem, the statement summed up realistically the areas decisive for human survival; but now, when half of that ten-year period has already passed, the present UN Secretary has this to say:

> The question now is whether sufficient progress can be made in the practical pursuit of both short- and long-term goals before the common problems which we face become completely unmanageable.

And he goes on to say:

> Many great civilizations in history have collapsed at the very height of their achievement because they were unable

to analyze their basic problems, to change direction and to adjust to the new situations which faced them. . . . Today the civilization that is facing such a challenge is not just one small part of mankind—it is mankind as a whole.

Hope—if any remains—is not in the impending emergence of world government in the place of nation-states. One can only work with what one has, that is, with states, their people and their leaders, and hope for the realization on the part of the decisive ones that—to mention only a few examples—radical arms reduction (not only nuclear but also conventional, not only production but also traffic) is needed not only to lessen the threat of war and increase the chances of détente but also to decrease the insane waste of resources that armaments entail, resources so urgently needed to meet the most elementary needs of a majority of mankind for food and other necessities of life; that stabilization of population may require giving priority to birth-control measures and policies even over improvement of health—something that, if need be, must be reflected in aid programs of the developed to the developing nations; not nationalization but rather internationalization of vital energy resources; making the resources of the ocean floor—that last resource frontier of mankind—a "global patrimony" to be used, under an international licensing authority, for development rather than for unregulated individual exploitation for the profit and gain of multinational corporations; establishment of an international "ocean patrol" to discover (and penalize) oil spills and similar pollution not only where nations are directly affected, near their coasts and beaches, but in the middle of the ocean where, so far, nobody seems to care.

All this requires new standards of international law, new procedures to agree on new law more rapidly than in the traditional, slow, and cumbersome conference procedure, new powers to be bestowed upon agencies that are to be put in charge. It by no means involves an antitechnological attitude. Just the opposite. All that science and technology can summon will be needed to promote global planning and practice of the required nature. That is obvious in areas such as agricultural technology for increased food production or the development of better means of birth control, but it applies everywhere. We cannot, in the romantic mood of the *Maschinenstürmer* of yore, return to a pretechnological age, but we must become *Maschinenbändiger*—that is, replace the unregulated, often cancerlike "growth" the machine has been used for by its use for the long-range and global purposes I have mentioned. Like the early atomic scientists who, flabbergasted about what their science had wrought, became imbued with a sense of responsibility for the results of applied science, everybody working in the field of science and technology must realize that he cannot escape moral responsibility for what his inventions, discoveries, and work are used for. Nor can social scientists be satisfied any longer with ivory-tower theorizing and abstractionism. Only that which concerns the survival problems of mankind deserves to be called relevant in an emergency situation such as ours. And as far as the political leadership of nations is concerned, I mention the example set by a man who truly turned Paul from Saul when he, after having functioned as one of the chief U.S. planners of the Vietnam war, became the head of an international organization trying to help the underdeveloped, ceaselessly preaching the gospel of "globalism"—Robert McNamara.

As for specific "national" policies, especially of the most powerful nations, I would like to see them develop policies of what one may call the "power surplus." Whenever a nation like the United States has satisfied itself that it possesses the armaments and other means for its own protection and self-preservation, it should, in the place of further extension of power-political interests, such as bases in faraway places or alliances with, and aid to, authoritarian and oppressive regimes, invest its "surplus" power and resources in promoting global development and similar programs, as well as protecting and assisting those nations that share the democratic values of humaneness and of the basic rights of individuals and groups. This would exclude the South Koreas, South Africas, Chiles, Brazils of the world under their present regimes, but involve maintaining and reinforcing the common bonds with Western Europe, the new Greece, Israel, and (hopefully still) India. To be sure, it would, in a way, mean interference with the "domestic affairs" of others in the traditional sense. But today domestic affairs are no longer separable from international ones (if they ever were). Foreign policy, at long last, would acquire a moral dimension.

In a country that has been the birthplace of three world religions it may, perhaps, be appropriate to conclude with a few words on the role of religion in a universalizing world. The basic idea of the monotheistic religions has been that "we are brothers (and sisters) because we have one father." For those of us who do not have strong ties to any of these religions, this idea may seem to belong to an earlier stage of development, since one need not feel closely related to other human beings merely because one belongs to one "family." In practice, this "family" feeling of religions has oftentimes meant exclusivism, if not hostility toward others or even persecution, crusades, "holy wars"; it also has frequently led to bonds with interests of wealth, alliances with particular social systems and political regimes, or doctrinaire backwardness in regard to global problems such as birth control. But the other element, the emphasis on our common brotherhood, has never ceased to play a role, and it seems that recently this role has become stronger and more intensely felt. Churches have not only "modernized" themselves internally but, in many instances and in many parts of the world, have stood in the forefront of the battle against inhumanity (such as police torture or terrorism) and for aiding the economically deprived and the socially or racially downtrodden. The universalist ethic of the great religions may well render them important and effective allies of all those who feel responsible for creating the conditions for a viable future of all people on earth.

12

PROLOGUE AS EPILOGUE: ARISTOTLE'S DREAM

This short piece appeared as Prologue to the third edition of
Gwendolen M. Carter and John H. Herz, *Government and
Politics in the Twentieth Century* (New York, 1973), pp.
ix–xiii. It is self-explanatory.

Reprinted by permission of Praeger Publishers, New
York.

M y dear Cleon:

Is life a dream? Is what we call our dreams our real life?
The other day I had the strangest incident of my life. I prelived
immortality. In my strangest dream, the gods showed me the
future of the human race. When I awoke, they told me that I
had been in torporlike sleep for almost forty hours. If every
minute of my sleep corresponded to a year, I saw in that dream
what happened to man, and the star on which he lives, for
more than two thousand years. And what I saw, even you, who
are not among the incredulous, will have a hard time believing.

I shall dwell only briefly on what happened in the times
closest to our own—tempting though this would be, for we are
most curious about that which is close and familiar.

Familiar yet strange was what had happened to our Hellas.

303

304/The Nation-State and the Crisis of World Politics

For the first time, I found it united but, alas, only under the rule of alien tyrants. Those barbarians from Graecia Magna, to whom our colonies had brought the light of reason, ruled us for centuries, but there was triumph, too: In ruling us, they fell under the spell of our customs, our way of life, our art, our thoughts. And, greater triumph still, the very words and concepts of our language entered their language and their minds and, from there, those of all generations in those millennia I witnessed. In that ultimate period I lived through in my dream, men everywhere on the globe still spoke of "politics" as we speak of what happens in our *poleis;* and, while they invented a new name for the political community, they still distinguished forms and types in familiar terms: democracy, aristocracy, oligarchy, monarchy. I am embarrassed to report that to the very science and method of thought, dialectic and logic, they had given the attribute of my name.

You may be surprised to hear me speak of "men on this globe." Indeed, my friend, what some of us had suspected in the teeth of unending ridicule (and I must admit I had been one of the ridiculers), was found true: This earth is not a flat pancake but a sphere, a star among stars, revolving on its axis around the sun. And now I must tell you the unbelievable: Men, at the end of these millennia I saw, had not only penetrated to the ultimate ends of the globe but learned to thrust themselves into the universe and set foot on the moon, ready to travel to other stars. Having told you about this achievement, you will be less surprised to hear that they also had learned to fly into the air that surrounds the globe, to travel from one place to another with unbelievable speed. They also speak to each other through the air over huge distances and, by looking into an illuminated box, are able to see what happens in far, distant places. As a matter of fact, I saw many of them, and most of the very young, for most of their lives sitting in front of the box and staring at what happened elsewhere. Had they thus attained the "good life" of which we philosophers debate on end?

I must tell you, my friend, that my impression of what they had achieved was strangely ambiguous. You remember, I once wrote that slaves would become unnecessary if men should ever invent inanimate contraptions that could perform the work of slaves. Men, using what we discovered—science, the laws of nature—have fashioned them. They call them machines, and the art of using them—again borrowing our terms—they call technology. Has this made them free to live the good life? I am afraid not; for, having freed the slaves by substituting machines, they have themselves become slaves to their machines. They toil without end to make them do what they want, make them transport them hither and yon, make them even think for them, but it does not seem to me that they have freed themselves thereby for leisure and contemplation— the only pursuits worthy of humans.

Had they at least solved the problem of ruling themselves in freedom, of living as true citizens? Alas, no. Do you remember that strange philosopher, Phaleas the Chalcedonian, who believed that all ills came from economic inequality and proposed the utopia of a society of equals, wherein class struggle would no longer occur because each had what he wanted? Over two thousand years later, a latter-day Phaleas became the prophet of a movement that made half of the people of the world accept his belief and set up communistic societies. Alas, what I had said about the Chalcedonian's theory proved true: "Since men are guilty of the greatest crimes from ambition, and not from necessity, that polity which Phaleas establishes would only be salutary to prevent little crimes." And I also had blamed him for forgetting relations with foreign nations and the ensuing danger of war. Those Phalean societies I found ruled tyrannically, and their coexistence with other countries beset by the threat of war. But what about these others? You remember that I once put my students in the Academy to work to engage in comparative politics? To compile the constitutions of all the *poleis* and to study their systems? Since latter-day men had covered the entire earth and established *poleis* (which they called states) everywhere, there was to be found an immense number of these, all with their own governments and institutions. In this letter, I cannot give you even the merest inkling of their great variety. So, I shall try to write up some of the impressions I have gained in a separate treatise. But one thing I must say already here:

Men, in that faraway eon, would boast interminably about the "progress" mankind had made since our times (about which, by the way, they were amazingly well informed). And, considering their having reached the stars, and all the other miracles they had accomplished, one might be tempted to agree with their boastful use of that strange term. But then I looked more closely at their lives, whether under the Phalean system or whether on the huge continent of Atlantis that our descendants, the Europeans, had discovered and settled, or on other continents. Their much vaunted "democracy" hardly came up to the standards I had set for the form of government I had called *Politeia;* it rather amounted to ochlocracy or plutocracy. And many did not even have that. They were ruled, as are so many of our states, by tyrants. It made me very sad to see our own dear Hellas so governed. True, it had become united and was no longer in that perennial state of discord and war. But discord and war had simply been transferred to the plane of the larger units. And the means of killing and maiming and destroying in war (again, thanks to technology) had become so refined that one major strife could wipe out entire countries and civilizations.

Living forever in the shadow of destruction, men could not be happy. They would seek to divert themselves from unhappiness by staring at the illuminated box, or by traveling in high speed from place to place, or by temporarily escaping reality by swallowing intoxicating substances. It seems to me that, in their intoxication with growth and expansion, with more and more in terms of production and people, with bigness, speed— in short, with "progress"—they had lost that which we Greeks had found to be the essence of humanity: *Sophrosyne*—Measure, Moderation. I once suggested that the right size of a manageable political community was a few thousand human beings. More becomes not only unmanageable but lifeless and mechanical, controllable only by huge organization, with its inevitable machinery of coercion. But, as human beings, we cannot forego the intimacy of personal relationship. We Greeks certainly had, and, indeed, still have, our goodly measure of strife and cruelty. But we are still at home with nature and our gods. Look at that green peninsula, our Attica, with its forests and glens, and the white temples shimmering in the sunlight. In that faraway era I dreamt of, I saw that the green of the woods had disappeared, an evil yellow fog covered Eleusis, and the brooks and the rivers and even the purple sea had become discolored with slime. That Attica, the name of which they had seen fit to give to one of their most cruel prisons, had become a dream in their remembrance of times past. Would they, with all their ingenuity and inventiveness, be able to survive? They had become so many that they filled the last nook of the planet and were about to suffocate in their own wastes. Measure—lost. No *sophrosyne* as standard of behavior (although they would endlessly study "behavior"), only the hubris of the strong and the despair of the weak. Although tired from my rush through so many centuries, I was extremely curious to know more. How would they extricate themselves from the danger of annihilating themselves and everything by applying the superweapon of which they told me, and which seemed to be based on what appears of utmost illogic to a Greek: the splitting of the world's basic substance, the atom?

At that point, I suddenly woke up. My servants have since told me that there had been the most terrible thunderstorm they ever witnessed, and that I woke at the moment of the most terrifying thunderclap of all. They had believed it was the end of the world and were amazed not only to have survived but to see me come to life again.